Roadmap
to the Regents:
Comprehensive
English

The Princeton Review

Roadmap
to the Regents:
Comprehensive
English

by Elizabeth Silas and Reed Talada

Random House, Inc.
New York

www.randomhouse.com/princetonreview

This workbook was written by The Princeton Review, one of the nation's leaders in test preparation. The Princeton Review helps millions of students every year prepare for standardized assessments of all kinds. The Princeton Review offers the best way to help students excel on standardized tests.

The Princeton Review is not affiliated with Princeton University or Educational Testing Service.

Princeton Review Publishing, L.L.C.
160 Varick Street, 12th Floor
New York, NY 10013

E-mail: textbook@review.com

Published in the United States by Random House, Inc., New York.

ISBN 0-375-76311-2

Editor: Russell Kahn
Director of Production: Iam Williams
Design Director: Tina McMaster
Development Editor: Rachael Nevins
Art Director: Neil McMahon
Production Manager: Mike Rockwitz
Production Editor: Lisbeth Dyer

Manufactured in the United States of America

9 8 7 6 5 4 3 2 1

First Edition

CONTENTS

INTRODUCTION

WHAT IS THE PRINCETON REVIEW?

The Princeton Review is an international test-preparation company with branches in all major U.S. cities and several cities abroad. In 1981, John Katzman started teaching an SAT prep course in his parents' living room. Within five years The Princeton Review had become the largest SAT coaching program in the country.

The Princeton Review's phenomenal success in improving students' scores on standardized tests was (and continues to be) the result of a simple, innovative, and radically effective approach: Study the test, not what the test claims to measure. This approach has led to the development of techniques for taking standardized tests based on the principles the test writers themselves use to write the tests.

The Princeton Review has found that its methods work not just for cracking the SAT, but for any standardized test. We've successfully applied our system to the SAT II, AP, ACT, GMAT, and LSAT, to name just a few. As a result of hundreds of hours of exhaustive study, we are now applying that system to the New York State Regents exams. This book uses our time-tested principle: Figure out what the test givers want, and then teach that to the test takers in a comprehensive and fun way.

WHAT IS THE REGENTS COMPREHENSIVE EXAMINATION IN ENGLISH?

You will probably take the Regents Comprehensive Examination in English in June of your junior year. Most of your score will be based on your written responses to four writing tasks. The rest of your score will be based on some multiple-choice questions. We have created a set of techniques and practice exams so that you can crack the types of tasks and questions that you will see on the exam.

The Regents Comprehensive Examination in English is administered over two days and is made up of four parts. Session One, Part A, involves a listening comprehension passage followed by multiple-choice questions and a composition. For Session One, Part B, you are given a written text and information in a table or graph. Based on that information, you answer some multiple-choice questions and write another composition. The second day of the test starts with Session Two, Part A, in which you read two passages, answer multiple-choice questions, and write an essay. Finally, Session Two, Part B, of the exam asks you to write an essay in which you discuss a quote using examples from two pieces of literature you have read.

There are specific ways you can approach each one of these sections to increase your score on the exam. We suggest that you work through this book one chapter at a time to build your familiarity with the test and your test-taking skills.

This book provides you with the two things you need in order to be well prepared for the new Regents Comprehensive Examination in English. Part I introduces you to each type of question on the test and teaches you techniques that will help you do well. Part II of the book consists of sample exams that allow you to practice your newly learned techniques. Each practice exam is followed by detailed explanations of the answers to each question.

USING THIS BOOK

As you read the Part I chapters that explain the test-taking techniques, you will find that sample test questions or writing tasks are used in each chapter as examples of how to approach each part of the exam. Try to use these chapters interactively by completing each exercise as it is explained before looking at the correct answers to the multiple-choice questions and sample responses to the writing tasks provided.

When you take the complete practice tests in Part II, take them under conditions similar to the real test. Make sure you will be undisturbed for a few hours: Go to the library, turn off the ringer on the phone, or let your family know that you are taking a practice test and that they should not disturb you. Take the Session One parts together, and a few days later, take the Session Two parts together, because the real exam will be administered on two separate days. Because listening requires different skills from reading, and Session One, Part A, is specifically a listening section, it is very important that you have someone read the speech aloud to you.

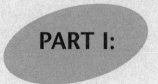

PART I:

HOW TO CRACK THE SYSTEM

CHAPTER 1
OVERVIEW OF THE REGENTS COMPREHENSIVE EXAMINATION IN ENGLISH

THE STRUCTURE OF THE EXAM

Session One

On the first day of testing for the English exam, you will take Session One, Parts A and B. You will have 3 hours to complete both parts. Part A requires you to listen to a text, answer five or six multiple-choice questions about it, and write a composition related to what you heard. Part B asks you to read a text with some accompanying visuals, answer eight to ten multiple-choice questions, and write a composition related to what you read. For both Parts A and B you will be assigned a specific composition topic and audience. However, you will have some flexibility in how you approach the assigned composition.

The Part A text that you hear and the Part B text and visuals that you read will be nonfiction works. The Regents test scorers will read your compositions to see if you understood the information and how well you applied it in a written response.

Session Two

On the second day of testing, you will take Session Two, Parts A and B. Again, you will have 3 hours to complete both parts. Part A asks you to read two literary passages from different genres, answer eight to ten multiple-choice questions, and write a composition that draws from both passages and from your own knowledge of literary devices. Part B consists of one quotation and requires you to write a composition giving your opinion on it, drawing evidence from two pieces of literature you have read. Again, your composition topics are assigned. However, you are able to develop your own controlling idea for each of these compositions. (See page 7 for further explanation of controlling ideas.)

Both parts of Session Two require you to use literary works to support your controlling ideas. That makes them significantly different from the Session One compositions, which ask you to write only about the provided nonfiction texts. Session Two compositions require you to be familiar with literary terms you use in English class, such as *plot, theme,* and *mood.* Regents test scorers will look to see how well you analyzed the literature that you wrote about in your compositions.

6 Hours?

Yes, this exam is a total of 6 hours—3 hours per day. You may be able to finish early, but if you do, you should take the extra time to read over your compositions and fine-tune them. You should not finish any session more than 30 minutes early. Taking the practice exams in this book will help you pace yourself so that you spend enough time on each step and do not run out of time.

THE SCORING OF THE EXAM

The teachers in your high school will score your compositions. Two different teachers will read each composition you write. Each teacher will give your composition a score ranging from 1 to 6. How does a teacher choose the number he or she gives your composition?

The teacher looks for certain qualities in your composition and judges it based on all of those qualities. These qualities—meaning, development, organization, language use, and conventions—are counted slightly differently for each part of the exam. As we teach you how to crack each part, we will explain how it will be scored.

The teacher will not give you scores for individual qualities, however. The teacher reading your composition will score it holistically, on the 1–6 scale. Holistic scoring means that the teacher will base your score on the overall impression that your composition makes. The test scorers do not start with 6 points and subtract points for errors that you make along the way. Although each of the qualities is important, no single quality determines your score.

You will receive two holistic scores for each composition you write. You will also get credit for each multiple-choice question you answer correctly. The compositions that you write will be worth twice what the multiple-choice questions are worth.

Thus, although we provide techniques for doing well on the multiple-choice items, we strongly encourage you to focus most of your preparation and test-taking time on the compositions.

GENERAL GUIDELINES FOR DOING WELL ON ALL THE COMPOSITIONS

There are important steps to follow that will help you to do well on all four of the compositions you will write for this exam.

Know Your Assignment

Each part of the Regents exam has a section that explains the task you have been assigned. Each part uses different terms to describe your assignment: Directions, Overview, the Situation, Your Task, Critical Lens, and Guidelines. These terms will be explained in the following chapters, but no matter which terms you see, pay close attention to the section that explains the assignment. Refer to it constantly. If you do not write the composition the test writers have assigned, you will lose points. The two most important parts of the assignment are the *audience* and the *controlling idea*.

Know Your Audience

Each assignment section tells you who will read your composition. Those people are your audience. Session One assignments tell you exactly who your audience is. They could be a school board, the readers of a newspaper, a room full of sixth-graders—almost anyone. Session Two assignments generally imply that your audience is your English teacher.

Keep your audience in mind; try to visualize writing directly to them. Think about what information they will need in order to understand what you have to say. Think about whether they will understand the words you are using and the way in which you present your ideas. This will help you write in a style that is appropriate for your audience—your writing should be more formal for newspaper readers and less formal for sixth-graders.

Know Your Controlling Idea and Purpose

In each of the test sections you will find either a stated or suggested controlling idea for your composition. Your English teacher has probably been using the term *controlling idea* in class. It refers to the main idea, or focus, of your composition. The Regents exam uses the term controlling idea, so that is the term we use throughout this book.

For all the compositions on the Regents exam, you must write about the controlling idea that is suggested or stated in the assignment. The purpose of each composition you write is to persuade the audience that the controlling idea is valid. The best way to make sure that you stick to the controlling idea is to make an outline or a map before you begin writing your composition.

Brainstorm and Make an Outline or Map

In the following chapters you will find many suggestions for how to come up with points to support the controlling ideas assigned to you. For any composition, however, you should always brainstorm and then organize your ideas before starting to write. This is particularly true in a testing situation, because you will not have an opportunity to revise or rewrite.

One way to brainstorm and organize your ideas is by creating an informal outline. Relax; this is not something that will be graded—for an informal outline you don't have to worry about Roman numerals or whether the letters need to be capital or lowercase. Instead, you can just create your own style to organize your ideas. Outlines are useful because they help you come up with a straightforward controlling idea and two or three major points that will support it.

Try creating an outline that could be used to write an essay about how to write compositions. Just jot down what you would say, and then arrange it into the best order.

_____

_____

_____

_____

_____

_____

_____

_____

_____

_____

_____

_____

_____

_____

_____

_____

_____

_____

Here is our outline:

WRITING A COMPOSITION

PLAN
read task carefully
brainstorm and ask yourself questions
organize with a concept map or outline

WRITE
introduce controlling idea
stick to one point per paragraph
explain supporting points
conclude in a final paragraph

PROOFREAD
look for your common errors
neatly correct mistakes

Another way to brainstorm and organize your points before writing is by mapping them. You may be familiar with this technique from school. Sometimes it is called clustering, concept mapping, or making a web. If you feel more comfortable organizing your ideas in a visual way, you may like this method better than writing an outline. You can start by writing your controlling idea in the middle of a blank page, then drawing a circle around it. You can then work outward from the controlling idea by connecting your supporting points to that central circle. Maps can be helpful to show you how your supporting points are connected to one another.

On the next page, try creating a concept map about how you will prepare for the Regents Comprehensive Examination in English.

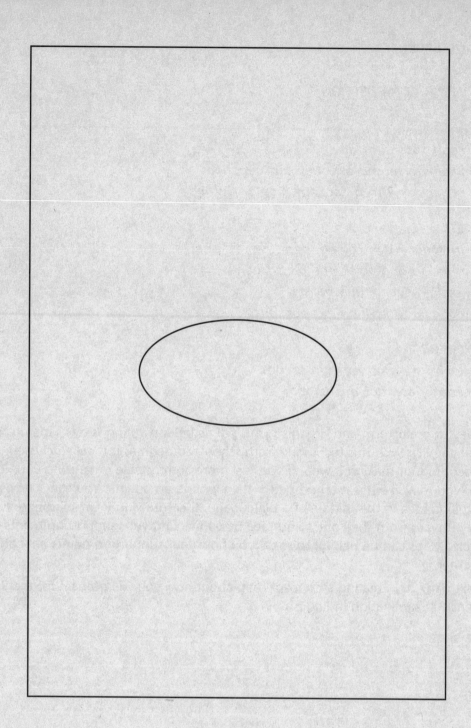

Now take a look at our concept map. Yours is probably much different, since you have only just started reading this book!

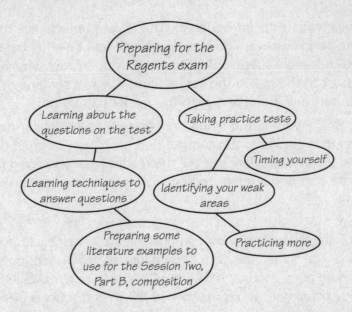

If you want to be particularly careful about planning to write your composition, you can draw a map to brainstorm and then write an outline to organize your ideas. However, because this is a timed test with many different parts, you should probably just choose one method for each composition. When you take the practice tests, try making an outline sometimes, and making a map other times, to see which method works best for you.

Write Your Composition

As you write, there are two items that you should constantly refer back to: your outline/map and the assignment.

Your outline or map will guide you as you write, and you should follow it all the way through your composition. Don't make the mistake of trying to stick in more details that you hadn't included in your outline or map while you are writing. Straying from your plan may cause you to lose focus, and when you lose focus, you lose points.

The assignment will also guide you. Keep referring back to it to make sure that you are actually writing the composition that has been assigned to you. The most important part of the assignment is the controlling idea that is suggested for your composition. Imagine that the test asks you to compare viewers of VH1 and MTV based on information from an article that is provided. The assignment directs you to use specific examples to highlight the two stations' differences. Imagine, also, that you are an avid fan of *The Real World*. If you don't keep the assignment in mind, you may write a composition that explains why MTV is far superior to VH1, rather than completing the task that was actually assigned to you. The task was to compare the two stations' viewers, not to persuade your reader that MTV is better than VH1. If you veer off track and do not follow the controlling idea that has been stated or suggested in the task, you will lose points no matter how well you can write.

THE THREE PARTS OF A GOOD COMPOSITION

Introduction

The first thing you will write is the introduction. This is your one chance to hook the reader, so try to be interesting and creative. The introduction should be a full paragraph that starts out general and becomes more specific. Begin by telling the reader why you are writing this composition. Refer back to the task in the instructions. The first sentence, while remaining very general, should start out strong and grab the reader's attention.

The following sentences of your introduction may provide more details, mentioning points you will develop later in the body of the composition. Don't get bogged down trying to expand any points in the introduction; just tell the reader what you are going to do in your composition and make him or her interested enough to want to read more.

Body

The paragraphs that form the body of your composition are extremely important. Remember to stick to your outline. You should use each body paragraph to present one point. You may have two, three, or more body paragraphs. Be sure that each one makes its own individual point. In a single body paragraph, you must do two things: introduce a piece of information, and most importantly, relate that piece of information to the controlling idea. If you fail to make the connection between the information you are presenting and the point you are trying to make, your composition will receive a low score. It is your responsibility, as the writer, to make sure that you develop each point and show how it supports the controlling idea.

Transitions

Keep your points in separate paragraphs, but link them with transition words. Transition words occur at the beginnings and ends of paragraphs to help your reader understand how one supporting detail relates to another. Sometimes two supporting details will have something in common that you can use to move from one paragraph to the next, as when they both come from one text. Sometimes they will have a chronological order, and then your transitions can be time-related, as in "*After* MTV captured viewers' interest by . . ." Sometimes you can contrast them, and point out their differences, as in "VH1 explored a *different* way of getting young people to tune in . . . ." Some standard transitional phrases are listed on the next page.

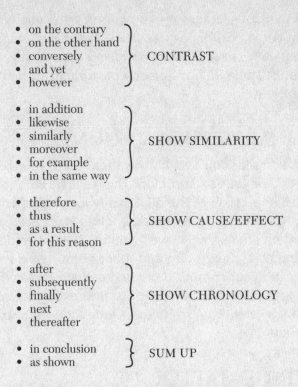

- on the contrary
- on the other hand
- conversely
- and yet
- however

} CONTRAST

- in addition
- likewise
- similarly
- moreover
- for example
- in the same way

} SHOW SIMILARITY

- therefore
- thus
- as a result
- for this reason

} SHOW CAUSE/EFFECT

- after
- subsequently
- finally
- next
- thereafter

} SHOW CHRONOLOGY

- in conclusion
- as shown

} SUM UP

These are phrases you can fall back on, but the best transitions emerge naturally from a logical sequence of points.

Conclusion

Your composition should end with a strong conclusion. Your conclusion should start out being specific, restating the points you made in your body paragraphs, and emphasizing the strongest points. As you move closer to the end, however, the conclusion should become more general, ending with an overall restatement of the main idea and its importance—this is what we call the kicker.

The kicker is something you can easily invent if you think about the implications of what you are arguing for in your composition. For instance, in the MTV/VH1 composition, you might conclude your discussion of the music television viewers by stating, "People like to see themselves in their art, and so any popular art form, including music videos, needs to represent many different types of individuals. MTV and VH1 have begun to do this by catering to two different groups of viewers, but we need further diversity."

To show you an example of a kicker for a literary composition, let's say that your composition argues that "characters in novels teach readers how to behave honorably or dishonorably." You state this argument in an introduction, and back it up in the body paragraphs by using examples from novels and your own experiences. You can conclude the composition with this kicker: "Thus, novel writers have an important responsibility to provide morally upright characters as models for readers to emulate." In this case, you've shown exactly why the main idea is important in the bigger picture by pointing out one of the results of the main idea.

Don't worry if you can't think of a kicker for every composition you write. Sometimes you just can't figure out what could possibly be important about the topic. In those cases, just make sure you have adequately restated your controlling idea. Always write some sort of conclusion, even if you must stop writing the body paragraphs to do it. It doesn't have to be long; it just has to be there.

FIRST AND LAST IMPRESSIONS COUNT

The two most important times for you to grab the attention of your readers are at the very beginning and the very end of your composition. The teachers who read your composition are likely to form an initial impression of the quality of your writing as they read your introductory paragraph. It is difficult to overcome a rough start, even if the subsequent portions of your composition are extremely well written. The impression you make on the readers in your concluding paragraph is also important because it is what they read immediately before assigning your composition a score. Keep these critical points in mind as you write. Do your best to make a good first and last impression on the reader by checking your spelling and mechanics carefully. Also try to include thoughtful content in both your introduction and conclusion.

THE LITTLE THINGS MATTER

Your compositions need to be well written and follow the assigned tasks. In addition, though, they need to be easy to read. The two teachers who will read and evaluate each composition will have graded hundreds of responses before and after yours.

What does this mean? It means that cosmetic factors—your handwriting, whether or not you indent when you start a new paragraph, how often and how neatly you correct errors in your writing—become important. If your compositions are exceptionally well written but your handwriting is illegible, your score will suffer.

When you write your compositions, you want to make sure that the teachers who read them will be able to appreciate their strong points rather than become frustrated with trivial weaknesses like appearance. Do the following:

- Write legibly and neatly. If you are able to print more neatly than you can write in cursive, then by all means, print.

- Indent generously when you start a new paragraph.

- Leave the margins of the lined paper clean and unmarked.

- Cross out your mistakes neatly with a single line.

- Plan your composition well to prevent having to insert large pieces of writing, which can often end up crammed illegibly into the margins.

The test scorers don't expect you to be perfect, but if your composition is neat and easy to read, it will be much easier for them to recognize your good writing.

HOW LONG SHOULD MY COMPOSITIONS BE?

There is no specific answer to this question. Your composition must have an introduction, a body, and a conclusion. It also must accomplish the task that is specified by the directions. As a general rule of thumb, a composition that is four paragraphs long (including the introduction and conclusion) is on the short side. If five or six paragraphs are enough space for you to do what the task asked you to do, then your composition is long enough. If you find yourself with an outline for a composition that will be more than seven paragraphs long, you may want to ask yourself the following two questions:

- Can I combine any of the paragraphs and make my point more strongly?
  If so, do it.

- Are all of my points directly related to the assignment, or do some points start to move away from the controlling idea?
  If some of your points aren't focused on the assigned task, delete them.

LANGUAGE USE

Language use is one of the qualities that scorers will be looking for in your compositions. You get full credit in this area not just for using language to make your point, but for using language *well.* Be sure to employ all those skills that English teachers have been drilling into your head for years, including staying aware of your audience and purpose and writing fluently.

Stay Aware of Your Audience and Purpose

Staying aware of your audience and purpose is a skill you can improve with a little practice. Focus on writing to your audience, whomever they are. Remain aware of why you are writing to them.

Sometimes the audience requires you to use a certain point of view. If your audience is the readers of a newspaper, and your purpose is to convince them to stop littering, you might use the second person "you," or the first person "we," when writing. When the audience is your English teacher, however, and your purpose is to convince him or her that two literary texts support your opinion that evil never triumphs, you should stick to the third person and avoid directly addressing the reader or mentioning yourself. Remember that in Session Two of testing, your English teacher will be the audience for both of your compositions. In Session One, your audiences may be different.

For the Regents compositions, your audience will always be somewhat public (since the test will never assign you to write to an audience of just your best friend), and thus your tone should be at least somewhat formal. That means that you must use standard written English, so avoid slang and your own dialect. Your manner of speaking and writing in informal situations is just as useful as standard written English, but the Regents exam tests only standard written English.

If you're like most people and you've picked this book up only a month or so before the exam, don't panic—you still have time to improve your language skills. You can best improve your use of language by practicing writing compositions like those on the Regents exam, and by doing the following while you write:

- Stay aware of your audience and your purpose.

- Avoid slang and informal styles.

Write Fluently

Writing fluently takes a lot longer to learn. You've been working on it every year you've been in school, actually. Using language well means choosing your words effectively and writing clearly and smoothly. There are a few simple things outlined below that you can do to help yourself become more fluent, but they take time.

Read

The first thing you should do is read more than you do now, and challenge yourself in your reading. If you read one book a month now, double that and read two. If you read only magazines now, try reading books as well. Ask your English teacher or other teachers to suggest books. At least some of the books and periodicals you read should contain words you don't know and have to look up in the dictionary. Reading is a long-term way to become more familiar with a variety of language styles. If your test is in a few months, start reading more now. Reading will help you with many more tests beyond just the Regents Comprehensive Examination in English.

Practice Writing

To show the Regents test scorers that you can write smoothly and in your own voice, you need to practice writing. Each time you do, show your composition to someone who can read it and tell you which parts he or she understands and which are unclear. If this person can also tell you which parts of the composition flow well and which are choppy, this will be a great help to you.

Learn New Words

Another way to increase your mastery of language is to be on the lookout for new vocabulary everywhere. New words pop up in all kinds of places—not just in your reading. You hear words that are unfamiliar to you on the radio and on television; you see them in advertisements and on signs. Be aware, and each time you hear or read a new word, jot it down on an index card (you can carry index cards with you anywhere). When you get home, look it up in the dictionary. Then write the definition on the back of the card, and write down a sentence that helps you remember what the word means. If you can make your sentence funny or include someone or something you know in it, you will remember the word easily.

Use Those New Words

Once you've learned some big vocabulary words, use them! Use them before you get to the Regents exam so that you can be sure you're using them correctly. If you're certain you know the meaning of a word, use it in your Regents compositions, if you can. In general, as you learn more words you will be able to express yourself more precisely, since each word you learn has a unique meaning. The bigger your vocabulary, the more meanings you have to choose from. In the real world, the bigger word is not always the best word, but on the Regents, a few big words used correctly can show off your arsenal (look that one up!) of vocabulary.

Write Simply

If you know you have trouble with sentence fragments or run-ons, you should not try to concentrate on creating sentences of varying length or structure. You should keep your sentences short and simple so that you can express your points without grammatical errors getting in the way.

Write in Your Own Words

Beware of the temptation to quote heavily from the text or passages provided. You may think that quoting the passage is the safest route to take—after all, a writer who is well known wrote those words. However, you will actually lose points for quoting the text or passages too much. A few direct quotes are okay, if you put quotation marks around them and if you explain how they support your controlling idea. Also, be careful that you do not use the words from the text by mistake.

Try to put the texts in your own words even before you begin writing. That way, your thoughts and voice will emerge, and the texts that you refer to will simply support your composition, instead of dominating it. If you can skillfully present the controlling idea by *using* the texts, you will successfully blend your opinion with the words that have been presented to you.

Write Creatively

We recommend a traditional organization of your ideas in a composition, with an introduction, a body, and a conclusion. Within this structure, however, you have the opportunities to write using fresh, original wording and to support your controlling idea in a number of inventive ways. You may decide to tell a short anecdote that will support your main idea, or use a metaphor to make your point. Write your composition the best way you can, and communicate your ideas as clearly and creatively as possible. Just keep in mind your overall controlling idea, and make sure that everything you write, and the manner in which you write it, contributes to making that main point.

CONVENTIONS

The test scorers are also looking to see if you've mastered the conventions of standard written English. Conventions include spelling, punctuation, capitalization, grammar, and usage.

Unless you've picked up this book far in advance of your exam, you will probably not be able to greatly improve your ability to follow these conventions before the test. Here's the good news, though: If your compositions are easily readable, your errors in spelling and grammar (and all the rest of the conventions) will not count against you much.

Because the test scorers have just a few minutes to read each composition, they cannot note every error you make, as some of your English teachers do when they correct your papers. They also know that this is a timed test, and you have no dictionary or reference materials available to you, so you can make a few errors and still get the highest composition score possible, 6 points.

The way you develop the controlling idea, the way you interpret the texts you are using to support that idea, and how well you organize the composition are much more important, and have a much bigger impact on the scorers, than how well you spell.

The only way your spelling, grammar, or punctuation can really get you into trouble is if your mistakes make your composition hard to understand. If this is so, you should try to get help from a teacher, a tutor, a parent, or handbooks. This book will not review basic conventions, and if errors make your composition unreadable, then you will need a thorough review of the basics.

If you just want to be sure that a few mistakes don't interfere with a good exam score, you can work on the errors you make often. Look at your old English papers and find the red marks your teacher made. What do they say? If you do not understand them, bring them to your English teacher and ask him or her which errors you make often. Then, as you practice with the tests in this book, be conscious of those errors when you proofread what you've written. (Do the same for any other writing you do.)

For example, if you often mess up "ie" and "ei" words, check your spelling especially for them. If you often write run-on sentences, make sure that each sentence expresses one (and only one) complete thought. Becoming aware of your most common mistakes will allow you to fix them before anyone else reads your writing. You can also try to avoid situations in which you know you will probably make an error. If you are trying to spell a word that you are unsure of, instead of trying to fudge it, just use another word. Likewise, if you know you have trouble with sentence fragments, write simple, clear sentences and check them for subjects and predicates.

Do your best to avoid making errors, but don't think about conventions too much while writing. The interpretations, development, organization, and focus in your essay are all much more important.

GENERAL GUIDELINES FOR DOING WELL ON THE COMPOSITIONS FOR SESSION TWO

What Makes These Compositions Different?

The compositions you write for Session Two are different from those in Session One because they require you to write about literary works. For a Session Two, Part A, composition, you are presented with two literary passages to write about. The Session Two, Part B, composition requires you to write about two literary works that you have read on your own. To write well about literary works, you need to be able to analyze them.

To analyze something means to pull the thing apart and look at its pieces and how they work together. If you take apart a telephone and look at the individual parts inside—the wires and the bell—and how they are connected, you may learn something about how the telephone works that you could not have learned if you had left it intact and never looked inside. Sure, you would know that it rings, and that you use it to speak to other people far away, but you wouldn't know how that happens. When you open it up and look at the pieces, you have a better idea. When you have someone next to you who knows a lot more about telephones and can explain how the wires make the bell ring, you'll learn even more.

This is what you've been doing in English class, except with written works of literature instead of telephones. At some point, everyone sits in an English class and says, "Why do we keep talking about this book? We've read it; now let's read something else." You keep talking about that same book because there are a lot of little parts that connect to make that book work. Your English teacher would like you to see them and get to know the parts, because if he or she can get you to understand how the parts of the book work, then you'll be able to apply that knowledge to another book. (Just like if you really understood how the parts of that ordinary telephone worked, you could apply that knowledge to a cordless telephone.) But what are the parts of a work of literature?

Granted, you can't see the parts of a work of literature the way you can see telephone wires. But you've come to know some of them: plot, character, theme, structure, style of language, point of view. If you think you've never seen these terms before, you should definitely ask your English teacher to help you with them. If you just need to brush up and see how to apply them to the Session Two compositions, then read through the list of common literary terms below to be sure you are familiar with them. Try to apply them to the works you review for the Session Two, Part B, composition. Also, as you take the practice exams in this book, try to apply them to the passages in the Session Two, Part A, sections.

Common Literary Terms

The following is a list of terms for many literary elements and techniques that you'll need to write about in the Session Two compositions.

Allegory—a story in which characters represent abstract qualities or ideas.
Example—In the fable "The Grasshopper and the Ant," the grasshopper represents flightiness, while the ant represents industriousness.

Allusion—an indirect reference to something outside the literary work. It could be a reference to a myth, an historical event, another literary work, a person . . . almost anything.
Example—If the narrator of a novel says that a character has made "Herculean efforts," then the novelist has used an allusion to tell you something about the character. This allusion is to the myth of Hercules.

Antagonist—a character who is the adversary of the protagonist.
Example—In "Little Red Riding Hood," the Big Bad Wolf is the antagonist because he is in conflict with Little Red Riding Hood.

Assonance—repetition of a vowel sound within or among words, usually within one line of poetry.

Characterization—the way an author presents the characters. Direct characterization is when the author tells you what a character is like. Indirect characterization is when the author allows you to draw your own conclusions about a character by showing you what a character is like.
Example—An author who shows a character who helps out at a nursing home and volunteers at a preschool is showing that the character is caring and kind.

Figurative language—language that is not literal, in that it does not mean exactly what it says. Metaphors and similes are both types of figurative language, as are many of the other terms included in this list.
Example—"He's a string bean" means that the man is very thin, but it does not actually mean that the man is a vegetable.

Foreshadowing—a hint to the reader, which may or may not be obvious during a first reading, about the general direction of the plot.
Example—A rainstorm in a story often foreshadows difficult times for characters later in the story.

Hyperbole—extreme exaggeration used to make a point.
Example—"I'm so hungry I could eat a horse."

Imagery—the use of descriptive language to appeal to one of the reader's senses (sound, touch, taste, smell, or sight).
Example—"The fudge melted in his mouth, swirling around his tongue with a rich, buttery flavor."

Irony—the expression of a certain idea by saying or showing just the opposite. Dramatic irony occurs when the audience or reader knows more than the character who is speaking, and thus the words mean something different to the audience or reader than to the character. Situational irony occurs when the opposite of what is expected takes place. Verbal irony occurs when someone says one thing but means the opposite.
Example—A character who says "I'm sure this will be fun," while walking into the dentist's office, is expressing verbal irony.

Metaphor—a comparison made without using the words "like" or "as."
Example—When Hamlet says, "I will speak daggers to her," he is comparing his hurtful words to daggers.

Onomatopoeia—the use of words that sound like what they mean.
Examples—"snap"; "pop"; "pow."

Organization—the general structure of a piece of writing. Organization can include how the writing is physically divided into paragraphs or stanzas, as well as the structure of the plot or the order in which ideas are developed.
Examples—One text may progress from a general to a specific treatment of one topic. Another text may focus on one character's view of an event and then another character's view of the same event.

Oxymoron—a phrase made up of two seemingly opposite words.
Examples—"sincere lie"; "deafening silence."

Paradox—two or more words or ideas that apparently contradict one another.
Example—The opening lines of Charles Dickens's *A Tale of Two Cities:* "It was the best of times, it was the worst of times. . . ."

Personification—giving human characteristics or abilities to nonhuman things.
Example—"The morning sunlight danced across his pillow."

Plot—what happens in a story.
Example—Plots can be very complex, as in *Romeo and Juliet,* in which the plot is the course of events leading to the two young lovers' deaths.

Point of view—how the narrator relates the events described in a piece of writing. A first-person point of view is one in which the narrator is a character and refers to himself or herself as "I." A first-person narrative might begin with an opening line such as, "I knew it would be a difficult day as soon as I awoke." The second-person narrative is much less common and might begin with "You knew it would be a difficult day as soon as you awoke." A third-person narrative refers to all the characters as "he" or "she." An example would be, "She knew it would be a difficult day as soon as she awoke." An omniscient third-person narrator also refers to all the characters as "he" or "she," but the omniscient narrator reveals information about the characters that a limited third-person narrator would not know, such as what many different characters are thinking.

Protagonist—generally the main character in a piece of writing, the character who is the focus of the plot and who changes in some way.
Example—In *The Catcher in the Rye,* the protagonist is Holden Caulfield.

Repetition—saying the same thing more than once or using the same sound or sentence structure over and over again.

Simile—a comparison made using the words "like" or "as."
Example—"She is as quick as a rabbit."

Stanza—a section of poetry separate from the sections that come before and after.

Symbolism—the use of an object to represent an abstract idea.
Examples—Hearts often symbolize love; the color white often symbolizes innocence.

Theme—a general idea expressed by a literary work. There can be more than one theme in a work.
Example—The theme of "The Tortoise and the Hare" is that slow, steady effort triumphs over natural but undeveloped talent.

Tone—the feeling an author conveys to the reader. Tone contributes to the overall mood of a work.
Example—Tone can be formal, serious, passionate, lighthearted, witty, sarcastic, or any other general expression of feeling.

CHAPTER 2
CRACKING SESSION ONE, PART A:
THE LISTENING SECTION

Session One, Part A, of the Regents Comprehensive Examination in English involves listening to a speech read aloud by your proctor and using the information you hear in the speech to answer multiple-choice questions and write a composition. The composition will be worth about twice as much as the multiple-choice questions toward your total score. You will not get the opportunity to read the speech, so you need to rely on your listening and note-taking skills to do well on this part of the exam. Learning and following The Princeton Review techniques outlined in this chapter will help you make the most of these skills and earn a higher score.

Session One, Part A, of the Regents exam requires you to do a lot with information that you get to hear only twice. When you listen to a teacher give a lecture in class, you probably also read about the same topic either before or after the lecture. During this exam, however, you can rely only on what you hear. You will not be allowed to read the text for yourself. Take a look at the following assignment for Session One, Part A, of a Regents exam.

SESSION ONE, PART A

> **Overview:** For this part of the test, you will listen to a speech about an author's memories of an island in South Carolina, answer some multiple-choice questions, and write a response based on the situation described below. You will hear the speech twice. You may take notes anytime you wish during the readings.
>
> **The Situation:** Your English class is learning about authors whose lives are strongly influenced by a specific place. Your teacher has asked you to write a composition about author Pat Conroy and the ways in which his life was influenced by a specific place. In preparation for writing your composition, you will listen to a speech Pat Conroy made about his memories of an island in South Carolina. Then use relevant information from this speech to write your composition.
>
> **Your Task:** Write a composition for your English class showing how Pat Conroy's life was influenced by a specific place.

Guidelines:

Be sure to

- Tell your audience what they need to know to help them understand how Pat Conroy's life was influenced by a specific place

- Use specific, accurate, and relevant information from the speech to support your discussion

- Use a tone and level of language appropriate for a composition for English class

- Organize your ideas in a logical and coherent manner

- Indicate any words taken directly from the speech by using quotation marks or referring to the speaker

- Follow the conventions of standard written English

That's all you get to read—the rest you have to listen to carefully as the proctor reads the speech. All is not lost, though. By using the following techniques, you will become adept at making the most of the time you have to listen to the speech. We'll take you step by step through Part A.

BEFORE THE SPEECH

Before your proctor begins reading the speech, he or she will read the "Overview" and the "Situation." These are basically the directions for Part A. Great time to tie your shoes and think about the weekend, right? Wrong. The Overview and the Situation are not ordinary test directions. The proctor is not just saying, "Okay, class, listen carefully." She or he is actually giving you information that is crucial to how well you will do on this entire section. She or he is telling you what to listen for in the speech that she or he will read. If you pay attention now, you will have a leg up on the test.

Overview

The Overview tells you what the speech will be about. Here is the Overview for the sample Part A that appears on pages 28–29:

> **Overview:** For this part of the test, you will listen to a speech about an author's memories of an island in South Carolina, answer some multiple-choice questions, and write a response based on the situation described below. You will hear the speech twice. You may take notes anytime you wish during the readings.

This description lets you know what the test writers think is most important in the speech. If you don't pay attention to this, you may waste the entire first reading trying to figure out what the main idea is.

As the proctor reads the Overview, follow along on your test paper. Underline the part of the Overview that tells you what is important about the speech, or what the main idea is. Underlining the main idea will make it easy for you to refer back to it. Now, look at the sample Overview above and underline the most important part.

You should have underlined "an author's memories of an island in South Carolina."

Notice, also, that the Overview tells you that there are multiple-choice questions as well as a composition, that you will hear the speech only twice, and that you may take notes. Make sure that you get plenty of scrap paper from your proctor so that you will not have to write in the margins of your paper or use really small print.

The Situation

The Situation is even more important than the Overview. The Situation tells you who the audience will be and what your task (your assignment) will be for the composition. This assignment will be restated under the heading "Your Task" after the Situation, but this is the first and most important mention of it, so pay attention.

The Situation also tells you who your audience is—the person or people who will read your composition—and addressing them is an essential part of scoring well. Now, you know that your real audience will always be the same—two English teachers from your school who each have about 2 minutes to read your composition and give it a score. However, you need to write your composition as if you really believe that your audience is whoever the Situation says it is. The Situation in the sample Session One, Part A, at the beginning of this chapter tells you that your audience is your English teacher, but the audience can vary from exam to exam—it won't always be an English teacher. The Situation may say that you are writing advice for junior high school students, an article for readers of a newspaper, or a report to present to an editorial board.

Your audience will determine how formally you write. Of the audiences listed in the paragraph above, which will require the least formal writing? If you said the junior high students, you are correct. Of course, you still need to be somewhat formal, using standard written English and avoiding slang, but your tone would be more conversational than it would be with an editorial board as your audience.

The audience also sometimes determines the approach you take to Your Task. Say your assignment is to write about the sports that present athletes with the greatest chance of being injured. If your audience consists of the readers of a health magazine, you might write an article discussing the pros and cons of those dangerous sports. However, if your audience is your younger sibling, you will probably write a more persuasive composition, emphasizing the hazards involved.

In addition to telling you about your audience, the Situation gives you your assignment for the composition. The sample Part A for this chapter says the following:

> **The Situation:** Your English class is learning about authors whose lives are strongly influenced by a specific place. Your teacher has asked you to write a composition about author Pat Conroy and the ways in which his life was influenced by a specific place. In preparation for writing your composition, you will listen to a speech Pat Conroy made about his memories of an island in South Carolina. Then use relevant information from this speech to write your composition.

As soon as you see the word "write" in the Situation, underline it and the words that follow it. The information that comes after the word "write" is Your Task—the assignment. You need to stick to this closely, and return to it many times to be sure you are fulfilling it. Examine each word—this is the most important information you get on your test paper. You should have underlined "write a composition about author Pat Conroy and the ways in which his life was influenced by a specific place."

Let's examine Your Task from the sample Part A. Did you notice that little "s" tacked on to the end of the word "way"? That means you need to write about more than one way in which Conroy's life was influenced. On the other hand, the paragraph also discusses "a specific place." That lets you know you should focus on only one place—and you already know something about the place from the Overview. It's an island in South Carolina. You should now write down what you know will be the focus of your composition, the controlling idea: "ways an island in South Carolina influenced Conroy's life."

All this preparation is important because now you know what to listen for and take notes on during the speech. Ideally, you'd be able to write the whole speech down as it was being read to you, but few of us can write as fast as a proctor can speak, so you will have to pick and choose what you write. Because you've listened to and read the Overview and the Situation, you now know what's most important to the composition.

The Situation may provide a little more information besides telling you the audience and the task. In the sample Part A, the Situation tells you that the speech was made by Conroy himself, and it reminds you to use what you learn from the speech in your composition.

Your Task

Now, you say, why do I have to do all that other stuff when I can just jump right to the task and see exactly what I have to do? Look at Your Task for the sample Part A:

> **Your Task:** Write a composition for your English class showing how Pat Conroy's life was influenced by a specific place.

Notice that not as much information is provided by Your Task as by the Overview and the Situation. Your Task is not as specific in its directions as the Situation. The wording does not let you know that the test writers expect you to mention more than one way that Conroy's life was influenced (remember that little "s" tacked on to "way" from the Situation). Finally, it does not mention what the specific place is.

So if you had just read Your Task, you wouldn't know as much as you could about what the test writers want your composition to be like, and you wouldn't know what to listen for in the speech. Being aware of exactly what you need to glean from the speech is the key to listening effectively, which will allow you to avoid writing down random bits and pieces that may not be useful in writing your composition.

What About the Multiple-Choice Questions?

If you feel more comfortable answering multiple-choice questions than writing compositions, then it's certainly understandable that you are eager to answer the multiple-choice questions first. However, keep in mind that they are worth only one-third of your score on this part of the exam. The composition is worth about two-thirds. Therefore, most of your time and energy during the two readings of the speech should be used to prepare to write your composition.

The Regents Board has decided that you cannot read the multiple-choice questions until after the speech is read twice. Do not try to read the questions while the proctor is reading the Overview and the Situation. You need that time to learn about your composition assignment so that you know what to focus on during the speech.

Remember that the multiple-choice questions are not nearly as important as your composition. Besides, if you take copious notes during the readings, you will have plenty of information to answer the questions with, even if you have not read them in advance. (If you aren't sure what "copious" means, look it up. It's never too early to start improving your vocabulary.)

DURING THE FIRST READING OF THE SPEECH

Below is the speech that accompanies the sample Part A for which we have given you the Overview, the Situation, and Your Task. Have someone read it aloud to you, if possible. If you must read it yourself, keep in mind that you will not be able to do so on the real test—it will only be read aloud by the proctor. (When you take the practice tests in this book, definitely have the speeches read aloud to you.) As someone reads the speech to you, take notes on a separate sheet of paper.

Ihave written, in part, to honor a landscape I carry with me wherever I go. Though I have traveled all over the world, it is the smell of the tides and marshes of Beaufort County, South Carolina, that identifies and shapes me. Its seeds and grasses grow along the margins of my books. Its soft mosses hang, like laundry, from my high-strung prose.

I sometimes feel that Fripp Island and I grew up together, formed a past of great intimacy during my final years of high school, and have maintained an alliance throughout my adult life despite many travels, false starts, and driftings of the spirit. A Marine colonel and his son first took me to Fripp on a fishing expedition the summer between my fifteenth and sixteenth year, and it was my first step on a sea island totally isolated from the mainland. It was an island as God made it, and nothing else, pristine as time itself. The sea islands of South Carolina shoulder up against the Atlantic, and the trees and the vegetation on these islands are wind-shaped and salt-burned and stunted by the great storms and swells resulting from this initial encounter with the continent. They are the first line of defense against hurricanes and those deep-throated storms out of the Northeast.

When I graduated from Beaufort High School, workers had just completed the bridge to Fripp Island, and I had a free run of the island that same summer. The president of the Student Council, Bruce Harper, sold real estate that first year land was for sale, and I remember him complaining that they would never sell a single lot with the prices so outrageously high. In my own memory, I think that oceanfront property was selling for $2,500 a lot during those hot, long-ago days. Bruce and I would golf when he got off work, then go for long swims in the ocean on a beach where not a single house had gone up. The sun would turn our bodies gold as it settled to the west of the marshes, and I thought I would be young forever.

My mother, Peg Conroy, walked the shoreline of Fripp every day for the last five years of her life and collected basketfuls of seashells that she would place in the clear globes of lamps. Those lamps are now treasures her children keep because we love to associate our mother with the sea, the crashing waves, the gathering up of beauty, and of light itself.

It was my mother who chose Fripp Island as our family beach, and it was where she was living when she died in 1984. She taught us that nature was simply another way of approaching God. When I asked her why buzzards never gathered over the corpses of loggerheads or pilot whales, she explained that the putrescence of red meat, and not seafood, is what attracted vultures to southern roadsides in the first place. "A matter of preference," she said, "Your father likes steak. I like shrimp."

My mother was afraid of hurricanes and bought her Fripp house near the golf course, so she could watch the small convoy of golfers sail past her house in the squat, pragmatic carts. That flow of humanity made her less lonely and provided her with an endless supply of free golf balls lost in the shrubbery of her yard. Years later, I bought my own house facing a saltwater lagoon where I watched osprey hunt fish in my backyard, then take their catch up into the trees to eat them heads first. I have seen great blue herons kill and eat snakes and huge eels. The alligators have developed a fondness for domesticated dog, and the raccoons find garbage cans better hunting ground than the toad-haunted wetlands. I woke up one bright fall morning and counted 300 egrets surrounding my lagoon in some mating ritual that looked like a dream of snow.

Because I came to Beaufort County when I was a boy, my novels all smell of seawater. I watch things closely here, and I try to get the details right. I write about the great salt marshes and pretend that I am that marsh. I do the same with the ocean, the horseshoe crab, the flock of brown pelicans, the beach-strewn kelp, the half-eaten stingray. I try to inhabit the soul of things, before I write them, the way my mother taught me.

There are other beaches, other oceans, but my mother staked out Fripp forever for her children. When she was dying, with her seven children gathered around her, Peggy, our mountain-born mother, said, "When I'm gone and you cross the bridge over to Fripp, look out toward the ocean. If you see whitecaps, that'll be me; that'll be your mother, waving, letting you know I'm still here with you."

What should you do during this first reading of the speech? Take notes! Don't concern yourself with making the notes into an outline with roman numerals and the like. Don't worry about your spelling, and don't try to write full sentences. If you've developed abbreviations from taking notes in class, that will help, but if you have not, be careful to take notes that will be understandable and legible when you write the composition.

Your notes should be phrases taken in the order that you hear them in the speech. Keep your notes in order so that you remember how the phrases are related to one another. Ordered notes will also help you with multiple-choice questions that ask you about the opening or closing lines of the speech.

If you write down a string of words exactly as the proctor says them, you should put quotation marks around them so that you remember they were taken directly from the speech. If you (either accidentally or on purpose) use too many direct quotes from the speech, you will lose credit. Try to understand each sentence and paraphrase it in your notes. If you must write your notes verbatim, you will have to be very careful to paraphrase once you are writing your composition.

As you take notes, listen for the essential points that you will use in your composition. Remember that the Situation told you that the focus of your composition will be ways an island in South Carolina influenced Conroy's life. Keep this controlling idea in mind as you listen and take notes. The speech may be uninteresting to you, but you must listen to it as though your grade depends on it (because it does).

Notice that the composition you have been asked to write is not a recap of the speech. You are not going to write a book report on the speech, saying, "Conroy said *X*, then he said *Y*, and then he closed with *Z*." You must use the speech as a resource—a place to get support for the controlling idea of your composition. Thus, although you are listening for ways the island influenced Conroy's life, the speech as a whole gives you a lot of other information as well. In the speech, Conroy tells you how he came to know the island, what he did there after high school, what his mother did there, his mother's philosophy of nature, what buzzards like to eat, and where his mother bought a house. Finally, he begins to tell you about his current life.

Although you should keep your controlling idea (ways an island in South Carolina influenced Conroy's life) in mind, you should not just wait, pen poised above the paper, until you hear the one or two points you need. You should note everything you can, but be particularly aware of the points you need. If you wait until the end of the Conroy speech to write anything, your notes will only tell you how his life is today—where he bought a house and how he tries to write. If you don't have notes on what the island is like and his mother's philosophy, you won't know what caused Conroy to buy a house on a saltwater lagoon and to write about the sea and the marsh. So keep your focus in mind, but write down the most important points, in case you can use them later.

AFTER THE FIRST READING OF THE SPEECH

When the proctor has finished reading the speech, look at your notes. What parts do you not understand? Where are the gaps? Do you feel like you can effectively write the composition? Reread the task that you underlined in the Situation and the notes you made on the controlling idea for your composition. Do you have examples from the speech that you can use to support the controlling idea? Make marks where you want to fill in more information in your notes.

The proctor is required only to give you a few minutes between the two readings. There is no set timing, so if your proctor gives you only 2 minutes and you would like a few more, don't be afraid to ask.

DURING THE SECOND READING OF THE SPEECH

Take notes again! If you reviewed your notes with the controlling idea in mind, you should have realized that there are a lot of things you missed the first time around. Try to fill in those gaps. Think specifically about which parts of the speech you want to use as examples to support your controlling idea. Make sure you've written them down.

For example, for the sample Part A, you need at least two ways that the island influenced Conroy's life. Do you have at least two ways? If you haven't already, try taking notes on a separate sheet of paper while the Conroy speech is read to you. When you are done, compare your notes to these:

Controlling Idea: ways the island in South Carolina influenced Conroy's life
writes to "honor a landscape"—Beaufort County, S.C.
"tides and marshes" influence his writing
Fripp Island—in Beaufort County?
remains dear to him
Marine colonel—first time to Fripp—fishing—15 or 16 years old
isolated island, undeveloped, no people
trees and plants protect against wind, salt, and storms
sea island of S.C.
graduated from H.S.—bridge to island built
friend sold real estate on island
Conroy golfed and swam there—still no houses
mother—Peg Conroy—walked around Fripp on the beach
she collected seashells and put them in lamps
mother associated with sea, waves, beauty, light
"family beach"
mother died 1984
mother: nature is "another way of approaching God"
buzzards like meat, not seafood—"preference"
mother's house near golf course
C. bought house on a "saltwater lagoon"
C. sees ospreys, herons, alligators, raccoons, toads, egrets
"my novels all smell of seawater"
C. watches carefully, looks at details
C. pretends he is a marsh, ocean, crab, pelican, kelp, stingray
C. tries to get inside things like his mother told him to
mother made Fripp important
7 children
mom said she'll be in the waves, waving

Don't worry if you didn't get as much information down when you took notes. You won't need all of these notes for your composition. You will mainly need to ask yourself, from your memory of the speech and your notes, what points you think you will use to support the controlling idea.

AFTER THE SECOND READING OF THE SPEECH

After the second reading, reread the controlling idea you underlined in the Situation. Mark those sections of your notes that will be most helpful in writing your composition. These should be points in the speech that you can use as support for the controlling idea. Mark them now in your notes or in the notes we have provided from the Conroy speech.

A NOTE ABOUT NOTES

If you don't think you can write your notes down as we've shown here, don't get discouraged. Practice note taking in classes, even when you don't really need to take notes on a lecture. Pretend you're going to have to write a composition on just 10 or 15 minutes of the lecture, and see how much of it you can take down. Work on abbreviating frequent words like "because," "with," and "causes."

You can also practice note taking by having a parent, sibling, or friend read articles or speeches aloud to you. If possible, have the reader tell you the main idea or subject of the passage before he or she begins. Again, pretend you must write a whole composition on a related topic.

You may also want to practice visualizing what the reader says as you take notes. For example, visualizing the island Conroy describes, his mother walking along the shore, and the sights he describes near his current home can help you remember what he says, even if you are not able to get it all on paper. As the proctor read the speech, if you pictured Conroy boating out to the island with the Marine officer and his son, fishing gear in tow, you could easily answer a question about why Conroy went out there the first time.

THE MULTIPLE-CHOICE QUESTIONS

Now that the two readings are finished and you've reviewed your notes, we recommend that you focus on the multiple-choice questions, get them out of the way, and earn some fairly easy points. There will be five or six questions.

Use Process of Elimination

In your notes, you probably haven't written every little thing the multiple-choice questions will ask you. That's okay. Using your notes and memory, eliminate as many wrong answer choices as you can, and then choose from the remaining options. Always choose an answer—you can only gain points!

Specific Detail Questions

The multiple-choice questions may ask you for very specific information from the speech. Here's an example of a "specific detail" question for the sample Part A.

▶ Pat Conroy's first trip to Fripp Island, at age 15, was for the purpose of
  (1) hiding
  (2) writing
  (3) fishing
  (4) studying

If you have this piece of information (why Pat Conroy made his first trip to Fripp Island) in your notes, you'll answer this question easily. Even if you do not, chances are you can eliminate a few answer choices and then choose. We never heard about Conroy hiding or studying. We did hear about him writing, but that was later. Therefore, the correct answer choice must be (3).

Imply/Infer Questions

Another type of multiple-choice question asks you to infer something from the speech or to state something the speech implies. When you make an inference or decide what is implied in the speech, you are taking what the speech hinted at and stating it outright in different words. Here's an example of a question that forces you to make an inference.

▶ Conroy implies that his house near the lagoon is a good place to
  (1) watch ships
  (2) entertain company
  (3) observe wildlife
  (4) play golf

Imply/infer questions will not ask you to jump too far from what was said in the speech. If you wrote down all the animals that Conroy sees from his house, you can easily answer this question. If you did not, eliminate the choices that you definitely did not hear about: watching ships and entertaining company. Then, think about when he mentioned golf—that was on Fripp Island, but not at his house. The correct answer choice must be (3).

Purpose Questions

Purpose questions ask you to explain why the author wrote something. It may be the entire speech, or just one part of the speech, that you are asked to explain. Think about the author's reason for writing those words, and use Process of Elimination to arrive at the best answer choice. For example:

▶ The speaker's opening lines serve to
   (1) list a series of problems
   (2) acknowledge a source of inspiration
   (3) describe a plan of organization
   (4) argue a point of view

Even if you did not note the opening lines, you know that there was no mention of problems and that the speaker was never seeking to argue a point of view. Think about the tone and focus of the speech. Look back at the notes for this speech. What was Conroy doing in the opening lines? The sample notes mention writing to "honor a landscape." He was acknowledging a source of inspiration, so the correct answer choice is (2).

CRAFTING THE COMPOSITION

You have already done much to plan for your composition. You investigated the Overview, the Situation, and Your Task to find the controlling idea the test writers want you to use. You listened carefully to both readings. You took notes to use for your composition. You made sure that you have supporting points for the controlling idea. Take a moment once again to note who the audience is and what controlling idea you have identified.

By this time you should have noticed that you cannot just turn your notes into sentences and call that a composition. You must use what you learned from the speech to build a composition around the controlling idea. To organize your thoughts, create a brief outline or map for your composition, separate from your existing notes.

Writing an Outline

Your outline should be very basic. If you follow traditional organization, it should consist of the following parts:

Introduction: Controlling Idea
Body Paragraph: Supporting Point
Body Paragraph: Supporting Point
Body Paragraph: Supporting Point
Conclusion: Restate Controlling Idea

Traditionally, the introduction begins with the controlling idea you pieced together from the Overview, the Situation, and Your Task, and then briefly describes the main supporting points you will make in the body paragraphs. This way, the introduction moves from a general statement to the specific details that will come.

If you feel confident that you can use a creative or different approach to constructing your composition, you may want to try it. The scoring system established for the Regents Comprehensive Examination in English rewards students who write very well, even if they take a nontraditional approach. If you feel that you can create a good composition without following a traditional structure, go for it, but to be safe, you should probably try it out on your English teacher before you take the real Regents exam. A good variation on the traditional structure might be opening with an anecdote that leads into the controlling idea; a potentially disastrous variation would be waiting until the conclusion to state the controlling idea.

The next part of the composition you need to outline is the body. There may be more or fewer body paragraphs than in the structure presented on page 34. The number depends on how many distinct points you make to support the controlling idea. You have already thought about which points you will make—just after the second reading, you marked the parts of your notes that you want to use.

As you list your points in an outline, keep in mind that you must show how each point supports the controlling idea. The outline stage is your time to make sure that each point is relevant to the controlling idea before you start writing. Look back again at the Situation and Your Task. Are you outlining a composition that will complete the assigned task? Each of your points should come from the speech, support the controlling idea, and allow you to explain how your composition supports the controlling idea. Explaining how each of your points does this will make up the bulk of your body paragraphs.

The conclusion restates the controlling idea. Note the conclusion in your outline so that you do not forget to include it in the composition! Always leave time to write a conclusion, even if you must stop developing supporting points in the body of your composition to do it. If you have time, do more than restate your controlling idea. Show how the controlling idea is important, how it relates to the world at large, or why you care about it.

Now write a brief outline for a composition in response to the sample task we've been using.

_____

_____

_____

_____

_____

_____

_____

_____

_____

_____

_____

_____

_____

_____

_____

Look at your points and see if there is a logical order in which to put them. Does point *B* flow from point *A*? Do the points have a chronological order? If no order occurs to you, see if you can think of a way to link your points, but if you still don't see one, don't worry. When moving between points, you can simply use standard transitional phrases like, "Another example of *X* is. . . ."

The outline allows you to arrange your information into a composition that fulfills the task in an organized way. Do not skip this step! It makes the difference between a focused composition and a rambling one.

Here is a sample outline for the Conroy composition. Because there are many ways to write this composition, yours may look completely different and still be effective. Just make sure the basic parts are there.

Sample Outline

INTRODUCTION: *Conroy's life was influenced by Fripp Island*

BODY PARAGRAPH 1: *He learned to appreciate nature there*
- *spent days out there alone*
- *learned to look at nature there*
- *learned to look at the details*

BODY PARAGRAPH 2: *He treasures his memories from there because he associates it with his mother*
- *mother walked along the beach there*
- *Conroy associates her with the sea*

BODY PARAGRAPH 3: *He writes about nature now, and tries to live as one with it, as his mother told him to*
- *tries to get inside living things, as his mother told him to*
- *lives on Fripp today*

CONCLUSION: *Fripp Island made Conroy aware of nature in his life and his writing*

Drawing a Concept Map

A concept map is helpful if you like to visualize the plan you are creating rather than read it. The one drawback, however, is that it does not leave you with a clear order for an introduction, body paragraphs, and a conclusion. You may want to draw a quick concept map first, and then put your ideas into an outline. See which method works for you as you practice. Try drawing a concept map for the Conroy speech in the diagram on the next page.

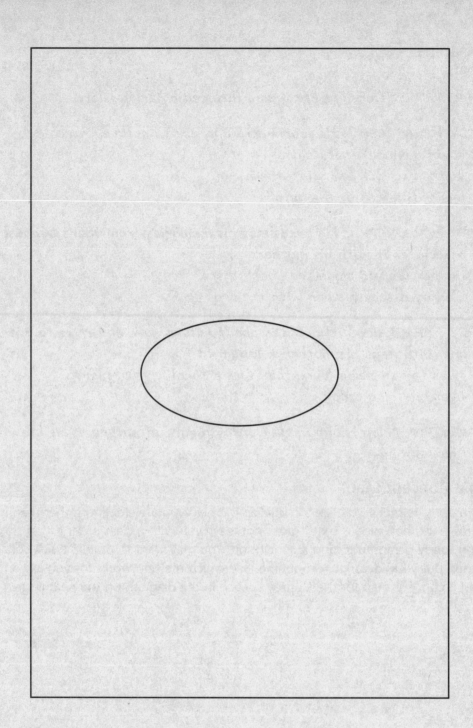

The following is a concept map equivalent to the sample outline you just saw. When you draw your map, you may have extra ideas that you put on the map and then decide not to follow up on. Just cross those out, and don't worry if your map doesn't look like this one. As long as you use some details from the speech to support the controlling idea, you're off to a good start.

Sample Concept Map

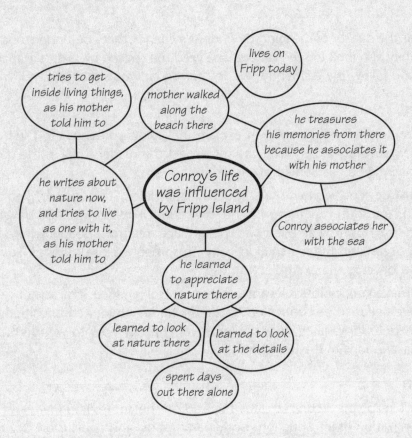

WRITING A HIGH-SCORING SESSION ONE, PART A, COMPOSITION

You will receive a score for your composition based on a 6-point scale. As you plan and write your composition, keep these five qualities in mind: meaning, development, organization, language use, and conventions. If your composition scores high in these five qualities, you'll receive full credit (6 points).

Meaning

Readers look for the quality of meaning by finding evidence that you understood the speech and the task. They also look to see that you analyzed the speech by taking it apart and using pieces of it. If you follow the techniques we've used so far, you should do well with this quality.

Development

Development is judged by how well you explain the points you chose to use from the speech. This is your responsibility. You cannot expect the reader to fill in the gaps by reading your mind or giving you the benefit of the doubt.

Your points must be specific. If you say, "Conroy really liked Fripp Island," you are not being specific enough. You must mention what he liked about Fripp Island, and develop the idea into something like, "Conroy enjoyed being in a place free from people where he could experience the ocean and the marsh alone or with someone close to him." Your notes should help you develop the examples you use.

You must also make your points relevant to your controlling idea. The sentence in the paragraph above needs to be connected to the main idea of your composition. You might go on to say, "Conroy translates his experiences on Fripp Island into wonderful novels that include vivid descriptions of the island."

Organization

Your outline will keep you organized. Stay focused on the controlling idea, and stick to the traditional organization of introduction, body paragraphs, and conclusion. Try to keep your points in a logical sequence, and connect them with transitions. If the transitions from paragraph to paragraph in your compositions seem forced or nonexistent when you practice, take a look at the section on transitions (page 12). If you find yourself straying from the main idea when you write, correct this problem by neatly crossing out the unnecessary information. Stay focused. Refer to the controlling idea and your outline as you write. Show off your organization with paragraph indents that readers can easily see.

Language Use

There are two different parts to language use. First, the reader is looking to be sure that you are aware of your audience and purpose. The proctor will tell you who your audience is and what your purpose is when he or she reads you the Situation and Your Task. In the sample Part A for this chapter, your audience is your English teacher, and your purpose is to convince him or her of the controlling idea of how Pat Conroy was influenced by a specific place. However, your audience for a different composition might be junior high school students with a purpose of convincing them of another interesting idea. Whoever your audience is, keep them in mind.

The language use quality also includes simply using language skillfully. This requires practice! You can find some hints for improving your ability to use language well in the language use section (page 15).

Conventions

These are the skills you've been learning since first grade—spelling, punctuation, capitalization, grammar, and usage. Look at old papers you've written and identify the errors you commonly make. Try to prevent them or catch them when you proofread. Take a look at the section on conventions (page 18) for more suggestions.

Try writing a composition of your own, based on your outline or concept map, for the sample Part A at the beginning of this chapter. Remember to refer back to the Situation and Your Task. Then read the following sample composition that received full-credit from the test scorers.

SAMPLE STUDENT COMPOSITION

Before you read this top-score student composition, write your own composition for the Session One, Part A, task at the beginning of this chapter. Then read the sample composition and the explanation of why it received full credit (6 points).

Score Level 6

> Almost everyone has a place that they long for—a place where everything seems perfect. This place can hold such a special place in the life of a person for various reasons. Maybe it reminds him of the innocence of his youth or his carefree teenage years. These treasured places oftentimes influence the lives of people, as was the case with author Pat Conroy.
>
> Conroy was attracted to the simplicity of Fripp Island. It was totally isolated from the mainland and seemed pristine. The most evident source of life was the plentiful vegetation that doubled as a line of defense against harsh weather, such as hurricanes and violent storms. Conroy was indeed happy in this simple world wasting hours

just swimming in the beautiful ocean or observing his surroundings. He more readily identified with the swell of the tides and marshes rather than things associated with the city. He felt as if he were transported into a magical land whenever he visited Fripp. This was evident because he felt closer to God and believed that he could remain a young man for all eternity. He learned to appreciate the things most people take for granted, such as nature and life in general.

Fripp also influenced the life of Conroy because it was there he had formed the fondest memories of his mother. She had been the one that had chosen Fripp for the family's beach. During the last few years of her life she walked along the shore collecting shells, a scene firmly etched into Conroy's mind. He thus began associating his beloved mother with his beloved sea. It was also the place his mother drew her last breath. It was time for Conroy to start developing some new memories.

Fripp was a haven for Conroy—a place to escape the worries of the everyday routine. This small island was very influential in making Conroy see how fabulous life was prior to the rise of industry, technology, and the like. There he learned to live life simply just as God had intended.

Why Did This Composition Get a 6?

The author of this composition shows a high level of understanding of the speech and is able to explain the ways in which places influence people. Two main points support the controlling idea: The island gives Conroy his love of nature, and the island is connected to Conroy's memories of his mother.

The composition uses specific details from the speech, but also stays focused on the controlling idea. The style and the level of language are appropriate, and the writer is skillful with words. He or she ends the composition with a nice kicker. There are few errors in conventions, and thus this composition receives full credit (6 points).

WHAT IF I RUN OUT OF TIME?

You have very little control over how long it takes your proctor to read the directions, the speech, and then the speech again. However, do not worry if he or she seems to be going slowly—you can use all that time to identify and underline the audience and controlling idea, take notes, and plan your composition. You should be concerned only if the proctor is moving too quickly.

Here is a general breakdown of how you should spend your time on Session One, Part A.

You will have approximately 90 minutes.

- 3–5 minutes—reading and understanding the Overview, the Situation, and Your Task, and underlining the most important parts, especially the audience and the task

- 5 minutes—taking notes while listening to the first reading

- 2–3 minutes—looking over your notes and thinking about how they relate to the task

- 5 minutes—taking notes while listening to the second reading

- 5 minutes—choosing and marking the points you want to use in your composition

- 5–10 minutes—answering the multiple-choice questions

- 10–15 minutes—planning your composition and writing the outline and/or creating a concept map

- 30 minutes—actually writing the composition

- 5 minutes—proofreading the composition

This schedule is only an estimate, because it may take your proctor more or less time to read the speech.

There are only two points at which you should check your timing during Session One, Part A—while you are answering the multiple-choice questions, and when you are nearing the 90-minute point.

The Multiple-Choice Checkpoint

You should spend about 90 minutes for all of Session One, Part A, so you should take no more than 10 minutes to answer the multiple-choice questions. There are only five or six questions, and the composition is worth more toward your score. Make sure you do not spend more than 10 minutes on these questions.

Closing In on the Finish Line

If you have spent about 80 minutes on Part A, and you have not yet started writing your conclusion, you should quickly finish the body paragraph you are working on and jot down a conclusion. Readers will be left dissatisfied with any composition, no matter how brilliant, if it lacks a conclusion.

If you can, try to think of some way to relate the controlling idea to the world at large. If you cannot think of some way to make a profound statement about your controlling idea, just restate it, referring to the support you have given it. In any case, always write something that wraps up the composition.

CHAPTER 3
CRACKING SESSION ONE, PART B: THE READING FOR INFORMATION SECTION

Session One, Part B, of the Regents Comprehensive Examination in English tests your ability to understand, interpret, and use information provided in a set of documents. The test gives you both a written text and a series of visuals—generally charts, tables, or graphs—each of which presents information about a specific topic or issue. You have approximately 90 minutes to answer a series of multiple-choice questions and write one composition based on this information. Here is a sample of the information you are given at the beginning of Session One, Part B.

SESSION ONE, PART B

Directions: Read the text and study the graphs on the following pages, answer the multiple-choice questions, and write a response based on the situation described below. You may use the margins to take notes as you read and scrap paper to plan your response.

The Situation: A community health clinic has invited students in your school to write health-related articles for its newsletter. You decide to write an article discussing factors that influence teenage smoking and the implications of those factors for reducing teenage smoking.

Your Task: Write an article for the community health newsletter. Using relevant information from the text and graphs, discuss the factors that influence teenage smoking and the implications of those factors for reducing teenage smoking.

Guidelines:

Be sure to

- Tell your audience what they need to know about the factors that influence teenage smoking

- Discuss the implications of those factors for reducing teenage smoking

- Use specific, accurate, and relevant information from the text *and* the graphs to support your discussion

- Use a tone and level of language appropriate for a community health newsletter

- Organize your ideas in a logical and coherent manner

- Indicate any words taken directly from the speech by using quotation marks or referring to the author

- Follow the conventions of standard written English

THE FIRST AND MOST IMPORTANT STEP

It may seem obvious, but the first step—reading the text and looking at the visuals—is also the most important. Take the time to read the text carefully, look at the visuals, and understand the information that is presented to you. If you don't take the time to really understand and interpret the given text and visuals, you will have difficulty with both the composition and the multiple-choice questions.

Read Actively

Consider the provided documents a big box of tools for you to use in writing your composition. As you read the documents, you should think of yourself going through the toolbox and inspecting one tool at a time. When you see something that looks useful or interesting, circle it, underline it, or put a star beside it to make it easy to find later on.

You may also find it useful to use a technique we call paragraph labeling. As you read the text, pause after each paragraph and write in the margin a very brief (between five and ten words should be sufficient) summary of what information is included in the paragraph. These paragraph labels make it easy for you to see, at a glance, the structure of the text. They also make it possible for you to quickly find answers to the multiple-choice questions because they can guide you straight to the information you need.

Look for Connections

Be sure to mark any connections between the information presented in the text and the information presented in the visuals. In many cases the visuals present specific examples or statistical information to support the more general topics covered in the text. The points where the text and the visuals connect are very important for you to include in your composition.

Be a Critic

As you read the text, decide which points are most and least convincing. You might, for instance, find the tobacco industry's claim that the increase in teenage smoking is due to teenagers' natural rebelliousness to be an easy point with which to disagree. The example of the student who buys only one brand of cigarette because of the coupons he saves might be the most compelling point from the text. Depending on the task you are given, these are excellent points to either support or attack in your composition.

Now that you know some things to think about and do as you read, here is a set of documents from the sample Session One, Part B, Regents Comprehensive Examination in English. Read through them and keep in mind everything we have just covered.

Researchers calculate that teenage smoking rates, after declining in the 1970s and leveling off in the 1980s, have climbed sharply over the last five years. Although everything from why the trend began to what might stop it is disputed, it adds up to a huge health problem for the country and a public relations disaster for the tobacco industry.

Teenage smoking rates are still lower than in the 1970s, but they are rapidly increasing. According to the most recent edition of the University of Michigan's Monitoring the Future survey, last year the percentage of twelfth-graders who smoked daily was up 20 percent from 1991. This annual study is widely followed by tobacco researchers. The rate among tenth-graders jumped 45 percent, and the rate for eighth-graders was up 44 percent between 1991 and 1996.

At current smoking rates, five million people now younger than 18 will eventually die of tobacco-related illnesses, according to the most recent projections from the Centers for Disease Control and Prevention in Atlanta.

Rising youth smoking rates have been cited by the Food and Drug Administration and President Clinton as evidence that the industry is marketing its products to youths and should be restricted by the Food and Drug Administration. The rates are also fueling demands in many states and nationally for higher taxes on tobacco, based on research showing that price increases typically discourage teen smokers.

Just what has caused the teenage smoking rate to rise so sharply is hotly debated. The tobacco industry says the increase is due to a broad range of social forces. Industry officials note that other kinds of risk-taking among teenagers, especially the use of marijuana and other drugs, have risen more sharply than tobacco use. The industry also cites teenagers' naturally rebellious reaction to the increasing efforts to stop them from smoking.

Critics of the tobacco industry agree that rebelliousness and other forces are at work. But they say the industry itself is the most important factor. The industry's spending on domestic advertising and promotions soared from $361 million in 1970 to $4.83 billion in 1994, a 250 percent increase after adjusting for inflation, according to the latest data published by the Federal Trade Commission.

Just how that huge pie has been divided is a secret closely guarded not only from critics but even among companies in the industry. Much of the money goes into promotions to encourage retailers to run sales or to display particular brands and signs more prominently. Tobacco companies say that they have adopted practices to focus their message on adults, like requiring that all models be—and look—older than twenty-five.

But critics like John Pierce, head of the Cancer Prevention Center at the University of California—San Diego, say it is most telling that spending rose most rapidly in the 1980s, when the decline in youth smoking was halted. They also point to research showing that children have been strongly attracted to some of the biggest marketing campaigns, notably R.J. Reynolds Tobacco's use of the ever-hip Joe Camel and Philip Morris's use of the rugged Marlboro Man and the Marlboro Adventure Team, a merchandise promotion.

The surge in teenage smoking in the 1990s coincided with a sharp expansion by both R.J. Reynolds and Phillip Morris in giveaways of items like T-shirts in return for coupons accumulated by buying their cigarettes. Research showed that the companies had limited success in preventing distribution of the merchandise to children—30 percent of teenage smokers have it—and that the items are just as appealing to teenagers as to adults.

Tobacco companies say critics grossly exaggerate the effects of their marketing. They point out that teenage smoking is also rising in countries where most forms of advertising have been banned.

The latest indicator of the distance between the two sides is Phillip Morris's creation of a record company—Woman Thing Music—to promote its Virginia Slims brand. The company will be selling bargain-priced compact discs by its female artists along with its cigarettes. Its first artist, Martha Byrne, a nonsmoking actress from the soap opera As the World Turns, is on a concert tour. She is appearing in venues where only those older than twenty-one are allowed.

Making matters worse, some critics say, is that Hollywood's long love affair with smoking seems to be heating up. Cigars are being widely used to symbolize success in movies like The Associate, with Whoopi Goldberg. And even though today's stars are not inseparable from their cigarettes the way Humphrey Bogart, Bette Davis, and James Dean were, actors who have shown up puffing on cigarettes include John Travolta and Uma Thurman as antiheroes in Pulp Fiction and Winona Ryder as a Generation X drifter in Reality Bites. Leonardo Di Caprio went so far as to light up as Romeo in last year's Romeo and Juliet.

Whether smoking in films contributes to the teenage trend or simply picks up on it is one of the many questions. Teenagers say that movie and music stars shape their sense of what is "cool" and that a desire to be cool is often a reason the youngest smokers first try cigarettes. But many researchers doubt that an effect can be readily measured.

Moreover, high school students who smoke regularly say it is so common that no one thinks of it as cool. Some concede that they enjoy doing something forbidden, but more often they cite a desire to relieve stress or to stay thin, the taste, or simply the need to fill time as reasons they kept smoking to the point of becoming addicted. Many, like David Bernt of Oak Park, agree with the industry's contention that its marketing has nothing to do with the decision to smoke but that it does influence brand choice.

"If I buy anything but Camel, it feels like I wasted money because I collect Camel cash," he said, referring to the coupons that can be redeemed for Camel merchandise.

The increased smoking rates since 1991 are expected to translate into tens of thousands of additional early deaths because one out of three teenage smokers is expected to develop fatal tobacco-related illnesses. About 46,000 more eighth-graders are smoking at least half a pack a day than in 1991, and 250,000 more have smoked within the last 30 days than in 1991, judging from the application of census data to results from the Monitoring the Future surveys. And, because of the rising smoking rate since 1991, an extra 110,000 tenth-graders are half-a-pack-a-day smokers, and nearly 366,000 more of them have smoked in the last 30 days.

—B. Feder

Graph 1

Half a Pack At an Early Age

Percentage in each grade who told surveyers that they smoke at least half a pack of cigarettes a day.

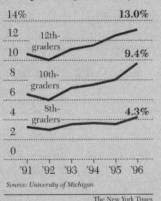

Source: University of Michigan

The New York Times

Graph 2

Teenage Smoking Makes a Comeback

The number of 12th-graders who try cigarettes has declined over the last two decades, but the number who smoke occasionally and who develop heavier habits has increased sharply in recent years.

Of 12th-graders surveyed:

Source: University of Michigan

The New York Times

CREATE SUMMARY NOTES

The next step, once you have read the text and looked carefully at the visuals, is to create a quick set of summary notes of the information. Write down, in as few words as possible, the conclusion or underlying message that you find in the documents. Then quickly jot down a list of the specific points of evidence that were presented in the text and visuals in support of that conclusion. Don't forget to include the information from the visuals in this list. Having these notes will help you easily find ways to write your composition based on the information given to you.

Write your summary notes for the documents on the lines below.

_____

_____

_____

_____

_____

_____

_____

_____

_____

_____

_____

_____

_____

_____

_____

_____

_____

_____

_____

Here are our sample summary notes. Don't worry if yours aren't exactly the same, but look to see if you included some of the same points we did.

C̲O̲N̲C̲L̲U̲S̲I̲O̲N̲: *Cigarette marketing has caused more teenagers to smoke.*
> *Evidence: Text—use of characters and major marketing campaigns*
> *Evidence: Text—Free merchandise to brand-loyal customers*
> *Evidence: Text—Hollywood's portrayal of smoking in film*
> *Evidence: Graph 1—From eighth through twelfth grade, more students are smoking at least half a pack of cigarettes a day.*
> *Evidence: Graph 2—Smoking among twelfth-graders declined from 1975 to 1990. It is now on the increase again.*

THE MULTIPLE-CHOICE QUESTIONS

You've read the documents and written your summary notes. Before you start actually writing your composition, you should tackle the multiple-choice questions. There will be eight to ten multiple-choice questions in Session One, Part B. Don't spend too much time on them because you'll need most of the time to plan and write a good composition. Plan to spend no more than 10 minutes working on the multiple-choice questions. If, after 10 minutes, you are still stumped by a question or two, just take your best guess and move on to the composition. You should always guess rather than leave a question blank. Here are some strategies to help you do well on the multiple-choice section of Session One, Part B.

This Is an "Open-Document" Test

Think of these questions as part of an open-book test you might take in one of your regular classes. On an open-book test, you refer to your textbook as you answer the questions. Be sure to do the same thing on this part of the exam. The documents, both text and visuals, are there for you, so you should use them. Don't rely on your memory to answer the questions.

Use Your Paragraph Labels

The brief paragraph labels you write as you read the text should serve as an excellent resource as you look back to find information to help you answer the questions correctly. Here's an example.

▶ Rising youth smoking rates have led the FDA to propose
  (1) a national antismoking campaign
  (2) a federal lawsuit against the tobacco industry
  (3) restrictions on marketing tobacco products to teenagers
  (4) denial of insurance coverage for smokers

The question asks about a specific detail related to the FDA. If you look back at the labels you wrote, you will likely see the FDA mentioned in your label for the fourth paragraph. Now read that paragraph again, looking for what the FDA has proposed in response to rising youth smoking rates. The paragraph mentions that "the industry is marketing its products to youths and should be restricted by the FDA." Which answer choice says the same thing? Choice (3). All it takes is a little detective work to answer these questions, and with some good paragraph labels to point the way, you should be able to find the correct answer choices quickly.

Two Kinds of Questions

The multiple-choice questions fall into two basic categories—general and specific.

General Questions

General questions ask you about the document as a whole. They likely include phrases such as "main idea" or "primary purpose." An excellent source of information to help you answer general questions is the summary notes you write after you finish reading the documents.

To show you how to answer these questions, look at a classic general question.

▶ What is the main purpose of the text?
   (1) to criticize the tobacco industry
   (2) to persuade readers not to smoke
   (3) to offer solutions to the problem of teenage smoking
   (4) to report on the increase in teenage smoking

This is not a question about a specific part of the text, but rather the text as a whole. Look at the summary notes you wrote. What did you pick out as the main idea? Hopefully it is something like, "Teenage smoking rates have climbed recently, in part because of cigarette marketing targeted at teens." Now look at the answer choices. The text does, at least indirectly, criticize the tobacco industry, and it does include some details that might persuade readers not to smoke, but which one of the answer choices is closest to your summary? Answer choice (4).

Specific Questions

The majority of the multiple-choice questions are likely to be specific. These questions ask you about a fact or detail found in either the text or the visuals, and generally tell you in which one the answer will be found. Answering these questions, if not always easy, is entirely straightforward. You should use your paragraph labels so that you can look back and quickly find the correct answer choice.

▶ The text implies that Hollywood may influence teenagers to smoke by

(1) shaping their sense of what is trendy

(2) indirectly advertising cigarettes in movies

(3) selling cigarettes in movie theaters

(4) giving them false information

The question asks about Hollywood and its influence on teenage smoking. Look back at those trusty paragraph labels for a mention of Hollywood. You find two paragraphs—the first starting at line 54 of the text and the second, one paragraph later, starting at line 61. By reading those two paragraphs, you find out that by showing actors smoking in films, Hollywood does shape teenagers' "sense of what is 'cool,'" (lines 62–63). The correct answer choice is (1).

If at First You Don't Succeed, Use POE

Remember that you want to move through the multiple-choice questions somewhat quickly. If you get stuck on a question and can't seem to find the correct answer choice, you can use Process of Elimination (POE) to eliminate wrong answer choices and then take a good guess. How can you spot a wrong answer choice? Look for choices that, for one reason or another, don't seem to answer the question. Check out the following examples:

▶ The text implies that one result of raising taxes on tobacco is that

(1) the FDA will restrict tobacco sales

(2) retailers will lower cigarette prices

(3) tobacco companies will advertise less

(4) teenagers will buy fewer cigarettes

Think about answer choice (2). Is a result of increasing taxes on tobacco that retailers will lower cigarette prices? Probably not. Retailers would be more likely to raise prices if taxes on tobacco were raised. So you can eliminate choice (2).

▶ According to the text, teenage smoking increased at the same time that the tobacco industry increased its promotion of

(1) long, slim cigarettes

(2) giveaway items

(3) more effective filters

(4) reduced nicotine cigarettes

Think about answer choice (1)—it might be possible, but long, slim cigarettes don't seem to have an obvious connection to teenage smoking. Eliminate it.

▶ The text implies that Hollywood may influence teenagers to smoke by

(1) shaping their sense of what is trendy

(2) indirectly advertising cigarettes in movies

(3) selling cigarettes in movie theaters

(4) giving them false information

You've seen this question before. Look at the answer choices. Which one can you most easily eliminate? Answer choice (3)—are cigarettes sold in movie theaters? Not lately.

▶ What does Graph 2 imply about twelfth-graders in 1995?

(1) About 40 percent of them did not smoke at all.

(2) About 40 percent of them developed tobacco-related illnesses.

(3) Twelfth-graders smoked primarily on weekends.

(4) Twelfth-graders started smoking in elementary school.

From even a quick look at the graph, you can see that there isn't any information about the days of the week on which teenagers smoke. You can eliminate answer choice (3) right away.

Using this kind of common sense can help you get rid of a few wrong answer choices and take more accurate guesses. The important thing to remember is to keep moving through the multiple-choice questions so that you will have plenty of time to write an excellent composition.

THE COMPOSITION

Start with a Plan

Before you begin writing your composition, take a few minutes to think carefully about what you are going to write. You should be sure to use the summary notes you wrote for the documents. Go back and reread the instructions for Session One, Part B, as you start to plan, paying special attention to the way Your Task is described.

Once you have all of these things firmly in mind, here are some important steps for you to follow.

Consider Your Audience

First consider your audience. The task or the guidelines given to you in the directions for Session One, Part B, will tell you for whom you are writing your composition.

As you prepare to write, keep your audience in mind and be sure to use an appropriate tone and level of detail. If the assignment tells you to write a composition for an audience that is already familiar with the topic, don't waste your time by giving too much introductory information. On the other hand, if you can't be sure your reader knows very much about the topic, provide whatever background is necessary for him or her to understand your points.

The Controlling Idea

Once you consider the information given to you by the test and the audience for whom you are writing, you are ready to decide what you want your composition to say. Before you take the next step, though, go back once again and read the task. Here you will find the underlying theme or controlling idea that you should use throughout your composition. Sometimes it is stated, and other times it is only suggested.

The concept of a controlling idea is an important one for this assignment. The documents provide you with a good amount of background information on a specific topic. Your job, in writing your composition, is to use this raw material to support the controlling idea. Be sure not to make the mistake of writing a composition that does not include evidence to support your main point. You will receive a lower score if you fail to provide evidence to support your point.

The task may ask you to discuss the general topic of the documents from a particular viewpoint or perspective. In this case, you should consider each of the supporting facts that you find in the text and visuals in light of that viewpoint. The sample composition assignment on teenage smoking is an excellent example of this sort of task. The documents provide information about the increase in teenage smoking and the link to cigarette marketing, and the task asks you to write an article discussing "factors that influence teenage smoking and the implications of those factors for reducing teenage smoking." The controlling idea, or perspective in this case, is suggested by "the implications of those factors taken from the documents for reducing teenage smoking." Your approach would be to briefly mention the factors that influence teenage smoking, and add to them by discussing how each one might be used in an effort to reduce teenage smoking.

A slightly different task may provide you with similar background information, but ask you to make an argument for or against one side of a debate. In this case, you should use as many of the supporting facts as possible from the text and visuals to make your argument.

There are many possible tasks that you may be given on your test. Don't spend time thinking in advance about what your task might be, but once you have the test in front of you, make certain that you know what the task is. If you are unclear, go back to the directions, find it, and underline it. If you have a good understanding of the task, your composition will have more focus.

Use All Documents

As you plan your composition, it is important for you to use information from both the text and the visuals in your response. Your composition is scored on a 6-point scale, but if you fail to address one of the documents, your composition may receive a score no higher than 3. This is one reason that the connections between the text and the visuals are so incredibly important.

Make an Outline or a Concept Map

Keeping in mind your audience and the controlling idea, you are finally ready to begin an outline or a concept map to serve as a plan for your composition. An outline is an easy way to organize information in an ordered, start-to-finish format. By now you're familiar with outlines from Session One, Part A, so you definitely have at least a general sense of how to make one.

Concept maps, as we mentioned in Chapter 1, give you more freedom to organize your thoughts, and in Session One, Part B, they may be useful when you don't quickly see the connections between different ideas you found in the documents. If you prefer to use a concept map, you can usually start with a general concept and then build outward from there. Each separate path that comes from your general topic should turn into one paragraph in your composition.

If you choose to create an outline, always start with an introduction where you briefly explain the general topic or argument of your composition and introduce some of the evidence or points that relate to your controlling idea.

The second part of your outline should include the body paragraphs where you introduce and discuss some or all of the key supporting facts from the text and visuals. You can easily create this part of your outline by looking back at the summary notes you made from the text and visuals. While keeping in mind the task you have been given, try to include as many of the supporting facts as you can. If there are some supporting facts included on the test that don't apply to the task, leave them out.

The final part of your outline is the conclusion. In one or two paragraphs at the end of your composition, you should bring together all of the points you made in the context of the controlling idea. In the conclusion, be certain to restate the purpose of your composition, which should incorporate the controlling idea specified by the task. You can also repeat one or two of the most powerful points you made in your composition.

On the next two pages, try making an outline first and then a concept map for the task about teenage smoking. You probably won't always create both while you take the Regents Comprehensive Examination in English, but in this case it will give you a good sense of which one you find more effective for organizing your thoughts.

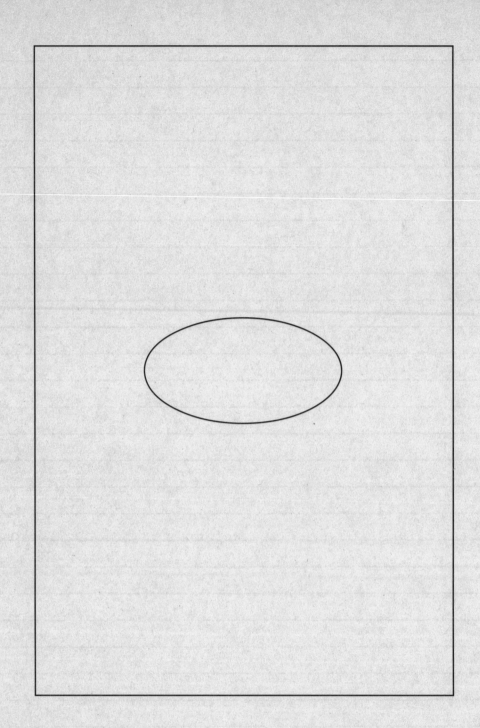

Here are our samples, which are probably different from the ones you made. It's okay if they're different as long as you included the major points that relate to the task.

Sample Outline

INTRODUCTION
- Teenage smoking on the rise
- Include statistics from Graphs 1 and 2
- Examining reasons why teens smoke can help to reduce teenage smoking

BODY PARAGRAPH 1
- Cigarette companies are targeting teens with ads
- Mention $ spent on promotions—Camel cash, etc.
- Propose that cigarette companies' advertising plans and budgets be reviewed to limit their appeal to teens

BODY PARAGRAPH 2
- Hollywood and other entertainment media show smoking in a favorable light
- Mention films showing cigarette and cigar smoking as either "cool" behavior or a sign of success
- Mention Virginia Slims record label and concert promotions
- Propose that restrictions be implemented to change the way smoking is portrayed by entertainers, especially those who appeal to teenagers

BODY PARAGRAPH 3
- Children are starting to smoke at an earlier age
- Mention Graph 1, showing that the percentage of students who smoked at least half a pack a day increased more between grade 8 and grade 10 than between grade 10 and grade 12
- Antismoking campaigns need to target students at young ages because many students start to smoke before they begin high school

CONCLUSION
- Limitations on the cigarette industry's rights to advertise and promote its products are important
- Smoking has been proven to kill people (include statistics from text) and the best way to reduce smoking is to stop children from ever starting
- Early prevention campaigns, limitations on advertising and promotion, and a general change in the way smokers appear in the media are the best ways to reduce teenage smoking

Sample Concept Map

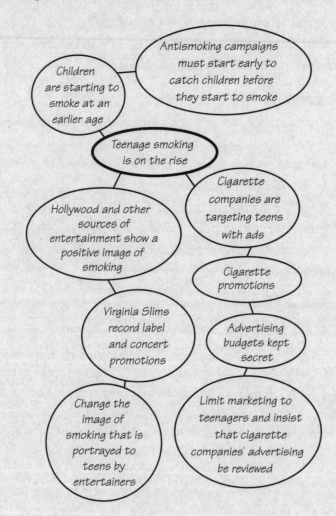

If you choose to make a concept map instead of an outline, you must remember to include a thorough introduction and conclusion. Also, remember not to focus so heavily on the concepts in the documents that you forget what the task asked you to do. Notice in this example that the final oval in each chain is the most important one because it makes the connection between the information provided and the task assigned.

You may be tempted to think that you can skip making an outline or a map and go straight to writing your composition. Don't fool yourself! Making a good outline or map will take you no more than 5 or 10 minutes (if you made a good set of summary notes of the text and visuals after you read them). With a strong guide, your composition will have the focus and organization necessary to earn a good score.

Once you finish your outline or map, make a final check to see that you covered both the written text and the visuals. If one of the documents is missing, go back and incorporate it in an appropriate place.

WRITING A HIGH-SCORING SESSION ONE, PART B, COMPOSITION

As with the Session One, Part A, composition, you will receive a score for your composition based on a 6-point scale. As you plan and write your composition, keep these five qualities in mind: meaning, development, organization, language use, and conventions. If your composition scores high in these five qualities, you'll receive full credit (6 points).

Meaning

Meaning is based on how well you understand the information provided in the documents and how clearly you relate that information to the assigned task. Remember the toolbox analogy here. Your job is to go through the documents, look at each piece of information as a tool, and then use those tools to complete the task you have been assigned. You will do well if you stay focused. You can be a little bit creative, but don't try to use a screwdriver to hammer in a nail.

Development

To do well in this area, you need to develop your ideas clearly and effectively, using specific evidence to make your points. One of the most important things to bear in mind here is that your composition must include specific evidence. If you write using only vague generalities, even if they are drawn from the documents, you will lose points. If the documents give you statistics or examples that help make your point, use them. Remember that your audience has not read the documents, so you should not be shy about repeating any relevant evidence as long as you also refer to its source.

Organization

If you take the time to create a good outline, you will have no trouble with organization. In addition to the basics of the introduction, body, and conclusion, remember to stay focused and make use of transitions. Your composition must have an underlying purpose, as specified in the task. Make sure your writing sticks to this purpose. If you stay focused, logical transitions between ideas and paragraphs should come naturally. You can refer to the general composition guidelines beginning on page 6 for more information about organization and transitions.

Language Use

The Regents test scorers look for language that is both sophisticated and appropriate. To receive a high score for language use, try to use some impressive vocabulary words. However, don't throw words into your composition that you don't know how to use or spell. A misused or misspelled word, no matter how impressive it may be, always sticks out like a sore thumb. Also, keep your audience in mind as you look for opportunities to use some of those impressive words you learned in your English class. Don't use terms that are too advanced or too technical for the purpose of your composition (which is indicated in Your Task). If this area concerns you, the general composition guidelines section beginning on page 6 will give you more detailed information about language use.

Conventions

Ever since you took your first spelling test and learned the difference between a subject and a predicate, you have been learning the things necessary to do well with conventions. Much more information about some common mistakes to watch for can be found in the general composition guidelines section beginning on page 6.

SAMPLE STUDENT COMPOSITION

Before you read this top-score student composition, write your own composition for the Session One, Part B, task at the beginning of this chapter. Then read the sample composition and the explanation of why it received full credit (6 points).

Score Level 6

TEENAGE SMOKING

There is an epidemic on the rise in the youth of America today. Researchers conclude that teenage smoking rates, after declining and leveling off in the 1970s and 1980s have increased sharply in the last five years. The tobacco industry, its critics, and even teenagers themselves, all have ideas about the factors that influence smoking.

The tobacco industry attributes the increase to "a broad range of social forces." The industry says that other drug-use and risk-taking procedures by teenagers have risen more sharply than tobacco use. The industry also believes that teenage smoking has increased because of the rebellious attitudes of teens towards increasing efforts to stop them from smoking.

The industry's critics, however, disagree with this hypothesis. The critics believe that the industry's huge increase in spending on domestic advertising and promotions, from $361 million in 1970, to $483 billion in 1994, is to blame. Most of the money goes into promotions that encourage stores to run sales or more prominently display particular brands and signs. Spending by the industry increased most rapidly in the 1980s when the decline in youth smoking was halted. Teens are also attracted to the advertising campaigns that use Joe Camel or the Marlboro Man. The giving-away of items, such as T-shirts, for coupons received when buying cigarettes, also attracts teens. Phillip Morris even created a record company to promote its Virginia Slims brand that is a draw to teens. Hollywood's use of cigarettes and cigars is also becoming more prevalent and is subliminally encouraging teens to take up smoking because it is trendy and "cool."

Teenagers say that a desire to be cool is often a reason young smokers try cigarettes. Teenagers also say that smoking is a way to relieve stress, stay thin, and a way to fill time. Teenagers also say they are drawn to smoking because of their desire to do something forbidden.

This trend in teenage smoking must end. The growing smoking rates are expected to translate into additional early deaths due to tobacco-related illnesses. This trend can be ended by increasing the cost of cigarettes, making them too expensive for teens to buy. Hollywood should also place a ban on the use of cigarettes and cigars in their films, so as not to project the message that smoking is cool. More awareness can made to teens about the effect that smoking would have on their bodies in the future. The tobacco industry should also not be allowed to use advertising that is intended to draw teens to their products. This epidemic of increased smoking by teens must end and it takes an effort by all to end it. Join the battle to end teen smoking!

Why Did This Composition Get a 6?

The author does an excellent job of organizing the composition by viewpoint: first the viewpoint of the cigarette companies, then that of their critics, then of teenagers themselves. This structure permits a smooth transition from one paragraph and set of ideas to the next. All the mechanical details—grammar, spelling, sentence structure, and language use—are in great shape. The author does a terrific job of using the documents to make strong points in the composition. Finally, the composition is written with a sense of its audience, particularly the concluding sentence, which is a nearly perfect example of a kicker.

WHAT IF I RUN OUT OF TIME?

Time is definitely an important factor to consider when thinking about Session One, Part B, of the test. You have 90 minutes to read the documents, answer the multiple-choice questions, and write your composition. Here is a general breakdown of how you should spend the time you are given.

- 20 minutes—reading and understanding the documents, including writing paragraph labels

- 5 minutes—writing a brief summary of the documents

- 10 minutes—answering the multiple-choice questions

- 5 minutes—reading and understanding the composition task

- 15 minutes—planning your composition, including writing an outline and/or creating a concept map

- 25 minutes—actually writing the composition

- 5 minutes—rereading your composition for clarity and mechanics

This schedule allows you an extra 5 minutes, but as you can see, you've got a lot to do and not a lot of time in which to do it. There are two points during this section where you should think about your timing.

The Multiple-Choice Checkpoint

First, as you begin the multiple-choice questions, glance at your watch and add 10 minutes to the time. This tells you when you should be moving on to the composition portion of the task. Make sure you don't take more than 10 minutes to complete this section because the composition is worth more toward your final score.

Closing In on the Finish Line

Your second checkpoint should be 10 minutes before the test is over. If you reach the point at which you have 10 minutes left and you have not yet started your conclusion, wrap up the body paragraph you are working on and go directly into your conclusion. It is better to leave one or two points from your outline unmade than it is to submit an essay without a conclusion. Don't become so preoccupied with time, though, that you waste precious minutes figuring out how much time is left on the test. Stay focused and follow the schedule above, and you should be just fine.

CHAPTER 4
CRACKING SESSION TWO, PART A: THE LITERARY PASSAGES SECTION

Session Two, Part A, of the Regents Comprehensive Examination in English focuses on two passages in different genres written about a similar topic or theme. The genre of each passage usually appears within the directions. You may be presented with passages of the following types: a composition, an excerpt from a story, a poem, or a section of a play. Here is a sample of the information you are given at the beginning of Session Two, Part A.

SESSION TWO, PART A

Directions: Read the passages on the following pages (a poem and an excerpt from a story) and answer the multiple-choice questions. Then write the essay described in **Your Task.** You may use the margins to take notes as you read and scrap paper to plan your response.

> **Your Task:** After you have read the passages and answered the multiple-choice questions, write a unified essay about the effects of war on the soldiers who do the fighting, as revealed in the passages. In your essay, use ideas from both passages to establish a controlling idea. Using evidence from each passage, develop your controlling idea and show how each author uses specific literary elements or techniques to convey that idea.

Guidelines:

Be sure to

- Use ideas from both passages to establish a controlling idea about the effects of war on the soldiers who do the fighting, as revealed in the passages

- Use specific and relevant evidence from each passage to develop your controlling idea

- Show how each author uses specific literary elements (for example: theme, characterization, structure, point of view) or techniques (for example: symbolism, irony, figurative language) to portray the effects of war on the soldiers who do the fighting

- Organize your ideas in a logical and coherent manner

- Use language that communicates ideas effectively

- Follow the conventions of standard written English

HOW TO READ

The two reading passages for Session Two, Part A, always represent two different genres. A readily apparent "unifying theme" always connects both texts. The task and guidelines above show you that part of the controlling idea is the effects of war on soldiers. It is your job to read the passages to determine what effects war has on soldiers, based on what the two pieces of writing have in common. It sounds a little confusing, but the important thing to remember is that the task and guidelines will always tell you what to look for as you read. As you read each passage, first make note of the text's genre. Are you reading a piece of drama? A poem? A composition? Then, think about its main theme.

Create Summary Notes

As you read, write a brief set of summary notes for each passage. When writing your summary notes, use your own words to answer the following two questions.

- What is the message? What does the author want the reader to remember after reading the passage?

- How do I know what the message is? What clues, found in both the specific language the author uses and the structure of the passage, show you the author's message? What figurative language does the author use? What are the parts that are most powerful? What is repeated? Are there symbols? Imagery?

First go back and reread the directions, task, and guidelines, and then read the two passages that follow.

Passage I

Our brains ache, in the merciless iced east winds that knive us . . .

Wearied we keep awake because the night is silent . . .

Low, drooping flares confuse our memory of the salient

Worried by silence, sentries whisper, curious, nervous,

5   But nothing happens

Watching, we hear the mad gusts tugging on the wire,

Like twitching agonies of men among its brambles.

Northward, incessantly, the flickering gunnery rumbles,

Far off, like a dull rumour of some other war.

10   What are we doing here?

The poignant misery of dawn begins to grow . . .

We only know war lasts, rain soaks, and clouds sag stormy.

Dawn massing in the east her melancholy army

Attacks once more in ranks on shivering ranks of gray,

15   But nothing happens.

Sudden successive flights of bullets streak the silence.

Less deadly than the air that shudders black with snow

With sideling flowing flacks that flock, pause and renew,

We watch them wandering up and down the wind's nonchalance,

20   But nothing happens.

Pale flakes with fingering stealth come feeling for our face—

We cringe in holes, back on forgotten dreams, and stare, snow-dazed.

Deep into the grassier ditches. So we drowse, sun-dozed,

Littered with blossoms trickling where the blackbird fusses.

25   Is it that we are dying?

Slowly our ghosts drag home: glimpsing the sunk fires, glozed

With crusted dark-red jewels; crickets jingle there;

For hours the innocent mice rejoice: the house is theirs;

Shutters and doors, all closed: on us the doors are closed,—

30   We turn back to our dying.

Since we believe not otherwise can kind fires burn;

Nor ever suns smile true on child, or field or fruit.

For God's invincible spring our love is made afraid;

Therefore, not loath, we lie out here; therefore were born,

35   For love of God seems dying.

Tonight, His frost will fasten on this mud and us,

Shrivelling many hands, puckering foreheads crisp.

The burying-party, picks and shovels in their shaking grasp,

Pause over half-known faces. All their eyes are ice,

40   But nothing happens

—Wilfred Owen

Passage II

They carried USO stationery and pencils and pens. They carried Sterno, safety pins,
trip flares, signal flares, spools of wire, razor blades, chewing tobacco, statuettes of
the smiling Buddha, candles, grease pencils, The Stars and Stripes, fingernail
clippers, bush hats, bolos, and much more. Twice a week, when the resupply
5 choppers came in, they carried hot chow in green mermite cans and large canvas
bags filled with iced beer and soda pop. They carried plastic water containers, each
with a two-gallon capacity. Mitchell Sanders carried a set of starched tiger fatigues
for special occasions. Henry Dobbins carried Black Flag insecticide. Dave Jensen
carried empty sandbags that could be filled at night for added protection. Lee Strunk
10 carried tanning lotion. Some things they carried in common. Taking turns, they
carried the big PRC-77 scrambler radio, which weighed thirty pounds with its
battery. They shared the weight of memory. They took up what others could no
longer bear. Often, they carried each other, the wounded or weak. They carried
infections. They carried chess sets, basketballs, Vietnamese-English dictionaries,
15 insignia of rank, Bronze Stars and Purple Hearts, plastic cards imprinted with the
Code of Conduct. They carried diseases, among them malaria and dysentery. They
carried lice and ringworm and leeches and paddy algae and various rots and molds.
They carried the land itself—Vietnam, the place, the soil . . . the stink of fungus, and
decay, all of it, they carried gravity.

—Tim O'Brien

Now write your own summary notes for each passage. Ask yourself the following two questions: What is the message? How do I know? Use a separate sheet of paper if you need more space.

_____

_____

_____

_____

_____

_____

_____

_____

_____

_____

_____

_____

_____

_____

_____

_____

_____

_____

_____

_____

_____

_____

_____

_____

_____

Now that you've given it a try, here is a sample set of summary notes to show you some of the things you might have included. Don't worry if yours are not identical to ours, but check to make sure you included the kinds of details we show below.

Sample Summary Notes

PASSAGE I: POEM

WHAT IS THE MESSAGE?
- War is painful and unreal to the soldiers

How do I know?
- Weather imagery: painful winds, soaking rain, mad gusts of wind
- Repetition at the end of stanzas 1, 3, 4, and 8: "But nothing happens"
- Mood: restlessness, fear, and uncertainty

PASSAGE II: ESSAY

WHAT IS THE MESSAGE?
- War is heavy for the soldiers, both literally and figuratively

How do I know?
- Repetition of words "they carried"
- Organization goes from literal items (USO stationery, the PRC-77 scrambler radio, fatigues, tanning lotion) to figurative ones (memory, the land itself, decay, gravity)
- Structure (one paragraph) emphasizes the heaviness of all that the soldiers carried without a break

LITERARY VOCABULARY

Both the multiple-choice questions and the essay ask you to refer to a variety of literary elements and techniques. These are terms you have, no doubt, heard in your English classes. In case you need a quick review, refer to the list in the first chapter for the most important literary elements and techniques to know. Make sure you understand each of these, and if you are unfamiliar with any, ask your English teacher for further explanation.

THE MULTIPLE-CHOICE QUESTIONS

You've read the documents and written your summary notes. You should now tackle the multiple-choice questions, which count for roughly one-third of your overall score on Session Two, Part A. As in the other parts, do not ignore the multiple-choice questions—they can give you some quick and easy points. However, don't spend too much time on them, because you'll need time to plan and write the composition. Don't plan to spend more than 10 minutes working on the multiple-choice questions. If, after 10 minutes, you are still stumped by a question or two, take a guess and move on to the composition. You should always guess rather than leave a question blank. Here are some strategies to help you do well on the multiple-choice section of Session Two, Part A.

One Passage at a Time

The multiple-choice questions for Session Two, Part A, are divided very clearly into two sections, one based on each passage. This is good news because it makes it very clear which passage you should refer to in order to answer each question. There's more good news: Most of the multiple-choice questions ask about vocabulary in context and literary elements from the passages. These questions include references to specific lines, paragraphs, or stanzas, so you will need to spend very little time searching through the passages for the answers, making it much easier to stick to the suggested 10-minute time limit.

The test does you another favor by presenting the questions roughly in the order they appear in the passages. This allows you to start with number 1, search the literary selection far enough to find the answer, then go on to number 2 and read down further, and so on.

Using the first sample passage as an example, look at question 1.

1 The mood conveyed in the first stanza is one of
   (1) mystery
   (2) foreboding
   (3) peacefulness
   (4) confusion

What will you read to find the correct answer choice? Of course, you know the answer is in the first stanza! What is the mood conveyed in the first stanza? Although there is a mention of confusion, because the stanza refers to the soldiers as "wearied," "worried," "curious," and "nervous," the best choice is foreboding—answer choice (2).

Once you select an answer choice for question 1, check out question 2.

2 Lines 13 and 14 (Dawn . . . gray) refer to
   (1) storm clouds
   (2) advancing soldiers
   (3) hungry rats
   (4) enemy tanks

Instead of skipping straight to lines 13 and 14 to read two random lines, start reading from the end of the first stanza (where you left off). Continue on through lines 13 and 14 and the next few lines if necessary. Which answer choice is correct? Choice (1). Once you have enough context clues to answer question 2, do so and move on to question 3, picking up where you left off in the passage.

Get the idea? This approach means that you will read each passage a second time, from start to finish, as you answer the questions. This second reading helps you not only choose the correct answer choices for the multiple-choice questions but also become more familiar with the passages. That extra familiarity will be useful as your write your composition.

Tips for Avoiding Tricky Answer Choices

One literary technique that can sometimes make a question tricky is figurative language. Some questions may ask you to determine what is represented by a description that uses either symbolism or figurative language. Let's take another look at question 2 from sample passage I, along with the lines of text the question asks about.

> The poignant misery of dawn begins to grow. . .
>
> We only know war lasts, rain soaks, and clouds sag stormy.
>
> Dawn massing in the east her melancholy army
>
> Attacks once more in ranks on shivering ranks of gray,
>
> > But nothing happens.

▶ Lines 13 and 14 (Dawn . . . gray) refer to

   (1) storm clouds

   (2) advancing soldiers

   (3) hungry rats

   (4) enemy tanks

First, eliminate answer choice (3), "hungry rats," because it has nothing to do with the specific lines that you read or the general theme of the passage. A careful reading of what comes before the specific reference in lines 13 and 14 shows you that the author is talking about the weather, and rain in particular. The subject of these lines is "Dawn"; therefore, the "melancholy army" is a figurative way of describing the onset of a stormy dawn. The correct answer choice, therefore, is (1). If you failed to read carefully and consider what the author was trying to say, it would be easy to fall into the trap and select either answer choice (2) or (4) because they seem related to the general theme of war. When you answer figurative language questions, make sure you have a firm grasp of what the author is saying. This will allow you to avoid some of these tricky answer choices.

THE ESSAY

Planning Your Essay

Before you actually begin to write your essay, take a few minutes to think about what you want to say. Then brainstorm and plan a coherent and organized structure for the essay using one or both of the techniques we discuss below.

The Controlling Idea

Your Task gives you the start of the controlling idea that you must use to write your essay. The controlling idea can be supported by proof from both passages. Both passages share some common ground, or a unifying theme. Expect the two passages to approach the unifying theme from different perspectives.

Let's apply this to our sample task. The task gave you the start of the controlling idea for your essay—the effects of war on soldiers. By reading the two passages, you found that the unifying theme is that war is miserable, monotonous, and heavy for soldiers. Based on this unifying theme, you can complete the controlling idea. In this case, the controlling idea for your essay is that war takes a great toll on soldiers, both emotionally and physically, because it is miserable, monotonous, and heavy.

So to recap, the task starts the controlling idea for you, you read the two passages and find their unifying theme, and finally you use that unifying theme to complete the controlling idea you use to write your essay. You must—absolutely must—make sure that you carefully read what the task says about the controlling idea and understand it thoroughly. If you misunderstand or neglect the controlling idea, your essay will suffer and you will not receive a high score.

Search for Connections

Once you have a firm grasp of the controlling idea, start looking for connections between the two literary passages. If you utilize these connections you will write a more unified essay. That means you must refer to both passages when discussing the controlling idea. To find connections between the two passages, make an outline or create a concept map.

Whether you decide to make an outline or a concept map, think about two different components of each passage. First and foremost, consider what the passage says. Include quotes and specific examples that help support the controlling idea. Second, include the literary elements and techniques that the passage uses. Consider how each passage is structured and how it makes its points. A well-written Session Two, Part A, essay includes a discussion of not only what the passages say but also how the authors say it.

The outline is good way to brainstorm for ideas and visualize connections. You should follow the same introduction, body, and conclusion format you used on earlier parts of the exam.

Your introduction should, as always, start with a general restatement of the controlling idea, followed by more specific references to the points you will make in the body. Each body paragraph should discuss one of the connections between the controlling idea and the specific details or literary elements of the passages. Finally, your conclusion should summarize your points, restate your approach to the controlling idea, and add any final thoughts that will help tie everything together.

On the lines that follow, write your own outline for the Session Two, Part A, essay about the effects of war on soldiers.

_____

_____

_____

_____

_____

_____

_____

_____

_____

_____

_____

_____

_____

_____

_____

_____

_____

_____

_____

_____

_____

One possible outline for the sample task is shown below. Remember that there are many ways to structure your Session Two, Part A, essay, and one is not necessarily better than another.

Sample Outline

INTRODUCTION

- War is more than exciting espionage, heart-pounding battles, and thrilling intrigue

- You have to have lived it to understand it

- War is a lifestyle of uncertainty, monotony, and heaviness

BODY PARAGRAPH 1: THE MONOTONY OF WAR
- Passage 1: "But nothing happens" repeated at the end of three stanzas
- Passage 2: Repetition of sentence structure and imagery associated with carrying a heavy load (physically and emotionally)

BODY PARAGRAPH 2: THE UNCERTAINTY OF WAR
- Passage 1: Questions at the end of stanzas
- Passage 2: The things that the soldiers carry reflect uncertainty of where they are going (starched fatigues and Codes of Conduct vs. lice, ringworm, fatigue, etc.)

BODY PARAGRAPH 3: THE HEAVINESS OF WAR
- War is heavy in many ways
- Passage 1: Physical pain and emotional uncertainty for soldiers
- Passage 2: The soldiers carried many things, tangible (the radio and its battery) and intangible (the land, gravity)

CONCLUSION
- War is not glamorous or action-packed; it is monotonous, uncertain, and painful for those who live it
- Ordinary people do not understand a soldier's life

A concept map allows you to jot down points from each passage quickly and then connect these points to each other and to the controlling idea. Try making a concept map to show the controlling idea, the elements of the unifying theme that you found in the passages, and the literary techniques used in both passages. Review the list of literary terms in the first chapter if you don't know what elements and techniques to look for.

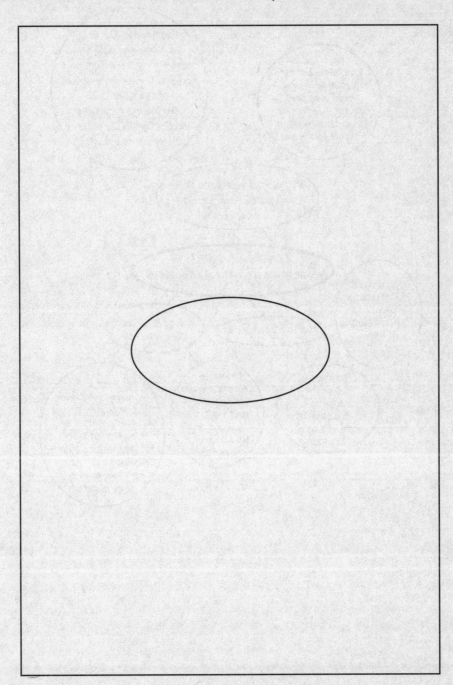

The concept map below is strong because it connects examples from both passages to each of its three primary points. Your concept map may not be so symmetrical, which is not a problem. Just be sure that you always include examples from both passages in the overall concept map.

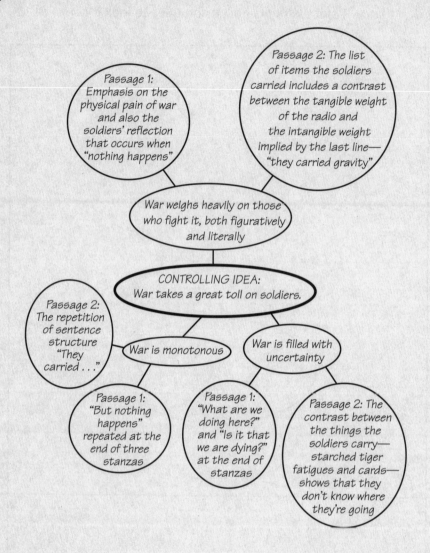

WRITING YOUR ESSAY

You will receive a score for your essay based on a 6-point scale. As you plan and write your composition, keep these five qualities in mind: meaning, development, organization, language use, and conventions. If your composition scores high in these five qualities, you'll receive full credit (6 points).

Meaning

Your essay is judged for meaning based on how well you understand what the passages said, how they said it, and how clearly you relate that message to the controlling idea. If you use the summary notes that you write for each passage to identify connections between the two passages, and then discuss these connections and the literary devices used to create them, you can expect to do well in this area.

Development

If you develop your ideas clearly and effectively, using specific evidence to make your point, you will do well in this area. One of the most important things to keep in mind here is that your essay must include specific evidence—facts and proof from both passages. Be sure to include relevant quotes from both passages to make your points clear to the reader. If you write using only vague generalities, even if they are drawn from the passages, you will lose points.

Organization

If you create a structured outline, you will have no trouble writing a well-organized essay. In addition to the basics of the introduction, body, and conclusion, remember to maintain focus and use transitions. Your essay must have an underlying purpose (as provided in the task), and you should stick to it. Do you make logical transitions from one idea or paragraph to the next? If you stay focused, these transitions should come naturally.

Language Use

The Regents test scorers look for you to use sophisticated and appropriate language. To receive a high score for language use, insert some impressive vocabulary words in your essay. Don't throw words into your essay that you don't know how to use or spell. A misused or misspelled word, no matter how impressive it may be, always sticks out.

Conventions

Ever since you took your first spelling test and learned the difference between a subject and a predicate, you have been learning the skills necessary to do well in this area. These skills include using correct spelling, grammar, and punctuation.

SAMPLE STUDENT ESSAY

Here is a sample high-scoring student essay in response to the task for Session Two, Part A, provided at the beginning of the chapter. Be sure to write your practice essay before reading the sample and the explanation of why it received a high score (5 points).

Score Level 5

The effects of war on soldiers are terrible. The description of pain, disease, stress, and unhappiness are present in both passages. Feelings of dread surround each work of literature.

In passage I, the soldiers' pain is shown in poetic form. Each stanza poses the fact that these people are unhappy, and frightened. At the beginning of the poem it states "our brains ache," and "wearied we keep awake." The poem describes the weather, and how dark, cold and silent the night is. At the end of most of the stanza's is a statement: "But nothing happens." This statement describes how the soldiers are waiting for the war, but nothing happens. This language tells the reader how expectant the soldiers are. The dread is incesant throughout this work. In stanza two the speaker speaks of the wind and how they hear "the mad gusts tugging on the wire . . ." He goes on to state that its like "twitching agonies of men among it's brambles." This image of death is a horrid one, and these soldiers must deal with it day after day. The effect of war upon these people is great. We know this by the way in which the speaker states that "We only know war lasts," and refers to dawn with "her melancholy army," which are storm clouds. Also, the speaker personifies snow flakes as "bullets." This imagery caused by the use of language is truly effective for getting across the authors point of how horrible war can be.

The second passage however takes a different form. This paragraph states the efforts of war in an entirely different manner; but poses the same answer. Throughout the paragraph the author uses monotonous language; and after repetition. He states the things that soldiers from Vietnam carried during the war. He begins by stating reasonable things that a soldier would be expected to carry: "They carried Sterno, Safety pins, trip flares, signal flares . . ." and many other reasonable items. This language and even the fact that the work is a paragraph tells the reader how monotonous and scary a soldier's life was. The effect of war on a fighting soldier is harsh; as portrayed in this paragraph. They had many things to "carry" and not are of them *were inanomit objects. The author states: "They carried each other, wounded or weak. They carried infections." The author also states that even through all this the soldier still maintained their pride. They held purple hearts, and codes of conduct. This use of language gives the reader the feeling that these were good men; they didn't give up their pride. The author concludes by using figurative language, stating the soldiers also held "gravity." This is symbolic of the weight the soldier had on their shoulder.*

Indeed, both of these works of literature provide insight to the reader on the effects of war. By using personification, verse form, and the successfull use of language the reader understood these attrocities.

Why Did This Essay Get a 5?

Overall this is a very good essay; its ideas are well developed and clearly expressed. The author has done a great job choosing details and quotes from the passages to include in his or her essay. Language use is also strong and the inclusion of some literary terms in the concluding paragraph is an excellent touch.

The essay transitions well from one topic to the next, but structurally it might be easier to read if the second and third paragraphs were each broken up into two smaller paragraphs. There are also a few mechanical errors (use of a semicolon in place of a comma, for instance) and spelling errors ("incesant," "inanomit," and two errors in the final sentence of the essay). These problems cost the author 1 point, but overall the essay is very well written.

WHAT IF I RUN OUT OF TIME?

Time is definitely an important factor to consider when thinking about this part of the test. You have 90 minutes to read the passages, answer the multiple-choice questions, and write your essay. Here is a general breakdown of how you should spend the time you are given.

- 15 minutes—reading and understanding the passages

- 10 minutes—writing a brief set of summary notes for the documents, using the questions "What is the message?" and "How do I know?" to organize your notes

- 10 minutes—answering the multiple-choice questions

- 5 minutes—reading and understanding the task, making sure that you identify and understand the controlling idea

- 15 minutes—planning your essay, including creating an outline and/or a concept map

- 25 minutes—actually writing the essay

- 5 minutes—reviewing your essay for clarity and mechanics

This schedule allows you an extra 5 minutes, but as you can see, you've got a lot to do and not a lot of time in which to do it. There are two points during the task where you should think about your timing.

The Multiple-Choice Checkpoint

As you begin the multiple-choice questions, glance at your watch and add 10 minutes to the time. This will tell you when you should move on to the essay portion of the test. Make sure you don't take more than 10 minutes answering the multiple-choice questions because they count less toward your final score than the essay does.

Closing In on the Finish Line

Your second checkpoint should be about 1 hour and 20 minutes into the test—10 minutes before you need to begin Session Two, Part B. If you have 10 minutes left but have not started your conclusion, wrap up the body paragraph you are working on and go directly into your conclusion. It is better to leave one or two points from your outline unmade than to submit a composition without a conclusion. Don't be so preoccupied with time, though, that you waste precious moments figuring out how much time is left for this task. Stay focused and follow the schedule above, and you should be just fine.

CHAPTER 5
CRACKING SESSION TWO, PART B:
THE CRITICAL ESSAY SECTION

The last part of the Regents Comprehensive Examination in English is a breeze, as long as you prepare for it. There are no multiple-choice questions, so all you have to do is write one more essay, and you are done.

Look at the following Session Two, Part B, task.

SESSION TWO, PART B

Your Task: Write a critical essay in which you discuss *two* works of literature you have read from the particular perspective of the statement that is provided for you in the **Critical Lens.** In your essay, provide a valid interpretation of the statement, agree *or* disagree with the statement as you have interpreted it, and support your opinion using specific references to appropriate literary elements from the two works. You may use scrap paper to plan your response.

Critical Lens:

"The best literature is about the old universal truths, such as love, honor, pride, compassion, and sacrifice."

—William Faulkner (adapted)

Guidelines:

Be sure to

- Provide a valid interpretation of the Critical Lens that clearly establishes the criteria for analysis

- Indicate whether you agree *or* disagree with the statement as you have interpreted it

- Choose *two* works you have read that you believe best support your opinion

- Use the criteria suggested by the Critical Lens to analyze the works you have chosen

- Avoid plot summary. Instead, use specific references to appropriate literary elements (for example: theme, characterization, setting, point of view) to develop your analysis

- Organize your ideas in a logical and coherent manner

- Specify the titles and authors of the literature you choose

- Follow the conventions of standard written English

WHAT YOU REALLY NEED TO DO

This composition is no more difficult than the others, but you do need to be familiar with the terms mentioned in Your Task. Although the terms may sound vaguely familiar to you, you need to fully understand them in order to write a successful composition. For instance, what the heck is a Critical Lens? How do you know if you've got a valid interpretation? What are literary elements?

Let's figure out what these terms mean now so that you don't have to waste time trying to decipher them on the day of the test. First, *Critical Lens* is merely the name the test writers apply to the quotation. Ignore the term and just look at the quotation itself. If you really think about what the given quotation means, you should be able to put it in your own words, and you will have a valid interpretation. If you have trouble, phrase the quotation several different ways. The key to interpreting the quotation is putting it in your own words. For the quotation above, you might paraphrase it by saying, "The books people like the most are those that involve feelings that everyone has experienced."

You need to do the following things in the essay:

- Explain what the quotation means to you.

- Agree with it or disagree with it.

- Support your opinion with examples from two pieces of literature.

If you've taken the steps we suggest in order to get a valid interpretation, then you can already explain what the quotation means to you. Let's look at the other two things you need to do.

Agree or Disagree with the Quotation

You can choose to agree or disagree. First, think about how you agree with the quotation, jot down a list of examples from literature you've read, and think about how you could use each one to support your opinion. Then, think about how you disagree, and make a similar list. Decide which way to argue based on how many examples you can think of and how well you can explain them in an essay.

This will take a few minutes, but it is an important step in planning your essay. The extra time you spend in this step will make writing your essay much easier.

Try to think of how you can argue either for or against the Faulkner quote in the sample task for Session Two, Part B, that we just saw.

Here's one example of a student list:

AGREE	DISAGREE
The Great Gatsby—love, sacrifice	?
To Kill a Mockingbird—honor, compassion	
Romeo and Juliet—love, sacrifice	
King Lear—pride	

In this case, it's easier to think of literary works that involve the universal qualities that Faulkner lists than to think of ones that don't. You might want to argue that Faulkner is wrong, but you would need to think of two works that are great despite the absence of these feelings. Because it is difficult to come up with any examples of serious literary works that do not include at least one of these feelings, it may be easier to agree with the quotation than it is to disagree with it.

Support Your Opinion with Two Examples from Literature

This is the part you need to start preparing now. How? The quotation given on the Regents Comprehensive Examination in English is always vague enough to accommodate almost any of the works you read in English class: novels, plays, poems, and nonfiction works. Thus, you can arm yourself in advance with a few pieces of literature you know well. You need to know more than just "what happened" in these works. You need to have paid attention to the *literary elements* of the work that your teacher spoke about in class or had you write papers about. Literary elements are things like characterization, theme, structure, point of view, and so on. Look back to pages 20–22 for more terms to refresh your memory. If you can analyze the piece of literature and write about its literary elements, then you know it well enough to use in your composition.

In the weeks leading up to the test, go back to your notes and papers from English class—this year's and last year's—to refamiliarize yourself with the literary works you've read. Look at the notes you took on those literary elements and think about how you could apply them to an essay. For example, if you read Harper Lee's *To Kill a Mockingbird,* make sure that you can discuss more than just what happened in the story. Go back to your notes and see what you learned about the overall theme of the novel, how Lee develops the characters, and how the style of language varies throughout the book. Think about from whose point of view the story is told, and how that affects the story. You probably talked or wrote about all of these things in class, so review your notes. If you no longer have the notes, see if you can prepare with a friend who does. You may also be able to jog your memory with a commercial study guide or study notes for the book, but this will only help you if you have actually read the book. Do not use movies, paperback romances, or other pop cultural pieces as your "works of literature." Prepare to use only pieces of serious literature, like those you read in English class.

Try to choose the works you like the most. If you enjoyed a work, it will be easier to remember its literary elements. Become familiar with four pieces of literature and you'll be prepared no matter what kind of quotation the exam throws at you. On the day of the test, you'll need to write about only two of these works to support your opinion.

Write down everything that you know about each literary work on a piece of paper. Make sure you include the following:

- Title

- Author

- Type of work (novel, short story, poem, play, composition, memoir)

- Setting (time and place)

- Main characters (their roles and a few adjectives to describe them)

- Minor characters (their roles and a few adjectives to describe them)

- Characterization (how you know what the characters are like)

- Point of view (who told the story)

- Plot (in one or two sentences)

- Important scenes

- Primary conflict or opposition

- Organization (the way the work was arranged)

- Theme(s)

- Mood

- Symbols

- Repetition

- Imagery

- Any other parts of the work, or techniques the author used, that you noticed or talked about in class (Take a look at the list of literary elements and techniques on pages 20–22 to refresh your memory.)

- Information about the author and the historical context of the work

Make four or five of these review sheets now, before you read any further. You cannot take these lists into the exam with you, but you should create them to help you review and remember each work's key elements.

Once you've prepared everything you know about a few pieces of literature, the next important step is using that material in your composition. You cannot just drop everything you know about a literary work into your composition. Perhaps if the task said, "Tell us everything you know about two works of literature," you could just spew all that information out. But it doesn't. You must use specific references to literary works to support your opinion of the given quotation.

Thoroughly reviewing the literary elements of a few works will help you earn a high score on this part of the Regents exam. Read on to learn how to apply this knowledge on the day of the test.

CRAFTING THE ESSAY

There are several ways you can plan your essay on paper, but the two easiest and most helpful ways are by using an outline or a concept map.

Writing an Outline

Your outline should be basic. It should consist of the essential parts listed below.

Introduction: Your interpretation of the quotation and your opinion of it

Body Paragraph: Supporting point from work #1

Body Paragraph: Supporting point from work #2

Conclusion: Restate your opinion

In the introduction, you need to show the Regents test scorers that you understand the quotation. To do this, put the quotation in your own words, and explain what it means to you. You can, of course, use the actual quotation, but you must also explain what it means to you.

The introduction should also contain your opinion of the quotation, which is your controlling idea for this composition. You can also mention the two works of literature that you will use to support your opinion so that the introduction gives a hint about the specific details you will cover in the body paragraphs.

The next part to outline is the body. If you plan to write about more than one element of each literary work, you should have more than just two body paragraphs, which is what we used in the example above. Even if you think you will have only two body paragraphs, you should provide yourself with some detail in your outline. Write more than just the title of the book you'll be using; make note of how that book supports your opinion.

The outline stage is your chance to make sure that each literary work you are thinking about using actually supports your opinion. Keep in mind that you must show how the works support your opinion, not just give a summary of the works' storylines. Make sure you outline an essay that uses both of the literary works to support an opinion of the quotation. Explaining how each of your literary examples backs up your main point will take up most of your body paragraphs.

The conclusion will restate your opinion. Note the conclusion in your outline so that you do not forget to write it! Always leave time to write a conclusion, even if you must stop developing ideas in the body of your essay to do it. If you have time, try to do more than restate your opinion. Explain why your opinion is important, how it relates to the world at large, or why you care about it. (Look back to the first chapter for more help on writing a "kicker" in your conclusion.)

Now look at your points and see if there is a logical order in which to put them. If no particular order occurs to you, see if you can think of a way to link your points, but if you still don't see it, don't worry. When making points between the paragraphs, you can simply use standard transitional phrases like, "Another example of X is . . . ."

Having an outline allows you to organize what you know about two literary texts into an essay that fulfills the Session Two, Part B, task. Do not skip this step! It could make the difference between a focused essay and a rambling one. If you are really uncomfortable with the outline structure, you can draw a concept map, which we'll discuss next. Right now, try writing a brief outline for an essay in response to the task at the beginning of this chapter.

The organization we've suggested you use may seem traditional—that's because it is. The individuality of your essay will come from how you interpret the quotation, which literary texts you choose, and how you use them to support your opinion. The organization of your points is something you can do in a traditional manner to make sure the test scorers see that you know how to organize your thoughts.

Here is a sample outline for an essay that addresses the task about the Faulkner quotation. Yours may look very different, depending on the literary works you choose.

INTRODUCTION: The best stories are about the things everyone experiences, because they make people feel connected to the characters—I agree

BODY PARAGRAPH 1: THE GREAT GATSBY
- *Character demonstrates*
  -love
  -compassion
  -sacrifice
- *Theme*
  -modern America losing honor
- *"Truths" (love, compassion, honor) make people care about the main character*

BODY PARAGRAPH 2: KING LEAR
- *At beginning, character has*
  -pride
- *At end, character has*
  -love
  -compassion
- *These "truths" (love, compassion) make readers start to like him*

CONCLUSION: The best literature needs these "truths" to build characters and make readers care about them

Drawing a Concept Map

A concept map is helpful if you prefer to visualize the plan you are creating. It can also help you see connections easily. The one drawback, however, is that it does not leave you with a clear order for an introduction, body paragraphs, and a conclusion. So if you like concept maps, you may want to draw a map first, and then put your ideas into an outline. See which method works for you as you practice. Use the diagram on the next page to make a concept map for the task at the beginning of this chapter.

This is a sample concept map that corresponds to the outline on page 92. When you draw your map, you may have extra ideas that you put on the map and then decide not to include in your essay. Just cross them out. That's the beauty of a concept map—it helps you organize more ideas than you may need!

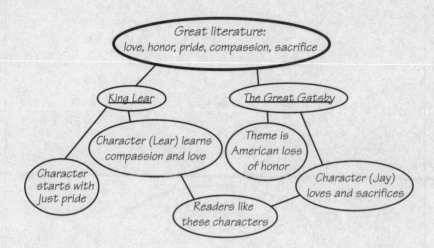

WRITING A HIGH-SCORING SESSION TWO, PART B, ESSAY

You will receive a score for your composition based on a 6-point scale. As you plan and write your composition, keep these five qualities in mind: meaning, development, organization, language use, and conventions. If your composition scores high in these five qualities, you'll receive full credit (6 points).

Meaning

Readers look for the quality of meaning by finding evidence that you understand the quotation and express an opinion of it. They also look to see that you analyze the literary texts you choose by taking them apart and using pieces of them to support your opinion. If you follow the techniques we've explained, you will do well.

Remember, your essay should not just summarize the literary texts that you write about. You must think about the various elements of each text, and choose parts of it to mention in your essay to support your opinion. The focus of your essay is your opinion of the quotation; while you are proving your opinion to be valid, you will happen to show off what you know about some literature.

Development

Development is judged by your effectiveness in describing how the points you choose to use from each literary work support your opinion. It is your responsibility to explain how the works show that the quotation is either right (if you agree with it) or wrong (if you disagree with it).

Your points must be specific. If you say, "Gatsby was in love," you are not being specific enough. You must tell the reader how Gatsby's love makes the novel great literature. You need to develop the idea into something like, "Gatsby's love for Daisy and his willingness to sacrifice for her are what make him an interesting character." Your preparation of literary examples in advance is crucial to your ability to develop the examples you use.

You must also make your points relevant to your controlling idea. The more specific sentence in the example above needs to be connected to the contolling idea of your essay, and so you might go on to say, "Since Gatsby is the main character, he is central to the success of the novel. If Fitzgerald had not characterized Gatsby as selfless and loving, readers would not be interested in him, and the novel would not be as great as it is."

Organization

Your outline or concept map will keep you organized. If you stay focused on the controlling idea and stick to the traditional organization of introduction, body paragraphs, and conclusion, you will be able to concentrate on supporting your opinion. If you find yourself straying from the main idea when you write, correct this problem by neatly crossing out the unnecessary information. Remain focused. Refer to the quotation and your outline as you write. Show off your organization with paragraph indents that readers can easily see.

Try to keep your points in a logical sequence, and connect them with transitions. If the transitions from paragraph to paragraph seem forced or nonexistent when you practice, review the section on transitions in Chapter 1 for some tips.

Language Use

There are two different elements of language use. First, the test grader looks to be sure that you are aware of your audience and purpose. Your audience for the Session Two, Part B, essay is always your English teacher. Your purpose is always to convince your English teacher that your opinion is correct, and that you have substantial reasons for holding your opinion, using relevant examples from literary works you have read.

The quality of good language use also includes simply using language skillfully. This requires practice! You can find some hints on how to improve your use of language in Chapter 1.

Conventions

These are the skills you've been learning since first grade—spelling, punctuation, capitalization, grammar, and usage. Look at old papers you've written for the errors you commonly make, and try to prevent them or catch them when you proofread. Take a look at Chapter 1 for more suggestions.

SAMPLE STUDENT ESSAYS

Here is a sample top-score student essay in response to the task for Session Two, Part B, provided at the beginning of the chapter. Be sure to write your practice essay before reading the sample and the explanation of why it received full credit (6 points).

Score Level 6

William Faulkner once said, "The best literature is about the old universal truths, such as love, honor, pride, compassion, and sacrifice." He couldn't be more right. The reason these truths are necessary is that they evoke emotions of the reader. They develop characters. Without these truths involved in one way or another, the story lacks substance. It's difficult to have a protagonist and an antagonist when these truths are completely ommitted.

The truths Faulkner talks about can be brought into a work of literature in one of two ways. The first way is directly. In a direct presentation, the plot is about someone's quest or conflict with one of the truths. In an indirect presentation of truths, the plot may not contain the truths but they might be used in another aspect such as character development.

In F. Scott Fitzgerald's <u>The Great Gatsby</u>, both presentations are used. The storyline is about a man who wishes to turn back time and convince his former girlfriend to marry him. The story contains love (Jay's love for Daisy), compassion (Jay's efforts to get sick and to marry Daisy), and sacrifice (Jay's willingness to give up his honor and convictions in order to get what he wants). The underlying theme also contains such truths. The theme is about how twentieth century America is losing its love and righteousness all for wealth. Without the truths Faulkner speaks of, <u>The Great Gatsby</u> would not be much of a story. No one would want to read about some rich guy that throws parties in his house every night.

In William Shakespeare's <u>King Lear</u>, truths are also a necessary part of the story. The plot here is about the fall of a king and the changes he undergoes during the fall. In the beginning of the story, Lear lacks every truth but pride. The reader thinks unfavorably of him at this point. But as the play continues on, Lear gains more truths such as compassion and love. As he does the reader is lead to like Lear and he becomes the protagonist.

In conclusion, the truths that Faulkner speaks of are necessary to build a story up. Without them, there is no character development. There is no plot, either. It is difficult to write a good piece of literature without this.

Why Did This Essay Get a 6?

This essay writer has done everything necessary to receive full credit (6 points). The essay begins with a clear statement of the writer's opinion and an interpretation of the quotation. The writer then analyzes two ways in which the quotation can be true, and uses two literary texts to support his or her opinion.

In addition, the writer explains how the literary texts support his or her opinion. This creates a strong essay, which is also well organized. The essay stays focused and combines opinion with literary analysis. It also benefits from the inclusion of a few choice literary terms. Finally, the essay is easy to read because the writer uses language well and makes few errors.

WHAT IF I RUN OUT OF TIME?

Here is a general breakdown of how you should spend your time during Session Two, Part B. You have approximately 90 minutes.

- 5 minutes—reading and understanding Your Task and the Critical Lens quotation

- 30 minutes—planning your essay and making a concept map, writing an outline, or both

- 40 minutes—writing the essay

- 10 minutes—proofreading the essay

This schedule leaves you 5 extra minutes. You may even finish early in this section, but you should use the extra time to proofread carefully. There are two points at which you should check your timing during Session Two, Part B, to make sure you will have time for every step.

Planning Your Essay

Planning your Session Two, Part B, essay takes a long time because all of your supporting points must come from your memory of literary works. As you begin planning, check your watch. Make sure that within 25 or 30 minutes, you have finished planning and are ready to begin writing.

Closing In on the Finish Line

If you have only 10 minutes left and you have not yet started writing your conclusion, you should quickly finish the body paragraph you are working on and write a conclusion. Test scorers will be left dissatisfied with any essay that lacks a conclusion.

If you can, try to think of some way to relate your opinion to the world at large. If you cannot think of some way to make a profound statement about your controlling idea, just restate it, mentioning the support you have given for it. In any case, write something that wraps up the essay.

With practice and proper preparation, you should have no problem completing Session Two, Part B, within the allotted time, and then you will have finished the entire Regents Comprehensive Examination in English.

Now you can practice the techniques you have learned on the practice exams in Part II.

PART II:

PRACTICE EXAMS WITH
ANSWERS AND
EXPLANATIONS

PRACTICE EXAM A

IMPORTANT NOTE:

The listening section, which starts the exam, requires you to listen to a passage read by someone else. It is essential that you have someone read this passage to you. The listening passage appears on pages 103–104. To best prepare for the Regents Comprehensive Examination in English, you should have someone read the passage aloud to you rather than reading it yourself. It's important to take the practice exams just as you'll take the actual exam. Listening skills are different from reading comprehension skills, so the best way to prepare for the listening section of the Regents Comprehensive Examination in English is to *listen* to the passage.

SESSION ONE, PART A

Overview: For this part of the test, you will listen to a speech about an author's memories of her early days as a writer, answer some multiple-choice questions, and write a response based on the situation described below. You will hear the speech twice. You may take notes anytime you wish during the readings. **Note: Have someone read the listening passage on pages 103–104 aloud to you.**

> **The Situation:** Your English class is learning about authors who faced obstacles as they pursued their careers in writing. Your teacher has asked you to write a composition about author Virginia Woolf and the obstacles she overcame as a female writer. In preparation for writing your composition, listen to a passage, adapted from a speech Virginia Woolf gave in 1942, about her early experiences with writing. Then use relevant information from the speech to write your composition.

Your Task: Write a composition for your English teacher showing how Virginia Woolf overcame the obstacles she faced as a female writer.

Guidelines:

Be sure to

- Tell your audience what they need to know to help them understand the obstacles Virginia Woolf faced as she began her career as a writer

- Use specific, accurate, and relevant information from the speech to support your discussion

- Use a tone and level of language appropriate for a composition for English class

- Organize your ideas in a logical and coherent manner

- Indicate any words taken directly from the speech by using quotation marks or referring to the speaker

- Follow the conventions of standard written English

Directions: Have someone read the listening passage on pages 103 and 104 to you now. Have the person read it to you a second time after you think about it for a few minutes. You may take notes on a separate piece of paper. When you have heard the passage twice, answer the multiple-choice questions that begin on page 104.

Listening Passage

When your secretary invited me to come here, she told me that your group is concerned with the employment of women, and she suggested that I might tell you something about my own professional experiences. Many famous women, and many more unknown and forgotten, have been before me, making the path smooth, and regulating my steps. Thus, when I came to write, there were very few material obstacles in my way. Writing was a reputable and harmless occupation. The family peace was not broken by the scratching of a pen. No demand was made on the family purse. For ten and sixpence one can buy enough paper to write all the plays of Shakespeare. The cheapness of writing paper is, of course, the reason why women have succeeded as writers before they have succeeded in the other professions.

But to tell you my story—it is a simple one. You have only got to imagine a girl in a bedroom with a pen in her hand. She had only to move that pen from left to right—from ten o'clock to one. Then it occurred to her to do what is simple and cheap enough after all—to slip a few of those pages into an envelope, fix a penny stamp in the corner, and drop the envelope into the box at the corner. It was thus that I became a journalist; and my effort was rewarded on the first day of the following month—by a letter from an editor containing a check. But to show you how little I deserve to be called a professional woman, how little I know the struggles and difficulties of such lives, I have to admit that instead of spending that sum up on bread and butter, rent, or butcher's bills, I went out and bought a cat—a beautiful Persian cat, which very soon involved me in bitter disputes with my neighbors.

What could be easier than to write articles and to buy Persian cats with the profits? But wait a moment. Articles have to be about something. Mine, I seem to remember, was about a novel by a famous man. And while I was writing this review, I discovered that if I were going to review books I should need to do battle with a certain phantom. The phantom was a woman, and when I came to know her better I called her after a heroine of a famous poem "The Angel in the House." It was she who used to come between me and my paper when I was writing reviews. It was she who bothered me and wasted my time and so tormented me that at last I killed her. You who come of a younger and happier generation may not have heard of her—you may not know what I mean by the Angel in the House. I will describe her as shortly as I can. She was intensely sympathetic, immensely charming, and utterly unselfish. She sacrificed herself daily. If there was chicken, she took the leg; if there was a draft, she sat in it—in short she was so constituted that she never had a mind or wish of her own, but preferred to sympathize always with the minds and wishes of others. Above all—she was pure. Her purity was supposed to be her chief beauty—her blushes, her great grace. In those days—the last of Queen Victoria—every house had its Angel. And when I came to write I encountered her with the very first words. The shadow of her wings fell on my page; I heard the rustling of her skirts in the room. As soon as I took my pen in hand to review that novel by a famous man, she slipped behind me and whispered: "My dear, you are a young woman. You are writing about a book that has been written by a man. Be sympathetic; be tender; flatter; deceive; use all the arts and wiles of our sex. Never let anybody guess that you have a mind of your own. Above all, be pure." And she made as if to guide my pen.

I now record the one act for which I take some credit to myself, though the credit rightly belongs to some excellent ancestors of mine who left me a certain sum of money—so that it was not necessary for me to depend solely on charm for my living. I turned upon her and caught her by the throat. I did my best to kill her. My excuse, if I were to be had up in a court of law, would be that I acted in self-defense. Had I not killed her she would have killed me. She would have plucked the heart out of my writing. I found directly when I put pen to paper, you cannot review even a novel without having a mind of your own, without expressing what you think to be the truth about human relations, or morality. All these questions, according to the Angel in the House, cannot be dealt with freely and openly by women; they must tell lies if they are to succeed. Thus, whenever I felt the shadow of her wing or the radiance of her halo up on my page, I took up the inkpot and flung it at her. She died hard. Her fictitious nature was of great assistance to her. It is far harder to kill a phantom than a reality. She was always creeping back when I thought I had dispatched her. But it was a real experience, an experience that was bound to befall all women writers at that time. Killing the Angel in the House was part of the occupation of a woman writer.

Multiple-Choice Questions

Directions: Use your notes to answer the following questions about the passage read to you. The questions may help you think about ideas and information you might use in your writing. You may return to these questions anytime you wish.

1 In her opening lines, the speaker attributes her smooth entrance into her profession to
   (1) an encouraging editor
   (2) a lack of competition
   (3) guidance from friends
   (4) women writers of the past

2 Who does the speaker imply is the girl in the bedroom?
   (1) a family member
   (2) a female friend
   (3) the speaker herself
   (4) an imaginary writer

3 The speaker says she became a journalist
   when
   (1) an editor offered her a job
   (2) she sent an article to an editor
   (3) she applied for an advertised position
   (4) a friend submitted her writing to a
       publisher

4 In describing the angel as "pure," the
   speaker most likely means the angel is
   (1) young
   (2) frivolous
   (3) virtuous
   (4) plain

5 In "killing" the angel, the speaker was
   trying to preserve her own
   (1) status
   (2) integrity
   (3) sanity
   (4) history

6 The Angel in the House most nearly
   represents the
   (1) poetic muse
   (2) spirit of other women writers
   (3) author's approaching death
   (4) ideal woman of the time

After you have finished these questions, turn back to page 101. Review the **Situation** and read **Your Task** and the **Guidelines.** Use scrap paper to plan your response. Then write your response to Session One, Part A. After you finish your response for Part A, go on to Part B.

SESSION ONE, PART B

Directions: Read the article and study the tables on the following pages, answer the multiple-choice questions, and write a response based on the situation described below. You may use the margins to take notes as you read and scrap paper to plan your response. **Note: Use your own blank paper to write your response.**

> **The Situation:** You have been asked to write an article for your local newspaper about the gap between the salaries of men and women in the workplace. The newspaper has asked you to provide a brief history of the issue and to discuss the present state of pay inequality.

Your Task: Write an article to be published in your local newspaper. Using relevant information from the text **and** the charts, explain the background of the pay inequity issue, discuss how and why men's and women's salaries have become more equal over time, and talk about how the issue continues to be addressed today.

Guidelines:

Be sure to

- Tell the readers of the newspaper what they need to know about the issue of pay inequity between men and women

- Explain what efforts have been made to establish pay equity in the past and whether or not they have been successful

- Discuss the ways that pay inequities still exist today and propose measures to eliminate them

- Use specific, accurate, and relevant information from the text **and** the tables to support your argument

- Use a tone and level of language appropriate for an argument to be submitted to a newspaper editorial board

- Organize your ideas in a logical and coherent manner

- Indicate any words taken directly from the text by using quotation marks or referring to the author

- Follow the conventions of standard written English

Beyond the Glass Ceiling: Pay Equity

Women may perform different jobs than men in a company, but if their jobs are equally valuable to an organization, women should be paid comparably.

Three out of four American working women, including full-time and part-time workers, are paid less than $25,000 a year. About half of all women work in traditionally female jobs, such as nursing, clerical work, child care, cooking, cleaning, and library work, all of which are relatively low-paying. Although progress has been made in reducing the wage gap between men and women, women still earn 71 cents on average for each dollar that men earn. According to a recent Department of Labor survey, few women think that their wages reflect the real value of their work or what they need to support their families. Over a woman's lifetime, unequal pay has big consequences. It directly affects her social security or pension benefits. Women retirees receive only half the average pension received by men, in part because of their wage gap.

In April 1997, the White House took a symbolic first step in addressing the problem of unfair pay practices in the workplace by proclaiming a "National Pay Inequity Awareness Day." President Clinton called upon employers to review their wage-setting practices and to see that their employees, particularly women and people of color, are paid fairly for their work.

In his proclamation the President stated:

"Unfair pay practices exist at all education levels and in every occupation. Last year, women physicians and lawyers earned substantially less than their male counterparts. The problem is particularly acute in female-dominated professions and in jobs where minority groups are disproportionately represented. Though changing technologies and a growing demand for services have made their positions increasingly vital, America's child-care providers, secretaries, textile workers, telephone operators, social workers, and maintenance people are among those who bear the greatest wage discrepancies."

Fairness in the Workforce

Many women still work in jobs that are different from those that men do, even though the work may be of equal or equivalent value. Fair pay or pay equity means equal pay for work of equal value even when the work is different. Most Americans agree with this concept. Polls consistently show that 70 percent of Americans would support a law requiring the same pay for men and women in jobs requiring similar skills and responsibilities.

More progress toward fair pay has been made in the public rather than the private sector, partly because the wages and job descriptions of government employees are public information. Job evaluation studies that compare and measure actual job responsibilities can easily fit civil service systems. Also, laws governing collective bargaining and the civil service often refer to the importance of fair and equitable pay.

For nearly two decades, the state of Minnesota has led pay equity efforts in the nation. Minnesota was the first to provide pay equity for state government employees and the first to require pay equity for local government and school district employees. For some workers, it has meant the difference between being on the edge of poverty and being self-supporting. For example, a single mother earning $8,600 as a clerk/typist saw her wages rise to $23,000 and no longer had to depend on government assistance.

In another case preceding the institution of pay equity, general maintenance workers were paid more than the clerical staff, who were required to have more skills and training. When pay equity was implemented, it did not penalize the maintenance workers, and they continued to get raises. In fact, it is illegal to reduce pay for employees to remedy past imbalances.

A 1992 study of Los Angeles Children's Social Service workers (mostly women) indicated that they were getting paid 34 percent less than county probation officers (mostly men) even though their jobs required similar skills, effort, and responsibility, and had similar working conditions. Social workers were being paid about $35,000 a year; the probation officers received $55,000. The social workers' union pushed for and was awarded a 20 percent wage increase.

Source: U.S. Women's Bureau

TABLE 1

ANNUAL SALARY, 1996

Men	$32,144
Women	$23,710
Wage gap:	73.8%

Source: U.S. Women's Bureau

TABLE 2

Women's Earnings as a Percent of Men's, 1979–1997

Year	Hourly	Weekly	Annual
1979	64.1%	62.5%	59.7%
1980	64.8	64.4	60.2
1981	65.1	64.6	59.2
1982	67.3	65.4	61.7
1983	69.4	66.7	63.6
1984	69.8	67.8	63.7
1985	70.0	68.2	64.6
1986	70.2	69.2	64.3
1987	72.1	70.0	65.2
1988	73.8	70.2	66.0
1989	75.4	70.1	68.7
1990	77.9	71.9	71.6
1991	78.6	74.2	69.9
1992	80.3	75.8	70.8
1993	80.4	77.1	71.5
1994	80.6	76.4	72.0
1995	80.8	75.5	71.4
1996	81.2	75.0	73.8
1997	80.8	74.4	

Source: U.S. Women's Bureau

Multiple-Choice Questions

Directions: Select the best suggested answer to each question. The questions may help you think about ideas and information you might want to use in your writing. You may return to these questions anytime you wish.

7 One of the points made by the President in his proclamation is that
  (1) the federal government has eliminated pay inequity for its own employees
  (2) even in high-paying careers, women are frequently paid less than men
  (3) more women should become physicians and lawyers so that they will be paid more than they would in other fields
  (4) eliminating the pay inequity between men and women would be simple if more Americans supported the idea

8 Which of these is a result of pay inequity that is mentioned in the text?
  (1) Men's incomes have decreased.
  (2) Women prefer lower-paying jobs that do not require skills or training.
  (3) Women have begun to pursue careers in jobs formerly held mostly by men.
  (4) Women have less income after they retire than men who had similar jobs.

9 The author mentions the state of Minnesota is an example of an employer that
  (1) eliminated most of its low-paying jobs
  (2) increased the salaries of those employees who were making less than other employees with similar skills and responsibilities
  (3) contributes to the wage gap by paying men higher salaries than it pays women
  (4) offered government assistance to many of its employees who did not earn large salaries

10 In line 44, the word "preceding" is used to mean
  (1) prior to
  (2) exemplifying
  (3) following
  (4) separate from

11 The text compares general maintenance workers and clerical workers in order to provide an example of

(1) a situation in which the general maintenance workers took a pay cut in order to produce pay equity

(2) one reason that general maintenance workers should receive more job training

(3) an instance where workers who had more skills and training were paid less than those without similar skills and training

(4) why more general maintenance workers than clerical workers receive government assistance

12 The example of Los Angeles social service workers and probation officers is used to illustrate that

(1) people who worked in occupations that were considered more dangerous earned more than those in less dangerous jobs

(2) men who were social service workers were paid more than women who were also social service workers

(3) jobs traditionally held by women still paid less than jobs usually held by men

(4) probation officers had used collective bargaining to increase their salaries

13 According to Table 1, which of the following was true in 1996?

(1) The average female year-round, full-time worker made 73.8 percent of the salary earned by the average male year-round, full-time worker.

(2) A survey showed that 73.8 percent of all year-round, full-time workers believed that there was a wage gap.

(3) 73.8 percent of all the year-round, full-time workers were women.

(4) Women who earned $23,710 made up 73.8 percent of the year-round, full-time workforce.

14 According to Table 2, between 1992 and 1997 the wage gap between male and female hourly workers

(1) remained approximately the same

(2) substantially increased

(3) substantially decreased

(4) changed more than the gap between the same workers changed between 1982 and 1987

After you have finished these questions, review the **Situation** and read **Your Task** and the **Guidelines.** Use scrap paper to plan your response.

SESSION TWO, PART A

Directions: Read the passages on the following pages (a poem and a memoir) and answer the multiple-choice questions. Then write the essay described in **Your Task.** You may use the margins to take notes as you read and scrap paper to plan your response. **Note: Use your own blank paper to write your response.**

> **Your Task:** After you have read the passages and answered the multiple-choice questions, write a unified composition about how adults remember scenes from their childhoods, as revealed in the passages. In your composition, use ideas from *both* passages to establish a controlling idea about memories of childhood. Using evidence from *each* passage, develop your controlling idea and show how *each* author uses specific literary elements or techniques to convey that idea.

Guidelines:

Be sure to

- Use ideas from *both* passages to establish a controlling idea about how adults remember scenes from their childhoods, as revealed in the passages

- Use specific and relevant evidence from *each* passage to develop your controlling idea

- Show how each author uses specific literary elements (for example: theme, characterization, structure, point of view) or techniques (for example: symbolism, irony, figurative language) to portray memories of childhood

- Organize your ideas in a logical and coherent manner

- Use language that communicates ideas effectively

- Follow the conventions of standard written English

Passage I

My Mother Is Not Watching

from the door as I start my first
walk to school. I am not afraid

though this crisp eyelet
dress feels like someone else's skin

and these houses
tall faces turning

away. This morning
my mother gets to stay

where she chooses, raising
one shoulder, cradling the phone

so her hands are free to coat each
nail to a shield over each

pale finger. Smoke from her cigarette
curls across the table like the breath

of a visitor, the glamorous
woman she secretly loves.

In this dress I'm her dream
and no one's daughter.

School is a story whose ending
she tells me she doesn't know.

Now she opens the paper to follow
a war far away, while I march

into autumn, beneath the fences
and high windows which in time

I won't see, just
the blackboard worn thin

with words that vanish
each night. I will find my way

through their sounds, a song
unwinding, and one day

I will open a book and not
notice I'm reading.

—Leslie Ullman

Passage II

Silk Parachute

When your mother is ninety-nine years old, you have so many memories of her that they tend to overlap, intermingle, and blur. It is extremely difficult to single out one or two, impossible to remember any that exemplify the whole.

It has been alleged that when I was in college she heard that I had stayed up all night playing poker and wrote me a letter that used the word "shame" forty-two times. I do not recall this.

I do not recall being pulled out of my college room and into the church next door.

It has been alleged that on December 24, 1936, when I was five years old, she sent me to my room at or close to 7 p.m. for using four-letter words while trimming the Christmas tree. I do not recall that.

The assertion is absolutely false that when I came home from high school with an A minus she demanded an explanation for the minus.

It has been alleged that she spoiled me with protectionism, because I was the youngest child and therefore the most vulnerable to attack from overhead—an assertion that I cannot confirm or confute, except to say that facts don't lie.

We lived only a few blocks from the elementary school and routinely ate lunch at home. It is reported that the following dialogue and ensuing action occurred on January 22, 1941:

"Eat your sandwich."

"I don't want to eat my sandwich."

"I made that sandwich, and you are going to eat it, Mister Man. You filled yourself up on penny candy on the way home, and now you're not hungry."

"I'm late. I have to go. I'll eat the sandwich on the way back to school."

"Promise?"

"Promise."

Allegedly I went up the street with the sandwich in my hand and buried it in a snowbank in front of Dr. Wright's house. My mother, holding back the curtain in the window of the side door, was watching. She came out in the bitter cold, wearing only a light dress, ran to the snowbank, dug out the sandwich, chased me up Nassau Street, and rammed the sandwich down my throat, snow and all. I do not recall any detail of that story. I believe it to be a total fabrication.

There was the case of the missing Cracker Jack at Lindel's corner store. Flimsy evidence pointed to Mrs. McPhee's smallest child. It has been averred that she laid the guilt on with the following words: "'Like mother, like son' is a saying so true, the world will judge largely of mother by you." It has been asserted that she immediately repeated that proverb three times, and also recited it on other occasions too numerous to count. I have absolutely no recollection of her saying that about the Cracker Jack or any other controlled substance.

We have now covered everything even faintly unsavory that has been reported about this person in ninety-nine years, and even those items are a collection of rumors, half-truths, prevarications, false allegations, inaccuracies, innuendos, and canards.

This is the mother who—when Alfred Knopf wrote her twenty-two-year-old son a letter saying, "The reader's reports in the case of your manuscript would not be very helpful, and I think might discourage you completely"—said, "Don't listen to Alfred Knopf. Who does Alfred Knopf think he is, anyway? Someone should go in there and k-nock his block off." To the best of my recollection, that is what she said.

I also recall her taking me, on or about March 8, my birthday, to the theater in New York every year, beginning in childhood. I remember those journeys as if they were today. I remember *A Connecticut Yankee.* Wednesday, March 8, 1944. Evidently my father had written for the tickets, because she and I sat in the last row of the second balcony. Mother knew what to do about that. She gave me for my birthday an elegant spyglass, sufficient in power to bring the Connecticut Yankee back from Vermont. I sat there watching the play through my telescope, drawing as many guffaws from the surrounding audience as the comedy on the stage.

On one of those theater days—when I was eleven or twelve—I asked her if we could start for the city early and go out to LaGuardia Field to see the comings and goings of airplanes. The temperature was well below the freeze point and the March winds were so blustery that the wind-chill factor was forty below zero. Or seemed to be. My mother figured out how to take the subway to a stop in Jackson Heights and a bus from there—a feat I am unable to duplicate to this day. At LaGuardia, she accompanied me to the observation deck and stood there in the icy wind for at least an hour, maybe two, while I, spellbound, watched the DC-3s coming in on final, their wings flapping in the gusts. When we at last left the observation deck, we went downstairs into the terminal, where she bought me what appeared to be a black rubber ball but on closer inspection was a pair of hollow hemispheres hinged on one side and folded together. They contained a silk parachute. Opposite the hinge, each hemisphere had a small nib. A piece of string wrapped round and round the two nibs kept the ball closed. If you threw it high into the air, the string unwound and the parachute blossomed. If you sent it up with a tennis racket, you could put it into the clouds. Not until the development of the ten-megabyte hard disk would the world ever know such a fabulous toy. Folded just so, the parachute never failed. Always, it floated back to you—silkily, beautifully—to start over and float back again. Even if you abused it, whacked it really hard—gracefully, lightly, it floated back to you.

—John McPhee

Multiple-Choice Questions

Directions: Select the best suggested answer to each question. The questions may help you think about the ideas and information you might want to use in your essay. You may return to these questions anytime you wish.

Passage I (the poem) — Questions 1–5 refer to Passage I.

1 From the title through line 7, the narrator suggests that the child is feeling
  (1) fearful
  (2) eager
  (3) isolated
  (4) curious

2 Which poetic device is used in lines 5–6?
  (1) onomatopoeia
  (2) end rhyme
  (3) dramatic monologue
  (4) personification

3 The image of the "glamorous woman" (lines 15–16) suggests the mother's
  (1) elegant friend
  (2) former life
  (3) telephone caller
  (4) daydream self

4 In lines 17–18, the child seems to sense the mother's need for
  (1) fantasy
  (2) approval
  (3) patience
  (4) control

5 The child compares reading to
  (1) following a path
  (2) unraveling a thread
  (3) hearing a melody
  (4) performing magic

Passage II (the memoir) — Questions 6–8 refer to Passage II.

6　On a symbolic level, the silk parachute represents
　　(1)　the planes landing at the airport
　　(2)　the sandwich the author's mother had made him earlier in his childhood
　　(3)　the love of the author's mother
　　(4)　the author's desire not to live far from home

7　The phrase "Not until the development of the ten-megabyte hard disk" (line 68) is an example of
　　(1)　allusion
　　(2)　personification
　　(3)　symbolism
　　(4)　simile

8　The repetition of the phrase "It has been alleged" helps establish a feeling of
　　(1)　sadness
　　(2)　good humor
　　(3)　loneliness
　　(4)　excitability

After you have finished these questions, review **Your Task** and the **Guidelines**. Use scrap paper to plan your response. Then write your response to Session Two, Part A. After you finish your responses for Part A, go on to Part B.

SESSION TWO, PART B

Your Task: Write a critical essay in which you discuss *two* works of literature you have read from the particular perspective of the statement that is provided for you in the **Critical Lens.** In your essay, provide a valid interpretation of the statement, agree *or* disagree with the statement as you have interpreted it, and support your opinion using specific references to appropriate literary elements from the two works. You may use scrap paper to plan your response. **Note: Use your own blank paper to write your response.**

Critical Lens:

"It is a skill we learn early, the art of inventing stories to explain away the fearful sacred strangeness of the world. Storytelling and make-believe, like war and agriculture, are among the arts of self-defense, and all of them are ways of enclosing otherness and claiming ownership."

—William Kittredge

Guidelines:

Be sure to

- Provide a valid interpretation of the Critical Lens that clearly establishes the criteria for analysis

- Indicate whether you agree *or* disagree with the statement as you have interpreted it

- Choose *two* works you have read that you believe best support your opinion

- Use the criteria suggested by the Critical Lens to analyze the works you have chosen

- Avoid plot summary. Instead, use specific references to appropriate literary elements (for example: theme, characterization, setting, point of view) to develop your analysis

- Organize your ideas in a unified and coherent manner

- Specify the titles and authors of the literature you choose

- Follow the conventions of standard written English

ANSWERS AND EXPLANATIONS FOR PRACTICE EXAM A

Session One, Part A

WRITTEN RESPONSE

To get a score of 6, you must do well on all of the qualities we detail below. For a more comprehensive explanation of these qualities and how to crack them, refer to chapter 2.

Preparing the Written Response

Remember, the two most important parts of the task are the purpose and the audience. You should have underlined "write a composition about author Virginia Woolf and the obstacles she overcame as a female writer" as the purpose and "your teacher" as your audience. Then you should have listened for two things during the teacher dictation:

- what obstacles got in Virginia Woolf's way

- how she overcame them

Your notes should include most of these points:

- money—Woolf had no problem with it, and most women writers probably didn't because writing is cheap

- "The Angel in the House":

  - perfect Victorian woman

  - self-sacrificing

  - no thoughts of her own

  - virtuous, "pure"

  - Angel tells Woolf to lie and flatter

  - Woolf kills the Angel so that she can write

Organizing Your Composition

Your outline and/or concept map should have included the two major points in the task: what obstacles got in Woolf's way and what she did to overcome them. You should have used these two points to organize your composition by mentioning them in both your introduction and conclusion, and then elaborating on them in the paragraphs in between.

Understanding the Task and Developing Your Ideas

Your composition should have developed the two points just mentioned. One important part of that elaboration is interpreting the story Woolf tells about the Angel. You should have explained that the Angel is not really a ghost, but is a part of Woolf herself that does not allow her to write what she feels. Because she knows how women are "supposed" to feel and think, she is afraid of writing differently. Woolf needs to break through the bounds of what she has learned is her place as a woman. In doing so, she "kills" the Angel (the part of herself that wants her to be more like an "ideal" woman), but the feelings keep coming back, so she has to "kill" the Angel many times.

Addressing the Audience

You should have remembered to keep your writing at the level and tone appropriate for your English teacher—formal and serious.

Following the Conventions of Standard Written English

Ask your English teacher or another good writer to read your composition and tell you if it is clear and easy to understand. If errors in grammar, spelling, punctuation, usage, or other conventions make the composition difficult to understand, ask a teacher, tutor, or parent to help you improve these skills.

MULTIPLE-CHOICE QUESTIONS

We have provided explanations for all of the answer choices because the easiest way to choose the best answer is often to eliminate the other three. Did you remember to use Process of Elimination?

1 (1) Woolf mentions an editor later in the speech, but not in the opening lines.

   (2) Woolf does mention other writers in her opening lines, but she says that because they existed, it is easier for her to write.

   (3) Woolf does not mention friends at all.

   (4) **Correct.** Woolf says that many women have written before her, making it easier for her to become a writer.

2 (1) Woolf never mentions family members who write.

   (2) Woolf never mentions a friend.

   (3) **Correct.** Woolf says that she will tell you her story, asks you to imagine the girl in the bedroom, and then explains that that is how she became a writer.

   (4) This answer choice is not as good as (3) because Woolf has clearly started to tell the story of how she came to write when she mentions "the girl," and she soon returns to the first person ("I").

3 (1) The editor sent a check, but that is not the same as offering a job, which would be a longer-term commitment than one story.

   (2) Correct. Woolf mails the pages she wrote, and then says, "It was thus that I became a journalist."

   (3) There is no mention of advertisements.

   (4) Woolf never mentions a friend.

4 (1) Does youth have anything to do with "blushes" and "grace"? Not particularly. Anyone can be graceful or easily embarrassed.

   (2) *Frivolous* means lacking in seriousness. Does the Angel seem like she has too much fun? No.

   (3) Correct. *Virtuous* means having virtue and being chaste. Is that like being pure? Yes.

   (4) Does being plain have anything to do with being pure? No. In fact, Woolf says that purity contributes to the Angel's beauty.

5 (1) *Status* means position, usually a person's position in society. By "killing" the Angel, Woolf is going against society, since the Angel is the perfect woman by society's standards. This cannot be right.

   (2) Correct. The Angel tries to get Woolf to lie and write words that do not express what Woolf really thinks. Thus, she must "kill" the Angel in order to preserve her integrity, which is her honesty and truthfulness.

   (3) Woolf does not actually "see" an angel, so she is not in danger of losing her sanity. She is just using an angel as a personification of the pressure she feels to write in socially acceptable ways.

   (4) The Angel is threatening not her history, only her ability to write what she really feels and thinks.

6 (1) A muse is someone who inspires an artist. The Angel tries to stop Woolf from writing what she wants to write, so the Angel cannot be a muse.

   (2) Woolf sees other women writers as supportive, and the Angel is not.

   (3) Woolf does not mention death.

   (4) Correct. Woolf says that the Angel has all of the qualities that the perfect Victorian woman would have—she is self-sacrificing, sympathetic, and pure. That these qualities are the Victorian ideal is never directly stated; however, the other three answer choices can all be eliminated.

SESSION ONE, PART B

WRITTEN RESPONSE

To get a score of 6, you must do well on all of the qualities we detail below. For a more comprehensive explanation of these qualities and how to crack them, refer to chapter 3.

Preparing the Written Response

The task asks you to explain the background of the pay inequity issue and explain how it has been addressed in both the past and the present.

Your summary notes should include some or most of the following items:

- women, on the whole, are paid less than men

- a wage gap is when women are paid less than men for doing comparable work

- even in high-paying professions (doctors/lawyers), women are paid less than men

- Minnesota—equity for government employees

- achieve pay equity by increasing salary of those making less money

Organizing Your Composition

Your outline and/or concept map should have included the three major points of the task: some background, what has been done in the past (probably the largest section), and what is being done now to minimize the wage gap. Breaking down the written response into these three points is an easy way to organize this composition.

Understanding the Task and Developing Your Ideas

Your composition should have elaborated on these three points: background, the past, and the present. In discussing the background behind the issue of wage inequity, you might have used any of the statistics from paragraph two and from the tables to show the disparity between salaries paid to women and to men. The discussion of past efforts to address the issue could begin with the President's remarks and the White House's 1997 recognition of the problem. Finally, to address what can be done to continue to minimize the wage gap, you could have discussed ideas such as comparing workers with similar skills and responsibilities, and additional initiatives like Minnesota's.

Addressing the Audience

You should have remembered to keep your writing at the level and tone appropriate for an article for your local newspaper—formal and serious.

Following the Conventions of Standard Written English

Ask your English teacher or another good writer to read your composition and tell you if it is clear and easy to understand. If errors in grammar, spelling, punctuation, usage, or other conventions make the composition difficult to understand, ask a teacher, tutor, or parent to help you improve these skills.

MULTIPLE-CHOICE QUESTIONS

7 (1) The President does not discuss whether there is a wage gap for employees of the federal government.

   (2) **Correct.** The President mentions that even among physicians and lawyers, women earn less money than their male counterparts.

   (3) The President does not suggest that anyone change occupations, but rather that men and women who work in the same occupation should be paid similar amounts.

   (4) The President does not discuss whether the public supports measures to eliminate pay inequity.

8 (1) The text actually states that it is illegal to lower the wages of any worker because he or she makes more than another. Thus, men's wages could not be decreased.

   (2) Women do not naturally prefer lower paying jobs.

   (3) This might be one possible consequence of the wage gap, but it is not one that is mentioned in the text. Remember that you must look back at the text to find the correct answer.

   (4) **Correct.** The text specifically tells you that because they earn less, women have smaller pension plans and less money to depend on after retirement.

9 (1) Minnesota did not eliminate its low-paying jobs. It increased the salaries for jobs traditionally held by women, for which it was paying less than other similar jobs held by men.

   (2) **Correct.** See explanation for choice (1).

   (3) This was probably true at some point in the past, but the text uses the state of Minnesota as an example of an employer that has taken praiseworthy steps to eliminate the wage gap.

   (4) The text says that by taking steps to eliminate the wage gap among its employees, Minnesota actually helped many employees get off government assistance.

10 (1) **Correct.** *Preceding* means coming before, and since the case mentioned in the text is an excellent example of pay inequity, it follows that it came before pay equity was required.

   (2) The word *exemplifying* means making an example of.

   (3) The case of the maintenance workers and the clerical workers is an example of pay inequity, so it is incorrect to believe that it followed the institution of pay equity.

   (4) In the context of the passage, *separate from* does not make sense.

11 (1) General maintenance workers and clerical workers are used by the text as an example of two occupations where the wage gap was particularly obvious. The problem with this answer choice is that the maintenance workers did not take a pay cut (which the text tells you is against the law); rather, the clerical workers received a pay increase.

(2) The clerical workers were described as having more skills and training than the maintenance workers, but the text did not suggest that the maintenance workers should receive additional training.

(3) Correct. The clerical workers had more skills and training but were paid less than the maintenance workers. This was used by the text as an example of the wage gap.

(4) The maintenance workers, because of pay inequity, made more than the clerical workers. Therefore it is unlikely that maintenance workers would receive more government assistance than clerical workers.

12 (1) Nowhere does the text mention that the danger involved in an occupation should determine how people are compensated.

(2) This would be an example of a wage gap, but the text makes the point that probation officers (a traditionally male occupation) earned more than social workers (a traditionally female occupation).

(3) Correct. Probation officers (who are generally men), according to the text, earned more than social workers (who are generally women).

(4) The text does, at one point, mention collective bargaining, but it does not indicate that the probation officers' higher salaries were a result of collective bargaining.

13 **(1) Correct.** The wage gap is represented by the percentage of an average male salary that is earned by an average female. In this case, the average female's salary was 73.8 percent of what a similar male would have earned.

(2) The text did mention a public opinion survey about the wage gap, but this was not what was shown in the table.

(3) Table 1 includes information about the average salaries earned by men and women in 1996. It does not tell what percentage of the workforce was either male or female.

(4) $23,710 was the average income for women, which was 73.8 percent of the average income for men during that year. The table does not suggest that 73.8 percent of the workforce was made up of women earning exactly $23,710.

14 **(1) Correct.** In 1992 the average female hourly worker earned 80.3 percent of a similar male's salary and in 1997 she earned 80.8 percent. This is a change of only 0.5 percent over a 5-year period.

(2) The wage gap among hourly workers did not increase between 1992 and 1997.

(3) The wage gap decreased very slightly (only 0.5 percent) between 1992 and 1997. This is a good second-choice answer, but such a small decrease should not be considered substantial.

(4) There was only a small change in the wage gap between 1992 and 1997 (0.5 percent) and a much larger change between 1982 and 1987 (nearly 5 percent).

WRITTEN RESPONSE

To get a score of 6, you must do well on all of the qualities we detail below. For a more comprehensive explanation of these qualities and how to crack them, refer to chapter 4.

Preparing the Written Response

The task asks you to write an essay about how adults remember their childhoods. As you read through the text, you might have kept your eyes open for things like:

- feelings that are most memorable (e.g., loneliness and love)

- events and situations that are most memorable

- people who are most memorable from childhood

Your summary notes should include most of these points:

Poem:
- first day of school, girl all alone
- mother in a fantasy world, glamorous
- school—mother and daughter both unsure
- girl will learn to read—challenge (song)

Memoir:
- memories difficult to single out
- mother had very strong opinions and took action
- like mother, like son—mother saw herself through son
- birthday theater trips
- 11th or 12th birthday—airport
- silk parachute—thrown in air, comes sailing back

Organizing Your Essay

Your outline and/or concept map might have included headings like the following: mother/parents (since both passages deal with memories of parents), love (how it is expressed), and getting attention (protective or not). There are many other ideas and themes common to both passages, but these are excellent points to use in planning your composition.

Understanding the Task and Developing Your Ideas

Your essay should have discussed what things most commonly become memories—the happiness and sadness of life. It may have also dealt with the influence that parents have over the memories and development of their children. You might have talked about how the two mothers were different, one very protective of her son and one not terribly involved in her daughter's life. The poem has a much darker tone that perhaps reflects the way the girl feels about her mother's "not watching." You should have discussed some of the literary elements from both passages and related them to the controlling idea of your essay.

Addressing the Audience

You should have remembered to keep your writing at the level and tone appropriate for your English teacher—formal and serious.

Following the Conventions of Standard Written English

Ask your English teacher or another good writer to read your essay and tell you if it is clear and easy to understand. If errors in grammar, spelling, punctuation, usage, or other conventions make the essay difficult to understand, ask a teacher, tutor, or parent to help you improve these skills.

MULTIPLE-CHOICE QUESTIONS

1 (1) Nothing indicates that the child is afraid, and in line 2 she actually says, "I am not afraid."

  (2) The girl seems reluctant and tentative as she takes her first walk to school. There is no indication that she is feeling eager.

  (3) Correct. The girl is walking to school for the first time. Both the title, "My Mother Is Not Watching," and the image of the houses as "tall faces turning away" should indicate that the girl feels isolated.

  (4) There is nothing in the poem that tells you that the child feels curious.

2 (1) There is no sound described in lines 5–6. Onomatopoeia is the use of words that sound like the thing they describe (e.g., zoom, pop).

  (2) There is no rhyme in lines 5–6.

  (3) This poem is full of description but does not contain any direct speech. A dramatic monologue is a poem that consists of a speech that one character gives.

  (4) Correct. The houses are described as having "tall faces" as though they were people. This is personification.

3 (1) There is no mention of an elegant friend in the poem. "Smoke from [the mother's] cigarette curls across the table like the breath of a visitor" is a similie indicating that the mother is being distant, like a visitor, rather than like a mother.

  (2) The poem doesn't tell us anything about the mother's life in the past, so we don't know whether she was ever a glamorous woman.

  (3) The poem refers to the mother being on the telephone, but doesn't provide any information about the person on the other end of the call.

  (4) Correct. The mother imagines herself as a glamorous woman whom she "secretly loves" in her own daydreams.

4 **(1) Correct.** The child is describing her place in her mother's fantasy when she says, "I'm her dream."

  (2) There is nothing in the poem to indicate that the mother needs approval from her daughter or anyone else.

  (3) Nothing in the poem tells you that the mother needs patience.

  (4) Nothing in the poem tells you that the mother needs control.

5 (1) When she mentions the words on the blackboard, the child does say that she will "find my way," but adds "through their sounds, a song unwinding." This refers to something other than a path.

  (2) No thread is mentioned in the poem.

  (3) Correct. The words are described as a song, or a melody, through which the child will "find my way."

(4)   The poem does not mention magic.

6   (1)   The silk parachute did come from the airport, but it does not represent the planes that the author watched landing at the airport.

(2)   The story about the sandwich may stick out in your mind, but it is not what is represented by the silk parachute.

(3)   Correct. The author expresses his appreciation for his mother's love through the silk parachute. "Always, it floated back to you—silkily, beautifully—to start over and float back again. Even if you abused it, whacked it really hard—gracefully, lightly, it floated back to you" is meant to describe the parachute on a literal level and his mother's love on a symbolic level.

(4)   The author does not express a desire not to live far from home.

7   **(1)   Correct.** The "ten-megabyte hard disk" is a reference, or an allusion, to something that was invented later on, after the silk parachute.

(2)   Personification involves giving human traits or abilities to inanimate objects. The ten-megabyte hard disk is not compared to a person.

(3)   The ten-megabyte hard disk is not included to represent anything, so there is no symbolism here.

(4)   A simile is a comparison made using either "like" or "as." The ten-megabyte hard disk is not actually compared to anything.

8   (1)   The author's description of his interactions with his mother are generally humorous and the memoir does not really have a feeling of sadness.

(2)   Correct. The phrase "It has been alleged" has a legalistic tone. By using it to describe laughable incidents from his childhood, the author sets a generally humorous tone.

(3)   There is not a sense of loneliness in the passage.

(4)   This choice might appeal to you because the mother is portrayed as being somewhat excitable. However, this is conveyed through the particular memories the author shares rather than by the words "It has been alleged."

SESSION TWO, PART B

WRITTEN RESPONSE

To get a score of 6, you must do well on all of the qualities detailed below. Remember that on Session Two, Part B, of the exam, you are required to use literary works you have read in class or on your own. For a more comprehensive explanation of how to crack this part of the exam, refer to Chapter 5.

Preparing the Written Response

For any Session Two, Part B, task, you must do three things:

- explain what the quotation means to you

- agree or disagree with it

- support your opinion with examples from two works of literature

If you analyzed four pieces of literature in advance of the test, you should have been able to do these three things easily.

Organizing Your Essay

In your outline and/or concept map, you should have put your interpretation and opinion of the quotation in the introduction. The examples from literature should have made up your body paragraphs. Finally, the conclusion should have refocused on your opinion and interpretation and, if possible, included a kicker.

Understanding the Task and Developing Your Ideas

Doing a good job of developing your ideas depends on how well you have prepared your examples. We cannot stress this enough. You must review four literary works and be sure you know them really well. You need to know most of the literary elements and devices in each one—not just the plots. Review Chapter 1 for the list of elements that you need to study and understand for each literary work you plan to write about for this part of the test.

You should break down this task into two parts: understanding the quotation and developing your interpretation with the literary examples you reference.

The first part is easy—don't be afraid that your understanding of the quotation is wrong because it is different from someone else's. As long as you have not interpreted the quotation to support an alien-conspiracy theory, you should be fine. Everyone will have a slightly different interpretation. The quotations are chosen specifically for their flexibility.

This quotation by Kittredge is the most difficult in the practice tests in this book. One interpretation (not the only one) is that the quotation means that literature is created to explain the unknown.

Your two examples for this essay should support your opinion. Is it easier for you to agree or disagree with this quotation? If none of your four literary works are examples of explaining the unknown, then you should disagree with the quotation and explain your literary works as examples that show there is some literature that deals with what everyone is familiar with.

Addressing the Audience and Sticking to the Purpose

The audience for Session Two, Part B, is always your English teacher, so be sure to write a formal, serious essay. You should avoid saying "you" in this essay. In addition, your purpose is to convince your English teacher that your opinion and interpretation are correct. That's why you use the examples from literature to back up your argument. Were you persuasive? Did you stick to the topic, telling your audience only what he or she needed to know to understand how each literary work supported your idea? Or did you start reciting the entire plot?

Because you should be using established, well-known pieces of literature as your examples, you do not need to give extraneous information. You can assume the Regents test scorer has read the works. However, that does not excuse you from showing how the works you mention actually support your opinion.

Following the Conventions of Standard Written English

Ask your English teacher or another good writer to read your essay and tell you if it is clear and easy to understand. If errors in grammar, spelling, punctuation, usage, or other conventions make the essay difficult to understand, ask a teacher, tutor, or parent to help you improve these skills.

PRACTICE EXAM B

IMPORTANT NOTE:

The listening section, which starts the exam, requires you to listen to a passage read by someone else. It is essential that you have someone read this passage to you. The listening passage appears on pages 133–134. To best prepare for the Regents Comprehensive Examination in English, you should have someone read the passage aloud to you rather than reading it yourself. It's important to take the practice exams just as you'll take the actual exam. Listening skills are different from reading comprehension skills, so the best way to prepare for the listening section of the Regents Comprehensive Examination in English is to *listen* to the passage.

SESSION ONE, PART A

Overview: For this part of the test, you will listen to a speech about homelessness in America, answer some multiple-choice questions, and write a response based on the situation described below. You will hear the speech twice. You may take notes anytime you wish during the readings. **Note: Have someone read the listening passage on pages 133–134 aloud to you.**

> **The Situation:** You are writing a letter to your senator to express your feelings about the problem of homelessness in America. In preparation for writing your letter, listen to a speech delivered by writer Jonathan Kozol at the Boston College graduation ceremonies in May 1989. Then use relevant information from the speech to write your letter.

Your Task: Write a letter to your senator explaining to him or her why the problem of homelessness in America must be addressed and proposing some solutions that will help solve the problem. *Write only the body of the letter.*

Guidelines:

Be sure to

• Tell your audience what they need to know to help them understand the problems of homelessness and the solutions you propose

• Use specific, accurate, and relevant information from the speech to support your discussion

• Use a tone and level of language appropriate for a letter to a government official

• Organize your ideas in a logical and coherent manner

• Indicate any words taken directly from the speech by using quotation marks or referring to the speaker

• Follow the conventions of standard written English

Directions: Have someone read the listening passage on pages 133 and 134 to you now. Have the person read it to you a second time after you think about it for a few minutes. You may take notes on a separate piece of paper. When you have heard the passage twice, answer the multiple-choice questions that begin on page 135.

Listening Passage

If commencement is the American dream, there is also an American nightmare. I have lived that nightmare now for three long years and want to share it with you.

It began a couple of nights before Christmas in 1985.

I read a story in *The New York Times* about a little boy who died while he was homeless in New York. He had been born while his mother was living in a hotel converted into a homeless shelter. She'd had no prenatal care, was poorly nourished, and the baby was born premature. He lived only eight months. After a long and sleepless night, I flew to New York, found the mother of that little boy, and, in time, found my way into the shelter.

It was a huge and squalid building, tall, one block from Fifth Avenue, standing in the shadow of the Empire State Building, within the richest section of the richest city in the world. There, in that squalid building, were 2,000 people—two-thirds of them children, the average child only six years old.

I spent Christmas there and then New Year's, then much of the winter, spring, and summer. I went there for Thanksgiving that year. A homeless family asked me to share their Thanksgiving dinner with them. They had no stove, so they cooked on a hot plate on the floor. Then I was there for Christmas, another New Year's, winter, spring, summer, another Christmas—and in a sense I never found my way back home.

There are hundreds and thousands of homeless children in this nation—a fivefold increase in the years since 1981. Because they are scattered in a thousand different cities, they are easily unseen. Many of them will never live to tell their stories.

None of these children has committed any crime. They have done nothing wrong. Their only crime is being born in a rich nation.

Last year I met a homeless family in Los Angeles. The mother had come there from Ohio to search for rent that she could afford. The father—there was a father, none of these families fit the stereotypes, few people do—the father worked full-time for minimum wage, working in a sweatshop making blue jeans, earning $500 a month. They couldn't pay their rent and feed their child in Los Angeles on $500. The child was with them in the street—thirty-eight days old. I shook my head and asked myself, "Is this the best the United States can do?"

Dr. Martin Luther King Jr. told us, "I have been to the mountain." But almost every voice that we have heard for twenty years has counseled us to shut that mountain out of mind, and to direct our eyes instead to the attractive flatlands where careers are made, résumés typed, and profits maximized. Our culture heroes have been sleek and agile people; cynical and cold, streamlined for efficient malice, and unweighted by the excess burden of compassion.

"We owe a definite homage to the reality around us," Thomas Merton wrote, "and we are obliged at certain times to say what things are and give them their right names." The right name for the willingness of a rich nation to leave half a million homeless children in its streets is sheer betrayal of ourselves and our best values.

It has been a long winter. But as with the seasons, so too with a nation: Life renews itself.

I like to think another season of compassion is before us. We look to you who graduate this morning to renew this weary earth, to water the soil of the 1990s with the simple but forgotten values of the heart, to heal the ill, house the homeless, feed the hungry, and bring mercy to the frightened mother and her child.

It is not by standing tall, but by bending low—to reach a hand to those who are too frail to stand at all—that good societies are defined.

Multiple-Choice Questions

Directions: Use your notes to answer the following questions about the passage read to you. The questions may help you think about ideas and information you might use in your writing. You may return to these questions anytime you wish.

1 The contrast between the shelter and its surroundings serves to evoke a sense of
   (1) shame
   (2) awe
   (3) comfort
   (4) amusement

2 When the speaker says, "I never found my way back home," he most likely means that he
   (1) wandered from city to city
   (2) never left New York City
   (3) remained in the shelter
   (4) was changed by his experience

3 The speaker implies that one common stereotype of homeless families is that their
   (1) families live only in large cities
   (2) fathers are absent
   (3) families have several children
   (4) fathers are uneducated

4 The message in the quotation from Thomas Merton is that people should
   (1) take pride in their achievements
   (2) defend the economy
   (3) acknowledge the truth
   (4) overcome their laziness

5 The speaker suggests that good societies are characterized by
   (1) humility
   (2) education
   (3) wealth
   (4) compassion

6 What is the speaker's tone at the end of the passage?
   (1) nostalgia
   (2) optimism
   (3) anger
   (4) frustration

After you have finished these questions, turn back to page 131. Review the **Situation** and read **Your Task** and the **Guidelines.** Use scrap paper to plan your response. Then write your response to Session One, Part A. After you finish your response for Part A, go on to Part B. **Note: Use your own blank paper to write your response.**

SESSION ONE, PART B

Directions: Read the text and study the graph on the following pages, answer the multiple-choice questions, and write a response based on the situation described below. You may use the margins to take notes as you read and scrap paper to plan your response. **Note: Use your own blank paper to write your response.**

> **The Situation:** You have been asked to make a presentation to your school's parent/teacher organization in which you will discuss the reasons that more people aged eighteen to twenty-four live at home now than in prior years. You should prepare a speech in which you provide some background information about the issue and also discuss some of the reasons that more young adults are choosing to live at home.

Your Task: Prepare a speech to present to the organization about the increasing numbers of young adults who are living at home. Use relevant information from the text *and* the graph, explain why more young adults are living at home now than in prior years.

Guidelines:

Be sure to

- Tell the members of the parent/teacher organization what they need to know about the issue

- Explain why more young adults are choosing to live at home now than in prior years

- Use specific, accurate, and relevant information from the text *and* the graph to support your argument

- Use a tone and level of language appropriate for a presentation to be made to your school's parent/teacher organization

- Organize your ideas in a logical and coherent manner

- Indicate any words taken directly from the text by using quotation marks or referring to the author

- Follow the conventions of standard written English

Rent Forever

The tax laws passed in the early eighties also lowered some of the incentives for investment in rental housing by altering the way landlords depreciate their properties. To compensate for the accompanying loss in deductions, landlords have had to increase the rents they charge tenants. In fast-growing areas like the West, rents rose by 24 percent in real terms over a ten-year period, reaching a median of $427 a month by 1988. According to a study by Harvard University's Joint Center for Housing Studies, rent as a share of the median income of young Americans has jumped by 50 percent since the early seventies. By 1991, those under the age of twenty-five were shelling out 36 percent of their gross income on rent.

Since the higher percentage of income devoted to rent makes it that much more difficult to save money for a down payment on a house, young adults face an uphill climb in the pursuit of owning a home. The lower incomes, higher rents, and higher home prices facing [these young adults] prompted the authors of the Harvard study to remark that current trends threaten "to produce a permanent underclass of disadvantaged renters and to jeopardize the long-term financial security of future generations."

The Boomerang Effect

The most noticeable result of the lofty housing prices and rents and the corresponding declining incomes of [young adults] is that more and more of them are returning to their parents' homes to live. By 1988, 61 percent of men and 48 percent of women aged eighteen to twenty-four were living with their parents, more than at any time since the Great Depression. In addition, another 12 to 13 percent were living with other relatives, meaning that only one young man in four and just over one woman in three was living independently in that year. As sociologist Larry Bumpass of the University of Wisconsin noted in 1987, "There is a naive notion that children grow up and leave home when they're eighteen, and the truth is far from that."

Those a little older have also been increasingly unable or unwilling to set out on their own. The proportion of men and women aged twenty-five to thirty-four living with their parents has doubled since 1970. While economic trends are the driving force behind this development, some observers have not been sympathetic to the predicament. Cynthia Graves and Dr. Larry Stockman, authors of *Adult Children Who Won't Grow Up,* categorize such boomerangers as "excessively dependent" and "taking an unhealthy length of time to sever the ties of adolescence." An exasperated parent told *The New York Times* in 1988, "You think you've done your bit and put them through college and here they come." And in a 1990 article on the subject in *American Demographics* magazine, the writers claimed that there is no reason to feel for the young adults who find themselves in this situation, and rather that "if anyone deserves pity, it's the affluent parent who has feathered such a nice nest that the fledglings won't leave."

Whereas recent graduates in earlier times often stayed home with Mom and Dad for a year to save up for a house or a car, [today's young adults] do so to save money to pay off student loans or to simply wait for employment that pays enough for them to afford
40   a place of their own. A good job is certainly the key to being able to live on one's own, but while the stereotype of the lazy freeloader haunts these young adults, who in most cases haven't got the financial resources to live independently, the truth is that more than two-thirds of them do work, and most of the rest are in school. Representative of the group is someone like Desmond Moody, two years out of the University of
45   Massachusetts in 1986 and living with Mom and Dad. "College just wasn't the big ticket my parents and I expected it to be," he explained to *U.S. News & World Report.* For the time being, he was at work earning $260 a week at a photocopying store.

—Geoffrey T. Holtz

Percentage of 18- to 24-Year-Olds
Living at Home, 1960–1990

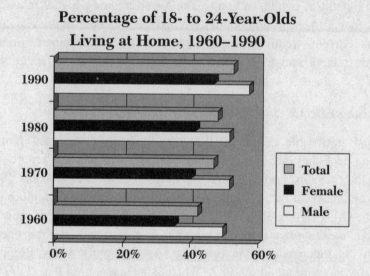

Source: U.S. Department of Commerce, Bureau of the Census

Multiple-Choice Questions

Directions: Select the best suggested answer to each question. The questions may help you think about ideas and information you might want to use in your writing. You may return to these questions anytime you wish.

7 The text suggests that a major reason for the increase in rents was
   (1) the additional demand for apartments that came along with higher numbers of eighteen- to twenty-four-year-old Americans
   (2) changes in the tax law
   (3) a fall in the stock market
   (4) the increased school taxes charged to property owners in many communities in the West

8 Which of the following is the best summary of the report of Harvard University's Joint Center for Housing Studies?
   (1) The income of the average eighteen- to twenty-four-year-old has increased 50 percent, while at the same time the average expense for rent has increased only 36 percent.
   (2) Any eighteen- to twenty-four-year-old who can earn 36 percent more than the average wage earned by eighteen- to twenty-four-year-olds can easily afford rent in any American city.
   (3) The percentage of income that the average eighteen- to twenty-four-year-old would need to spend on rent has increased dramatically.
   (4) If rents were decreased by an average of 36 percent, then eighteen- to twenty-four-year-olds would be able to earn 50 percent more than they currently earn.

9 The first sentence of paragraph two suggests that
   (1) fewer homes are for sale, since owners can now charge higher rents
   (2) because of the growth in the economy, rents are likely to continue to increase
   (3) young Americans would be better off to purchase a home than to rent an apartment
   (4) because of the large portion of income they must spend on rent, it is difficult for many young Americans to afford to purchase a home

10 In line 16, the word "lofty" is used to mean
   (1) high
   (2) difficult
   (3) decreasing
   (4) luxurious

11 The authors of *Adult Children Who Won't Grow Up* believe that young adults who live at home are
   (1) courageous
   (2) stubborn
   (3) overly reliant
   (4) wealthy

12 The final paragraph of the text suggests that one reason why more young adults live at home today than in prior years is that
(1) college tuitions are substantially higher than they were in prior years
(2) students without a college education are given no opportunity to buy a home
(3) young adults prefer to drive expensive cars
(4) fewer young adults get married while in college

13 The text mentions Desmond Moody in order to illustrate
(1) one reason that apartment rents are often too high for young adults to afford
(2) that $260 a week in salary is more than enough for a young adult to use to find a home of his or her own
(3) that careers in photocopy stores do not pay well
(4) an example of one young adult who could not afford to live away from home after college

14 The graph shows that the percentage of all eighteen- to twenty-four-year-olds living at home
(1) remained the same from 1960 to 1990
(2) increased steadily from 1960 to 1990
(3) decreased dramatically from 1970 to 1980
(4) fluctuated wildly from 1960 to 1970

15 Based on the information provided by the graph, which of the following statements is true?
(1) No more than 40 percent of eighteen- to twenty-four-year-old women lived at home between 1960 and 1990.
(2) A greater percentage of men aged eighteen to twenty-four lived at home than women in the same age group between 1960 and 1990.
(3) Less than 20 percent of men aged eighteen to twenty-four lived at home in 1960.
(4) The percentage of women aged eighteen to twenty-four who lived at home in 1990 is more than double the percentage of women aged eighteen to twenty-four who lived at home in 1960.

After you have finished these questions, review the **Situation,** and read **Your Task** and the **Guidelines.** Use scrap paper to plan your response.

SESSION TWO, PART A

Directions: Read the passages on the following pages (a poem and a memoir) and answer the multiple-choice questions. Then write the essay described in **Your Task.** You may use the margins to take notes as you read and scrap paper to plan your response. **Note: Use your own blank paper to write your response.**

> **Your Task:** After you have read the passages and answered the multiple-choice questions, write a unified essay about the influence that ancestors and family members have on children, as revealed in the passages. In your essay, use ideas from *both* passages to establish a controlling idea about these effects. Using evidence from *each* passage, develop your controlling idea and show how *each* author uses specific literary elements or techniques to convey that idea.

Guidelines:

Be sure to

- Use ideas from *both* passages to establish a controlling idea about how ancestors and other family members influence children, as revealed in the passages

- Use specific and relevant evidence from *each* passage to develop your controlling idea

- Show how *each* author uses specific literary elements (for example: theme, characterization, structure, point of view) or techniques (for example: symbolism, irony, figurative language) to portray the way ancestors or family members influence children

- Organize your ideas in a logical and coherent manner

- Use language that communicates ideas effectively

- Follow the conventions of standard written English

Passage I

Daughters

woman who shines at the head
of my grandmother's bed,
brilliant woman, i like to think
you whispered into her ear
5   instructions. i like to think
you are the oddness in us,
you are the arrow
that pierced our plain skin
and made us fancy women;
10 my wild witch gran, my magic mama,
and even these gaudy girls.
i like to think you gave us
extraordinary power and to
protect us, you became the name
15 we were cautioned to forget.
it is enough,
you must have murmured,
to remember that i was
and that you are. woman, i am
20 lucille, which stands for light,
daughter of thelma, daughter
of georgia, daughter of
dazzling you.

—Lucille Clifton

Passage II

Dear Mama,

It is Christmas eve and the year is passing away with calloused feet. My father, your son and I decorate the night with words. Sit ceremoniously in human song. Watch our blue sapphire words eclipse the night. We have come to this simplicity from afar.

5   He stirs, pulls from his pocket a faded picture of you. Blackwoman. Sitting in frigid peace. All of your biography preserved in your face. And my eyes draw up short as he says, "her name was Elizabeth but we used to call her Lizzie." And I hold your picture in my hands. But I know your name by heart. It's Mama. I hold you in my hands and let time pass over my face: "Let my baby be. She ain't like the others. She's rough. She'll
10   stumble on gentleness later on."

Ah Mama. Gentleness ain't never been no stranger to my genes. But I did like the roughness of running and swallowing the wind, diving in rivers I could barely swim, jumping from second story windows into a saving backyard bush. I did love you for loving me so hard until I slid inside your veins and sailed your blood to an uncrucified shore.

15   And I remember Saturday afternoons at our house. The old sister deaconesses sitting in sacred pain. Black cadavers burning with lost aromas. And I crawled behind the couch and listened to breaths I had never breathed. Tasted their enormous martyrdom. Lives spent on so many things. Heard their laughter at Sister Smith's latest performance in church—her purse sailing toward Brother Thomas's head again. And I
20   hugged the laughter round my knees. Draped it round my shoulder like a Spanish shawl.

And history began once again. I received it and let it circulate in my blood. I learned on those Saturday afternoons about women rooted in themselves, raising themselves in dark America, discharging their pain without ever stopping. I learned about women fighting men back when they hit them: "Don't ever let no mens hit you mo than once
25   girl." I learned about "womens waking up they mens" in the nite with pans of hot grease and the compromises reached after the smell of hot grease had penetrated their sleepy brains. I learned about loose women walking their abandoned walk down front in church, crossing their legs instead of their hands to God. And I crept into my eyes. Alone with my daydreams of being woman. Adult. Powerful. Loving. Like them. Allowing
30   nobody to rule me if I didn't want to be.

And when they left. When those old bodies had gathered up their sovereign smells. After they had kissed and packed up beans snapped and cakes cooked and laughter bagged. After they had called out their last goodbyes, I crawled out of my place. Surveyed the room. Then walked over to the couch where some had sat for hours and
35   bent my head and smelled their evening smells. I screamed out loud, "oooweeee! Ain't that stinky!" and I laughed laughter from a thousand corridors. And you turned Mama, closed the door, chased me round the room until I crawled into a corner where your large body could not reach me. But your laughter pierced the little alcove where I sat laughing at the night. And your humming sprinkled my small space. Your humming about your
40   Jesus and how one day he was gonna take you home . . .

Because you died when I was six Mama, I never laughed like that again. Because you died without warning Mama, my sister and I moved from family to stepmother to friend of the family. I never felt your warmth again.

But I knew corners and alcoves and closets where I was pushed when some mad woman went out of control. Where I sat for days while some woman raved in rhymes about unwanted children. And work. And not enough money. Or love. And I sat out my childhood with stutters and poems gathered in my head like some winter storm. And the poems erased the stutters and pain. And the words loved me and I loved them in return.

My first real poem was about you Mama and death. My first real poem recited an alphabet of spit splattering a white bus driver's face after he tried to push cousin Lucille off a bus and she left Birmingham under cover of darkness. Forever. My first real poem was about your Charleswhite arms holding me up against death.

My life flows from you Mama. My style comes from a long line of Louises who picked me up in the nite to keep me from wetting the bed. A long line of Sarahs who fed me and my sister and fourteen other children from watery soups and beans and a lot of imagination. A long line of Lizzies who made me understand love. Sharing. Holding a child up to the stars. Holding your tribe in a grip of love. A long line of Black people holding each other up against silence.

I still hear your humming, Mama. The color of your song calls me home. The color of your words saying, "Let her be. She got a right to be different. She gonna stumble on herself one of these days. Just let the child be."

And I be Mama.

—Sonia Sanchez

Multiple-Choice Questions

Directions: Select the best suggested answer to each question. The questions may help you think about the ideas and information you might want to use in your essay. You may return to these questions anytime you wish.

Passage I (the poem) — Questions 1–2 refer to Passage I.

1 The phrase "my wild witch gran, my magic mama" (line 10) is an example of which of the following literary devices?
   (1) alliteration
   (2) onomatopoeia
   (3) personification
   (4) foreshadowing

2 To which of the following people does "you" refer throughout the poem?
   (1) the author's daughter
   (2) the author's mother
   (3) the author's grandmother
   (4) the author's great-grandmother

Passage II (the memoir) — Questions 3–8 refer to Passage II.

3 Which literary device is used in the phrase "Watch our blue sapphire words eclipse the night" (lines 2–3)?
   (1) sensory imagery
   (2) figurative language
   (3) metonymy
   (4) symbolism

4 The passage is written from which of the following points of view?
   (1) that of an omniscient narrator
   (2) third person
   (3) second person
   (4) first person

5 The phrase "let time pass over my face" (lines 8–9) is an example of
   (1) figurative language
   (2) personification
   (3) simile
   (4) alliteration

6 The dominant literary device used in the fourth paragraph is
   (1) irony
   (2) dissonance
   (3) sensory imagery
   (4) foreshadowing

7 In line 28, the phrase "I crept into my eyes" refers to

(1) the fact that the author could not see the front of the church

(2) the author's retreat into her own imagination

(3) the dark atmosphere inside the church

(4) the absent look in the eyes of the women in the front of the church

8 The final words of the passage—"And I be Mama."—are meant to indicate

(1) that the author has found her own identity

(2) that the author has become a parent

(3) that the author has returned to visit the house where she lived as a young child

(4) that the author has become a poet

After you have finished these questions, review **Your Task** and the **Guidelines.** Use scrap paper to plan your response. Then write your response to Session Two, Part A. After you finish your response for Part A, go on to Part B.

SESSION TWO, PART B

Your Task: Write a critical essay in which you discuss *two* works of literature you have read from the particular perspective of the statement that is provided for you in the **Critical Lens.** In your essay, provide a valid interpretation of the statement, agree *or* disagree with the statement as you have interpreted it, and support your opinion using specific references to appropriate literary elements from the two works. You may use scrap paper to plan your response. **Note: Use your own blank paper to write your written response.**

> **Critical Lens:**
>
> "Sometimes failure is more beneficial than success."

Guidelines:

Be sure to

- Provide a valid interpretation of the Critical Lens that clearly establishes the criteria for analysis

- Indicate whether you agree *or* disagree with the statement as you have interpreted it

- Choose *two* works you have read that you believe best support your opinion

- Use the criteria suggested by the Critical Lens to analyze the works you have chosen

- Avoid plot summary. Instead, use specific references to appropriate literary elements (for example: theme, characterization, setting, point of view) to develop your analysis

- Organize your ideas in a unified and coherent manner

- Specify the titles and authors of the literature you choose

- Follow the conventions of standard written English

ANSWERS AND EXPLANATIONS FOR PRACTICE EXAM B

SESSION ONE, PART A

WRITTEN RESPONSE

To get a score of 6, you must do well on all of the qualities we detail below. For a more comprehensive explanation of these qualities and how to crack them, refer to Chapter 2.

Preparing the Written Response

Your Task gives you all the information you need. You should have underlined "Write a letter to your senator explaining to him or her why the problem of homelessness in America must be addressed and proposing some solutions that will help solve the problem." That sentence tells you your purpose and defines the audience.

You should have listened for two things during the teacher dictation:

- why we must do something about homelessness

- what we can do to improve the situation

Your notes should include most of these points:

- why is homelessness important?

- the rich do not help the poor

- many homeless people are children

- the people are not stereotypical—they work, they have families

- the people just can't afford to live on the money they make

- we have been ignoring the poor in order to further ourselves

- what can we do?

- find better role models than the self-obsessed ones we have now

- pay people a decent wage

- feel compassion for others and help them

Organizing Your Composition

Your outline and/or concept map should have included the two major points that are given to you in the task: why homelessness is important and what can be done to help the homeless. These two points provide an easy way to organize your composition. You should have mentioned both points in your introduction and conclusion, and then elaborated on them in the body paragraphs.

Understanding the Task and Developing Your Ideas

The task is easy to understand, but the ideas you presented might have been harder to develop. If you understood what Kozol said, and presented his ideas about why homelessness is such a problem, you were halfway there. You also needed to discuss solutions, and Kozol does not present any simple solutions beyond feel compassion and help people. However, if you understood some of the problems he discusses, you should have mentioned them and proposed your own solutions. Remember that you are writing a letter to a senator, so you must propose a more detailed solution than "Feel compassion."

For instance, one of the problems Kozol mentions is that homeless people often work, but still do not make enough money to pay rent. You could have proposed a number of ways that the government might help with this problem—raise the minimum wage, provide low-income housing, regulate rents, or provide job-skills training.

Another problem that Kozol points out is that many role models are entirely unconcerned with helping other people. You might have discussed the importance of promoting role models who are concerned with social issues.

Addressing the Audience and Sticking to the Purpose

Your letter should be written to a senator, so it should discuss in a formal tone why homelessness is a problem and what can be done about it.

Following the Conventions of Standard Written English

Ask your English teacher or another good writer to read your composition and tell you if it is clear and easy to understand. If errors in grammar, spelling, punctuation, usage, or other conventions make the composition difficult to understand, ask a teacher, tutor, or parent to help you improve these skills.

MULTIPLE-CHOICE QUESTIONS

1 **(1) Correct.** This answer may seem extreme, but it is the only possible one. The shelter is "squalid," or slumlike; the neighborhood is wealthy. This most likely serves to make the audience feel guilty.

(2) The wealthy surroundings should not inspire awe, or any positive feelings, since the wealthy are unfeeling toward the poor in their midst.

(3) The audience is not likely to feel comfortable while hearing about squalor.

(4) The audience is not expected to be amused at hearing about these housing conditions.

2 (1) There is no support for this idea in the passage. Kozol does not speak of wandering.

(2) Kozol later talks about meeting a family in Los Angeles, so this can't be right.

(3) Again, we know he later goes to Los Angeles, so this can't be true.

(4) Correct. Kozol speaks metaphorically, saying that he was never able to return to his old way of thinking. When he says, "in a sense," he is giving a clue that he is not speaking literally.

3 (1) What is Kozol talking about when he mentions stereotypes? He is talking about a father. He never brings up the topic of where most homeless families are located.

(2) Correct. When Kozol says that the Los Angeles family he met had a father, he then mentions that none of the homeless families fit the stereotypes, implying that the stereotypical homeless family has an absent father.

(3) Kozol does not mention the number of children at all.

(4) Kozol does not mention education.

4 (1) Neither the quotation nor the passage as a whole is about pride in achievements.

(2) Neither the quotation nor the passage as a whole is about the economy.

(3) Correct. The word *homage* in the quotation means duty. Merton says we have a duty to the reality around us. The quotation says that we need to look at how things really are, and admit the truth.

(4) The quotation is much more about the need to face reality than about laziness. Answer choice (3) is better.

5 (1) This may seem like a possible answer, but Kozol is not asking people to be humble. Keep looking for a better answer.

(2) Kozol does not mention education.

(3) Kozol points out that a wealthy society can still be heartless toward some of its people, and he sees that as bad.

(4) Correct. The last lines state that good societies are built on helping people who cannot help themselves.

6 (1) Kozol does not speak of a past time that he longs for, so he cannot be nostalgic.

(2) Correct. The end of the passage is optimistic, and Kozol expresses a hope that the audience will improve the world.

(3) Kozol may have sounded a little angry at the beginning or in the middle of the passage, but at the end he is hopeful.

(4) Kozol may have sounded frustrated at the beginning or in the middle of the passage, but at the end he is hopeful.

SESSION ONE, PART B

WRITTEN RESPONSE

To get a score of 6, you must do well on all of the qualities detailed below. For a more comprehensive explanation of these qualities and how to crack them, refer to Chapter 3.

Preparing the Written Response

The task asks you to prepare a speech that you will deliver to a parent/teacher organization about the increasing number of young adults who are living at home.

If you paid attention to the task, you should have included most of these points in your summary notes:

- changes in tax law led to higher rents

- 36 percent of young adults' income spent on rent

- high rent makes it hard to save for down payment on house

- more young adults living at home

- some critics are unsympathetic

- young adults cannot afford to live on their own

Organizing Your Composition

There are many ways to structure this response. Your composition might have been divided into sections about, first, the increase in rents, second, the income of young adults, and third, young adults' inability to afford their own housing. Or you might have first approached the issue from the landlords' perspective, then the young adults', and finally the parents'.

Understanding the Task and Developing Your Ideas

First, remember that your response must include details from the text *and* visuals. According to the task, your composition must explain the problems that face young adults looking for affordable housing and then explain the reasons many of them choose to live at home. You could have picked out the problems from the text and supported them with statistics from the visuals. If you were able to suggest ways to solve the problems you discussed, those solutions would have made an excellent conclusion.

Addressing the Audience and Sticking to the Purpose

Because your assignment is to write a speech, this audience is different from some of the others you have seen. In a speech, grabbing the attention of your audience early on with a compelling introduction is very important. In this case, you could have used some statistics to impress them.

Following the Conventions of Standard Written English

Ask your English teacher or another good writer to read your composition and tell you if it is clear and easy to understand. If errors in grammar, spelling, punctuation, usage, or other conventions make the composition difficult to understand, ask a teacher, tutor, or parent help you improve these skills.

MULTIPLE-CHOICE QUESTIONS

7 (1) Higher demand might well lead to higher rents, but that is not a reason suggested by the text.

 (2) **Correct.** The first paragraph refers to changes in the tax law that caused landlords to have to increase rents on apartments.

 (3) The stock market is not mentioned in the text.

 (4) This is an attractive answer even though it is incorrect. The text mentions a change in the tax law, but not specifically the school tax. The text also uses apartments in the West as an example, but does not limit the scope of the tax changes to landlords in the West.

8 (1) This answer choice refers to some of the statistics found in the text, but it does so incorrectly. It also does not provide a summary of the Harvard University report.

 (2) This answer choice also refers to some of the statistics that were given by the text, but like choice (1), it uses the statistics incorrectly and fails to summarize the Harvard report.

 (3) **Correct.** The Harvard report focuses on what fraction of a young adult's income is spent on rent, and this choice provides an excellent summary of the report's findings.

 (4) Again, this answer refers to statistics from the text, but does so incorrectly, and fails to summarize the Harvard report.

9 (1) This may be true, but it is not suggested by the first sentence of paragraph two. Be sure to look back at the text and to read carefully.

 (2) Paragraph two does not discuss growth in the economy. It discusses the fact that young adults are finding it harder and harder to afford to pay rent and also save for a down payment on a house.

 (3) You might logically assume this, especially because the second paragraph talks about the high percentage of income spent on rent, but this is not the main point of the first sentence of paragraph two.

 (4) **Correct.** Since young adults are spending more of their income on rent, it is more difficult for them to save enough money to afford the down payment on a house.

10 **(1)** **Correct.** The word "lofty" is used to refer to housing prices and rents in the text. Because the main point of the text is that rents have increased and are more difficult for young adults to afford, it is correct to say that housing prices and rents are high.

(2) This is a close choice: The high housing prices and rents do make it difficult for young adults to afford housing on their own, but the word "lofty" does not mean difficult.

(3) The text discusses the fact that housing costs and rents have increased, not decreased.

(4) The word "lofty" may bring to mind something luxurious, but in this case it refers to housing costs and rents that are high, not wealth or wealthiness.

11 (1) The title of the book, *Adult Children Who Won't Grow Up,* gives you an idea that the authors are most apt to consider young adults living at home in a negative light. Calling them courageous would be a compliment.

(2) The authors believe the reason young adults live at home is that they are, like children, too dependent on their parents. This has little to do with being stubborn.

(3) **Correct.** The authors of the book refer to young adults living at home as "excessively dependent," which means the same thing as overly reliant.

(4) The authors do not mention that the young adults who live at home are wealthy. Even if you did not refer to the passage, you could infer from the rest of the text that it would be factually incorrect to claim that young people are wealthy.

12 **(1)** **Correct.** The text tells you that one reason young adults have traditionally lived at home to save money is to repay student loans. Higher college tuitions make it more difficult to save enough money to repay those loans.

(2) The text discusses young adults who move home after college. Whether students without a college education have opportunities to buy homes is not relevant here.

(3) If this were true, it would be a reason that more young adults live at home today, since saving for a car is mentioned in the text. The text gives no evidence, however, that today's young adults prefer to drive expensive cars.

(4) Again, if this were true, it would be a possible reason for the increase in the percentage of young adults living at home. The text does not mention this, though.

13 (1) The text uses Desmond Moody as an example of a young adult with a college education who cannot afford to live away from home. His situation does not give a reason for high apartment rents.

(2) Read a few lines before the line in which Desmond Moody is mentioned. The text discusses the fact that many young adults have jobs, but not jobs that pay well enough to enable them to afford housing of their own.

(3) You might infer this from the information in the text, but the question asks why the text mentions Desmond Moody. The point is not to show the reader that working in a photocopy store does not pay well.

(4) **Correct.** The text refers to Desmond Moody as one example of a young adult who cannot afford a home of his own, in spite of the fact that he is a college graduate.

14 (1) The graph indicates that the percentage of all eighteen- to twenty-four-year-olds living at home (look at the total bar) increased from slightly more than 40 percent to more than 50 percent. It did not stay the same.

(2) **Correct.** The percentage of all eighteen- to twenty-four-year-olds living at home increased during each ten-year period shown by the graph.

(3) The graph shows, and the text emphasizes, that the percentage of young adults living at home increased; it did not decrease.

(4) Looking at the graph (look at the total bar for each ten-year period), you can see that the percentage of eighteen- to twenty-four-year-olds living at home increased slightly each year; it did not fluctuate wildly at all.

15 (1) In 1960, less than 40 percent of eighteen- to twenty-four-year-old women lived at home, but since then the percentage has been greater than 40 percent.

(2) **Correct.** By looking at the breakdown of men and women during each time period, you can see that there has consistently been a higher percentage of eighteen- to twenty-four-year-old men than women living at home.

(3) More than 20 percent of men in this age group have lived at home during each of the time periods shown in the graph.

(4) In 1960, roughly 35 percent of eighteen- to twenty-four-year-old women lived at home. In 1990, nearly 50 percent of this group of women lived at home. This is certainly an increase, but the percentage did not double.

SESSION TWO, PART A

WRITTEN RESPONSE

To get a score of 6, you must do well on all of the qualities detailed below. For a more comprehensive explanation of these qualities and how to crack them, refer to Chapter 4.

Preparing the Written Response

The task asks you to use both passages to write a unified essay about the influence ancestors and family members have on children.

Your summary notes on the passages should include most of these points:

Poem:

- great-grandmother
- made us fancy women (mother, grandmother)
- protect us
- author sees herself being influenced through generations

Memoir:

- daughter addressing grandmother who is absent, looks at picture
- Mama defended daughter—"Let my baby be."
- daughter knew gentleness, but preferred to be rough
- memories of childhood—visitors, church
- Mama died when girl was six—girl missed warmth
- girl wrote poetry—about Mama and family
- girl's life flowed from Mama
- Mama lives on through memory and words
- girl has become her own person

Organizing Your Essay

Your outline and/or concept map should have included primary themes such as family and generations. Both passages describe the authors developing their identities, so you could have chosen to use that as a primary theme as well. You could have discussed that both authors address an ancestor (the grandmother in the memoir and the great-grandmother in the poem) who is no longer living.

Perhaps the most direct way to approach this essay is to provide a general introduction in which you mention that both passages provide support for the saying "Like mother, like daughter." Your first and second body paragraphs could have each discussed one passage, focusing on how the author was influenced by her individual family members. Your third body paragraph could have discussed the fact that each author has become "her own woman" but still feels a strong connection to the influence of a relative. And finally, your conclusion could provide a basic summary and conclude with a kicker like, "We are all individuals, but we are also a product of those who came before us."

Understanding the Task and Developing Your Ideas

Your essay should make it clear that both pieces describe a very strong connection between the authors and their ancestors, in spite of the separation between them. The statement "My life flows from you Mama" from Passage II is an excellent reference to the connection between generations. Your essay could have discussed the traditional ways family members influence children (by giving them shelter and protection) and also the nontraditional ways, such as the great-grandmother's making the women in her family into "fancy women" or the grandmother in the memoir letting the daughter grow up "rough." You might also have mentioned the strong connections between women that are shown in these two passages.

Addressing the Audience and Sticking to the Purpose

You should have remembered to keep your writing at the level and tone appropriate for your English teacher—formal and serious. Your essay should also have stuck to the purpose assigned by the task: to write about the ways children are influenced by family members and relatives.

Following the Conventions of Standard Written English

Ask your English teacher or another good writer to read your essay and tell you if it is clear and easy to understand. If errors in grammar, spelling, punctuation, usage, or other conventions make the essay difficult to understand, ask a teacher, tutor, or parent to help you improve these skills.

MULTIPLE-CHOICE QUESTIONS

1 **(1)** **Correct.** The initial letters in "wild witch" and "magic mama" make this a good example of alliteration.

   (2) There is no sound expressed in this phrase, so onomatopoeia is not the correct literary device.

   (3) No inanimate object is given human characteristics or abilities here, so personification is incorrect.

   (4) This phrase is meant to provide the reader with a vivid visual image, not to represent something that will happen later in the poem.

2 (1) There is no reference in the poem to the author having a daughter of her own.

   (2) The author's mother is mentioned in the poem, but by using the final lines in the poem, you can trace "you" back a couple of generations earlier than her mother's.

   (3) The author's grandmother is mentioned, but by using the final sentence, you can trace the reference "you" back to a generation beyond grandmother.

  (4) **Correct.** The last sentence of the poem says that the author is Lucille. The author's mother is Thelma. The author's grandmother is Georgia, and the author's great-grandmother is "dazzling you."

3 **(1)** **Correct.** That the phrase starts with the word "watch" is a clear clue that the author is providing a visual image to the reader.

   (2) This phrase is very descriptive, but it is descriptive without using simile, metaphor, or any other figurative language.

   (3) Metonymy is the substitution of an attribute or feature for the name of the thing itself (as in "they counted heads"). There is no metonymy in this phrase.

   (4) Neither the words nor the night is used to represent anything else, so this is not an example of symbolism.

4 (1) The memoir is not told to the reader by a narrator who knows everything and can see into other people's heads.

   (2) A story told from a third-person point of view usually refers to all the characters in terms of "he" and "she." In this case, the author refers to herself as "I."

   (3) Pieces written in the second person are rare. In a work using the second-person point of view, the reader is addressed as "you" as though he or she were the main character.

  (4) **Correct.** The memoir is told from the author's perspective. She refers to herself as "I."

5 **(1) Correct.** This is an example of figurative language. The phrase is a metaphorical way of describing the author's act of remembering.

(2) Personification is a tempting choice because the phrase includes something intangible (time) performing an action (passing over my face), but the passing of time is not personification because it does not involve a nonhuman object performing a human function.

(3) A simile is a comparison made using either "like" or "as." The author does not use "like" or "as" here.

(4) This phrase does not include any repetition of the same sound at the beginning of more than one word, so alliteration is incorrect.

6 (1) The fourth paragraph describes one of the author's childhood memories, but does not include any instances of irony.

(2) Dissonance refers to words or sounds that are unappealing to the ear. The term is more commonly used to describe lines of poetry and is not a literary device used in this case.

(3) Correct. The fourth paragraph relates to the reader the sights and sounds she remembers from her youth.

(4) The fourth paragraph tells the reader some of the things the author recalls from her youth, but does not use those recollections to predict anything that happens later in the memoir.

7 (1) This answer is attractive because the author alludes to her vision to describe what happened to her in church; however, the phrase does not address what she can or can not see in church.

(2) Correct. The sentences following the phrase tell you that the author is "Alone with my daydreams of being woman," which indicates that she is in a world of her own, imagining herself as an adult.

(3) The author uses the phrase to express that she imagined herself as an adult rather than to describe the atmosphere or the lighting conditions in the church.

(4) If you read only the lines before the phrase "I crept into my eyes," you might have been tempted to choose this answer. Read a few lines after the phrase, though, and you will see that the author is describing her own imagination.

8 **(1) Correct.** You must read the few lines before the final line to develop a sense of context. Mama said "Let her be." Here the author is saying that she has now developed her own identity and that "she is."

(2) Taking the words very literally, without considering their context, you might interpret the phrase to mean "I am now a mother." By reading enough of the passage, though, you can see that the author is addressing her grandmother, not explaining that she has become a parent.

(3) The author describes her memories of the setting of her youth, but does not tell the reader anything about visiting the house where she grew up.

(4) The author does tell her grandmother about her early poems. These words at the end of the passage do not refer to her poetry, though.

Session Two, Part B

WRITTEN RESPONSE

To get a score of 6, you must do well on all of the qualities detailed below. Remember that Session Two, Part B, of the exam is the section in which you are required to refer to literary works you have read in class or on your own. For a more comprehensive explanation of how to crack this part of the exam, refer to Chapter 5.

Preparing the Written Response

For any Session Two, Part B, task, you must do three things:

- explain what the quotation means to you

- agree or disagree with it

- support your opinion with examples from two works of literature

If you analyzed four pieces of literature in advance of the test, you should have been able to do these three things easily.

Organizing Your Essay

In your outline and/or concept map, you should have put your interpretation and opinion of the quotation in the introduction. The examples from literature should have made up your body paragraphs. Finally, the conclusion should have refocused on your opinion and interpretation, and if possible, included a kicker.

Understanding the Task and Developing Your Ideas

This quotation is fairly easy to interpret. You could write that it means that sometimes when people seem to fail, they may actually learn more than if they had succeeded. Or, you may interpret the quotation to mean that what one person sees as a failure is not always a failure—it depends on what a person values.

Doing a good job of developing your ideas depends on how well you have prepared your examples. We cannot stress this enough. You must review four literary works and be sure you know them really well—not just the plots. You need to know most of the literary elements and devices in each one. Review Chapter 1 for the list of literary elements you need to study and understand for each literary work you plan to write about for this part of the test.

Your two examples for this essay must support your opinion. Is it easier for you to agree or disagree with this quotation? If you have two examples where characters fail at something and the experience turns out to be good for them, then you should agree with the quotation. If, instead, you have two examples prepared where characters fail and the experience is truly bad, then you can disagree.

Addressing the Audience and Sticking to the Purpose

The audience for Session Two, Part B, is always your English teacher, so be sure to write a formal, serious essay. You should avoid saying "you" in this essay. In addition, your purpose is to convince your English teacher that your opinion and interpretation are correct. That's why you use the examples from literature to back up your argument. Were you persuasive? Did you stick to the topic, telling your audience only what she or he needed to know to understand how each literary work supported your idea? Or did you start telling the whole plot?

Because you should be using established, well-known pieces of literature as your examples, you do not need to give extraneous information. You can assume the Regents test scorer has read the works. However, that does not excuse you from showing how the works you mention actually support your opinion.

Following the Conventions of Standard Written English

Ask your English teacher or another good writer to read your essay and tell you if it is clear and easy to understand. If errors in grammar, spelling, punctuation, usage, or other conventions make the essay difficult to understand, ask a teacher, tutor, or parent to help you improve these skills.

PRACTICE EXAM: JUNE 2001

HOW TO TAKE THE PRACTICE REGENTS EXAM

Three of the most recent Regents Comprehensive Examinations in English are reprinted in this book: June 2001, August 2001, and January 2002. Each exam has two sessions, and each session should take no more than three hours to complete.

The June 2001 Regents Comprehensive Examination in English begins on the next page. Try to take this practice Regents exam as if it were the actual Comprehensive Examination in English that you will take. That means that you should complete one session of the practice exam at one time. For example, if you begin Session One, don't stop until you are finished with the session. You should limit yourself to three hours for each of the two sessions on the exam because that's exactly how much time you'll have on the testing days. It's recommended that you complete Session One on one day and Session Two on the following day. While taking the practice Regents Comprehensive Examination in English, you should not have any books open. Also, you should not watch television, talk on the phone, or listen to music as you take this exam.

After you have taken the practice exam, check out the list of correct answer choices and explanations for each question. The answers and explanations for the June 2001 exam begin on page 191. Read the explanations for as many questions as you need to. Pay special attention to the explanations for questions that you answered incorrectly or had difficulty answering. If you take these steps, you should be prepared for anything the Regents can throw at you.

IMPORTANT NOTE:

The listening section, which starts the exam, requires you to listen to a passage read by someone else. It is essential that you have someone read this passage to you. The listening passage appears on page 167–169. To best prepare for the Regents Comprehensive Examination in English, you should have someone read the passage aloud to you rather than reading it yourself. It's important to take the practice exams just as you'll take the actual exam. Listening skills are different from reading comprehension skills, so the best way to prepare for the listening section of the Regents Comprehensive Examination in English is to *listen* to the passage.

SESSION ONE

The University of the State of New York
REGENTS HIGH SCHOOL EXAMINATION

COMPREHENSIVE EXAMINATION

IN

ENGLISH
SESSION ONE

Thursday, June 14, 2001 — 9:15 a.m. to 12:15 p.m.

This session of the examination has two parts. Part A tests listening skills; you are to answer all six multiple-choice questions and write a response, as directed. For Part B, you are to answer all ten multiple-choice questions and write a response, as directed. The answer sheet for the multiple-choice questions in this session is on page 177. You will write your responses on separate sheets of paper.

PART A

Overview: For this part of the test, you will listen to a speech about the value of book ownership, answer some multiple-choice questions, and write a response based on the situation described below. You will hear the speech twice. You may take notes on a separate piece of paper anytime you wish during the readings. **Note: Have someone read the listening passage on pages 167–199 aloud to you.**

> **The Situation:** The Board of Education for your school district is considering a proposal to provide personal copies of assigned novels for students to keep. You have been asked to prepare a presentation, to be delivered at the next board meeting, in favor of this proposal. In preparation for writing your presentation, listen to a speech given in 1940 by noted philosopher and educator, Dr. Mortimer Adler. Then use relevant information from the speech to write your presentation.

Your Task: Write a presentation persuading your local Board of Education to provide personal copies of assigned novels for students to keep.

Guidelines:

Be sure to

- Tell your audience what they need to know to persuade them of the value of book ownership

- Use specific, accurate, and relevant information from the speech to support your argument

- Use a tone and level of language appropriate for a presentation to the Board of Education

- Organize your ideas in a logical and coherent manner

- Indicate any words taken directly from the speech by using quotation marks or referring to the speaker

- Follow the conventions of standard written English

Directions:

Have someone read the listening passage on pages 167–169 to you now. Have the person read it to you a second time after you think about it for a few minutes.

You may take notes on a separate piece of paper. When you have heard the passage twice, answer the multiple-choice questions that begin on page 170.

Listening Passage

You know you have to read "between the lines" to get the most out of anything. I want to persuade you to do something equally important in the course of your reading. I want to persuade you to "write between the lines." Unless you do, you are not likely to do the most efficient kind of reading.

I contend, quite bluntly, that marking up a book is not an act of mutilation but of love. You shouldn't mark up a book which isn't yours. Librarians (or your friends) who lend you books expect you to keep them clean, and you should. If you decide that I am right about the usefulness of marking books, you will have to buy them.

There are two ways in which you can own a book. The first is the property right you establish by paying for it, just as you pay for clothes and furniture. But this act of purchase is only the prelude to possession. Full ownership comes only when you have made it a part of yourself, and the best way to make yourself a part of it is by writing in it. An illustration may make the point clear. You buy a beefsteak and transfer it from the butcher's icebox to your own. But you do not own the beefsteak in the most important sense until you consume it and get it into your bloodstream. I am arguing that books, too, must be absorbed in your bloodstream to do you any good.

There are three kinds of book owners. The first has all the standard sets and best-sellers—unread, untouched. (This deluded individual owns wood pulp and ink, not books.) The second has a great many books—a few of them read through, most of them dipped into, but all of them as clean and shiny as the day they were bought. (This person would probably like to make books his or her own, but is restrained by a false respect for their physical appearance.) The third has a few books or many—every one of them dog-eared and dilapidated, shaken and loosened by continual use, marked and scribbled in from front to back. (This person owns books.)

Is it false respect, you may ask, to preserve intact and unblemished a beautifully printed book, an elegantly bound edition? Of course not. I'd no more scribble all over a first edition of *Paradise Lost* than I'd give my baby a set of crayons and an original Rembrandt! I wouldn't mark up a painting or a statue. And the beauty of a rare edition or of a richly manufactured volume is like that of a painting or a statue.

Why is marking up a book indispensable to reading? First, it keeps you awake. (And I don't mean merely conscious; I mean wide awake.) In the second place, reading, if it is active, is thinking, and thinking tends to express itself in words, spoken or written. The marked book is usually the thought-through book. Finally, writing helps you remember the thoughts you had, or the thoughts the author expressed. Let me develop these three points.

If reading is to accomplish anything more than passing time, it must be active. You can't let your eyes glide across the lines of a book and come up with an understanding of what you have read. Now an ordinary piece of light fiction, like say, *Gone with the Wind,* doesn't require the most active kind of reading. The books you read for pleasure can be read in a state of relaxation, and nothing is lost. But a great book, rich in ideas and beauty, a book that raises and tries to answer great fundamental questions, demands the most active reading of which you are capable.

But, you may ask, why is writing necessary? Well, the physical act of writing, with your own hand, brings words and sentences more sharply before your mind and preserves them better in your memory. To set down your reaction to important words and sentences you have read, and the questions they have raised in your mind, is to preserve those reactions and sharpen those questions.

Even if you wrote on a scratch pad, and threw the paper away when you had finished writing, your grasp of the book would be surer. But you don't have to throw the paper away. The margins (top and bottom, as well as side), the end-papers, the very space between the lines, are all available. They aren't sacred. And, best of all, your marks and notes become an integral part of the book and stay there forever. You can pick up the book the following week or year, and there are all your points of agreement, disagreement, doubt, and inquiry. It's like resuming an interrupted conversation with the advantage of being able to pick up where you left off.

And that is exactly what reading a book should be: a conversation between you and the author. Presumably she or he knows more about the subject than you do; naturally, you'll have the proper humility as you approach her or him. But don't let anybody tell you that a reader is supposed to be solely on the receiving end. Understanding is a two-way operation; learning doesn't consist in being an empty receptacle. The learner has to question him- or herself and question the teacher. He or she even has to argue with the teacher, once he or she understands what the teacher is saying. And marking a book is literally an expression of your differences, or agreements of opinion, with the author.

There are all kinds of devices for marking a book intelligently and fruitfully. Here's the way I do it.

1. *Underlining*: of major points, of important or forceful statements.

2. *Vertical lines at the margin*: to emphasize a statement already underlined.

3. *Star, asterisk, or other doodad at the margin*: to be used sparingly, to emphasize the ten or twenty most important statements in the book.

4. *Numbers in the margin*: to indicate the sequence of points the author makes in developing a single argument.

5. *Numbers of other pages in the margin*: to indicate where else in the book the author made points relevant to the point marked; to tie up the ideas in a book, which, though they may be separated by many pages, belong together.

6. *Circling of key words or phrases*.

7. *Writing in the margin, or at the top or bottom of the page, for the sake of*: recording questions (and perhaps answers) which a passage raised in your mind; reducing a complicated discussion to a simple statement; recording the sequence of major points right through the books. I use the endpapers at the back of the book to make a personal index of the author's points in the order of their appearance.

The front endpapers are, to me, the most important. Some people reserve them for a fancy bookplate. I reserve them for fancy thinking. After I have finished reading the book and making my personal index on the back endpapers, I turn to the front and try to outline the book, not page by page, or point by point (I've already done that at the back), but as an integrated structure, with a basic unity and an order of parts. This outline is, to me, the measure of my understanding of the work.

You may say that this business of marking books is going to slow up your reading. It probably will. That's one of the reasons for doing it. Most of us have been taken in by the notion that speed of reading is a measure of our intelligence. There is no such thing as the right speed for intelligent reading. Some things should be read quickly and effortlessly, and some should be read slowly and even laboriously. The sign of intelligence in reading is the ability to read different things differently according to their worth. In the case of good books, the point is not to see how many of them you can get through, but rather how many can get through you—how many you can make your own. A few friends are better than a thousand acquaintances.

Multiple-Choice Questions

Directions (1–6): Use your notes to answer the following questions about the passage read to you. Select the best suggested answer and write its number in the space provided on the answer sheet. The questions may help you think about ideas and information you might use in your writing. You may return to these questions anytime you wish.

1 Which action does the speaker consider to be the *first* step toward full possession of a book?

(1) talking about it

(2) marking in it

(3) reading it

(4) buying it

2 The condition of the books that belong to the true book owner is best described as

(1) intact

(2) worn

(3) clean

(4) drab

3 According to the speaker, what is required for reading to result in learning?

(1) active engagement

(2) strong motivation

(3) a relaxed attitude

(4) a slow pace

4 In describing the empty space in a book as "not sacred," the speaker most likely means that the space is

(1) abundant

(2) necessary

(3) usable

(4) permanent

5 The speaker's devices for marking a book serve as both a stimulus and a

(1) record

(2) comfort

(3) distraction

(4) decoration

6 The use of the word "you" throughout the speech has the effect of

(1) stressing the speaker's importance

(2) appealing directly to the audience

(3) creating a humorous tone

(4) establishing a parallel structure

After you have finished these questions, turn back to page 166. Review **The Situation** and read **Your Task** and the **Guidelines.** Use scrap paper to plan your response. Then write your response for Part A on separate sheets of paper. After you finish your response for Part A, go to page 171 and complete Part B.

PART B

Directions: Read the text and study the graph on the following pages, answer the multiple-choice questions, and write a response based on the situation described below. You may use the margins to take notes as you read and scrap paper to plan your response.

> **The Situation:** The planning team in your school is interested in developing a school-to-work program in connection with businesses in your community. As a member of the career guidance class, you have been asked to write a letter to the school planning team in which you describe the benefits of school-to-work programs and the conditions needed to make such programs successful.

Your Task: Using relevant information from *both* documents, write a letter to the school planning team in which you describe the benefits of school-to-work programs and the conditions needed to make such programs successful. *Write only the body of the letter.*

Guidelines:

Be sure to

- Tell your audience what they need to know about the benefits of school-to-work programs and the conditions needed to make such programs successful

- Use specific, accurate, and relevant information from the text and the graph to support your discussion

- Use a tone and level of language appropriate for a letter to the school planning team

- Organize your ideas in a logical and coherent manner

- Indicate any words taken directly from the text by using quotation marks or referring to the source

- Follow the conventions of standard written English

School-to-Work Programs

Several years ago, faculty at Roosevelt High in Portland, Oregon, recognized that many of their students went directly from high school to low-paying, dead-end jobs. No wonder the school's dropout rate was 13 percent. Kids didn't see a reason to stay in school.

5   Determined to make school more relevant to the workplace, the faculty developed "Roosevelt Renaissance 2000." In their freshman year, students explore six career pathways: natural resources, manufacturing and engineering, human services, health occupations, business and management, and arts and communications. The following year, each student chooses one of the pathways and examines it in depth. The ninth and

10   tenth graders also participate in job shadow experiences, spending three hours a semester watching someone on the job.

During their junior and senior years, Roosevelt students participate in internships that put them in the workplace for longer periods of time. Internships are available at a newspaper, a hospital, an automotive shop, and many other work sites. "One student did

15   an internship with the local electrical union," says business partnership coordinator Amy Henry, "and some kids interested in law have been sent to the public defender or the district attorney's offices."

Win-Win Partnerships

For many schools, the school-to-work initiative is built around a series of partnerships. For example, Eastman Kodak, a major employer in Colorado, introduces

20   elementary students to business by helping them construct a model city using small cardboard structures. "The children use the models to decide on the best place to locate lemonade stands," says Lucille Mantelli, community relations director for Eastman Kodak's Colorado Division. Kodak representatives introduce math concepts by teaching fifth graders to balance a checkbook. They also provide one-on-one job shadowing

25   experiences and offer internships for high school juniors and seniors. "Students come to the plant site two or three hours a day," explains Eastman Kodak's Mantelli. "They do accounting, clerical, or secretarial work for us. We pay them, and they get school credit. We also give them feedback on their performance and developmental opportunities."

In these partnerships, everybody wins. The participating students tend to stay in school

30   and to take more difficult courses than students in schools that don't offer such programs. Business benefits by having a better prepared workforce. "It's a way for us to work with the school systems to develop the type of workforce we'll need in future years," continues Mantelli. "We need employees who understand the basics of reading and writing. We need them to be proficient in math and to be comfortable working on a team."

The Middle Years

While some schools start as early as elementary school, and others wait until high
school, it's in the middle grades where schools really need to catch students. Middle
school is the time when many students lose interest in school, explains Jondel Hoye,
director of the National School-to-Work Office. "Middle schools need to reinforce
exploration activities within the community at the same time they're reinforcing math
and reading skills in the classrooms."

In Texas, weeklong internships in the business community are currently offered to
seventh graders in the Fort Worth Independent School District. The Vital Link program
involves nearly 300 companies which offer students experiences in banking, accounting,
hotel management, engineering, medicine, government, the arts, communications,
education, nonprofit agencies, retailing, legal services, and printing.

"We target middle school students because research shows that at age 12 kids start
making choices that will affect them for the rest of their lives," explains coordinator
Nancy Ricker. Students are placed in internships that match their skills and interests.
Businesspeople come to the school to talk with the kids before the internships begin.
"They tell them about the business and what the people who work there do and what
their salaries are," Ricker explains. "They ask the students to fill out job applications and
explain why that's required."

When the students get to the job site, they are given the same introduction any new
hire receives. After a morning of "work," they return to their classrooms to talk about
their experiences. Their teachers reinforce the link between skills they have used in the
workplace and those learned in the classroom. Vital Link students take harder courses,
perform better on state-mandated tests, and have better attendance and discipline
records than students who are not part of the project.

In Milwaukee, Wisconsin, a school-to-work project introduced middle school
students to the intricacies of city planning. "Representatives from the city came into the
classroom and showed our students how math, science, writing, and communication
skills relate to building new structures," reports Eve Maria Hall, who oversees the
school-to-work initiative for the Milwaukee Public Schools.

Learning Reignited in High School

In Maryland, students can apply to the Baltimore National Academy of Finance, a
school-within-a-school located at Lake Clifton Eastern High School. In addition to
courses in history, English, math, science, and computer skills, students study financial
careers, economics, accounting, security operations, international finance, financial
planning, and banking and credit. "Every Friday," explains Kathleen Floyd, who directs
the academy, "we have a personal development day, when we teach interview skills,
résumé writing, business etiquette, how to dress for success, and how to speak to adults."

70   "Our philosophy is that they can learn as much outside the classroom as in," says Floyd. "It helps them see how classes relate to what's happening in the real world."

"All students have the ability to change the world, not just to live in it," comments Milwaukee's Eve Maria Hall. "To do that, they have to know how to solve problems and use critical thinking skills, and they have to be able to work in teams. They also have to

75   develop transferable skills because it's predicted that they may have to change jobs six or seven times in their lifetime."

From the time students enter school, "We need to encourage them to dream about careers that go beyond what they see today," concludes National School-to-Work's Hoye, noting that "a majority of our kindergarten students will have jobs that don't even exist

80   today."

— Harriett Webster

GRAPH

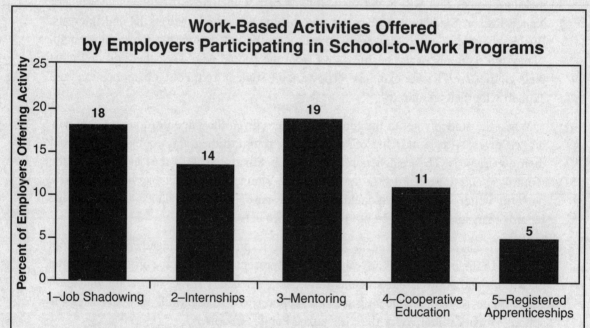

Work-Based Activities Offered by Employers Participating in School-to-Work Programs

1 A student follows an employee for one day or more to learn about a particular occupation or industry.

2 For a specified period of time, students work for an employer to learn about a particular occupation or industry. This may or may not include financial compensation.

3 An employee is assigned to guide a student and serve as a liason with the school on behalf of the student and the firm.

4 Students alternate or coordinate their academic and vocational studies with a paid or unpaid job in a related field.

5 Formal programs registered with the U.S. Department of Labor or with an approved state apprenticeship agency. Registered apprenticeships are typically paid work experiences.

Source: *National Employer Survey,* U.S. Bureau of the Census, 1994

Multiple-Choice Questions

Directions (7–16): Select the best suggested answer to each question and write its number in the space provided on the answer sheet. The questions may help you think about ideas and information you might want to use in your writing. You may return to these questions anytime you wish.

7   The author implies that the main purpose of "Roosevelt Renaissance 2000" was to
   (1)   strengthen connections between school and work
   (2)   attract new business to the community
   (3)   encourage students to take paying jobs in the community
   (4)   improve relations between students and teachers

8   Using the example of Eastman Kodak in Colorado, the author implies that a school-to-work program depends partly on the
   (1)   diversity of the school population
   (2)   involvement of local businesses
   (3)   availability of current technology
   (4)   cooperation of government agencies

9   According to Nancy Ricker (lines 45 through 46), the middle school years are appropriate for career internships because middle school students begin to
   (1)   experience physical growth
   (2)   form strong friendships
   (3)   develop academic skills
   (4)   make significant decisions

10   Lines 55 through 57 imply a correlation between internships and a student's
   (1)   behavior at school
   (2)   salary at work
   (3)   choice of college
   (4)   relationship with parents

11   In lines 59 through 62, Eve Maria Hall implies that Milwaukee students learned that city planning involves knowledge of
   (1)   economic systems
   (2)   social structures
   (3)   academic subjects
   (4)   political strategies

12   The term "transferable skills" (line 75) refers to skills that are
   (1)   easily learned by new workers
   (2)   likely to result in high wages
   (3)   highly technical in nature
   (4)   useful in different situations

13 Hoye's comment about kindergarten students (lines 77–79) implies that
(1) jobs will be scarce in the future
(2) young children learn quickly
(3) society's needs change rapidly
(4) teachers' skills are out-of-date

14 The author develops the text primarily by
(1) providing illustrations of existing programs
(2) examining advantages and disadvantages
(3) comparing opinions of proponents and opponents
(4) explaining ways to develop programs

15 From the graph, a reader can determine which activities are most likely to be
(1) successful
(2) available
(3) difficult
(4) expensive

16 According to the footnotes below the graph, which example illustrates an internship?
(1) Tamika follows a physical therapist for a day.
(2) José writes a research paper about law-related careers.
(3) Sue alternates 3 hours in class with 3 hours at a restaurant job.
(4) Tim works at a newspaper office for 2 weeks.

After you have finished these questions, turn back to page 171. Review **The Situation** and read **Your Task** and the **Guidelines.** Use scrap paper to plan your response. Then write your response to Part B on separate sheets of paper.

The University of the State of New York
REGENTS HIGH SCHOOL EXAMINATION

COMPREHENSIVE EXAMINATION IN ENGLISH
SESSION ONE

Thursday, June 14, 2001 — 9:15 a.m. to 12:15 p.m.

ANSWER SHEET

Student . . . .

School . . . . Grade . . . . Teacher . . . .

Write your answers to the multiple-choice questions for Part A and Part B on this answer sheet.

Part A	Part B
1 _____	7 _____
2 _____	8 _____
3 _____	9 _____
4 _____	10 _____
5 _____	11 _____
6 _____	12 _____
	13 _____
	14 _____
	15 _____
	16 _____

Your essay responses for Part A and Part B should be written on separate sheets of paper.

SESSION TWO

The University of the State of New York

REGENTS HIGH SCHOOL EXAMINATION

COMPREHENSIVE EXAMINATION

IN

ENGLISH
SESSION TWO

Friday, June 15, 2001 — 9:15 a.m. to 12:15 p.m.

This session of the examination has two parts. For Part A, you are to answer all ten multiple-choice questions and write a response, as directed. For Part B, you are to write a response, as directed. The answer sheet for the multiple-choice questions in this session is on page 189. You will write your response on separate sheets of paper.

PART A

Directions: Read the passages on the following pages (a short story and an excerpt from an autobiography). Write the number of the answer to each multiple-choice question on your answer sheet. Then write the essay on separate sheets of paper as described in **Your Task.** You may use the margins to take notes as you read and scrap paper to plan your response.

Your Task:

> After you have read the passages and answered the multiple-choice questions, write a unified essay about the meaning of human dignity, as revealed in the passages. In your essay, use ideas from *both* passages to establish a controlling idea about the meaning of human dignity. Using evidence from *each* passage, develop your controlling idea and show how the author uses specific literary elements or techniques to convey that idea.

Guidelines:

Be sure to

- Use ideas from *both* passages to establish a controlling idea about the meaning of human dignity

- Use specific and relevant evidence from *each* passage to develop your controlling idea

- Show how each author uses specific literary elements (for example: theme, characterization, structure, point of view) or techniques (for example: symbolism, irony, figurative language) to convey the controlling idea

- Organize your ideas in a logical and coherent manner

- Use language that communicates ideas effectively

- Follow the conventions of standard written English

Passage I

Mashenka Pavletsky, a young girl who had only just finished her studies at a boarding school, returning from a walk to the house of the Kushkins, with whom she was living as a governess, found the household in a terrible turmoil. Mihailo, the porter who opened the door to her, was excited and red as a crab.

5   Loud voices were heard from upstairs.

"Madame Kushkin is in a fit, most likely, or else she has quarreled with her husband," thought Mashenka.

In the hall and in the corridor she met maidservants. One of them was crying. Then Mashenka saw, running out of her room, Madame Kushkin's husband, Nikolay
10   Sergeitch, a little man with a flabby face and a bald head. He was red in the face and twitching all over. He passed the governess without noticing her, and throwing up his arms, exclaimed:

"Oh, how horrible it is! How tactless! How stupid! How barbarous! Abominable!"

Mashenka went into her room, and then, for the first time in her life, it was her lot to
15   experience in all its acuteness the feeling that is so familiar to persons in dependent positions, who eat the bread of the rich and powerful, and cannot speak their minds. There was a search going on in her room. The lady of the house, Madame Fenya Kushkin, a stout, broad-shouldered, uncouth woman, was standing at the table, putting back into Mashenka's workbag balls of wool, scraps of materials, and bits of paper. . . .
20   Evidently the governess's arrival took her by surprise, since, on looking round and seeing the girl's pale and astonished face, she was a little taken aback, and muttered:

"*Pardon.* I . . . I upset it accidentally. . . . My sleeve caught in it. . . ."

And saying something more, Madame Kushkin rustled her long skirts and went out. Mashenka looked round her room with wondering eyes, and, unable to understand it, not
25   knowing what to think, shrugged her shoulders, and turned cold with dismay. What had Madame Kushkin been looking for in her workbag? If she really had, as she said, caught her sleeve in it and upset everything, why had Nikolay Sergeitch, the master of the house, dashed out of her room so excited, and red in the face? Why was one drawer of the table pulled out a little way? The whatnot with her books on it, the things on the
30   table, the bed—all bore fresh traces of a search. Her linen-basket, too. The linen had been carefully folded, but it was not in the same order as Mashenka had left it when she went out. So the search had been thorough, most thorough. But what was it for? Why? What had happened? Was not she mixed up in something dreadful? Mashenka turned pale, and feeling cold all over, sank on to her linen-basket.

35   A maidservant came into the room.

"Liza, you don't know why they have been rummaging in my room?" the governess asked her.

"Mistress has lost a brooch worth two thousand," said Liza. "She has been rummaging in everything with her own hands. She even searched Mihailo, the porter, herself. It's a perfect disgrace! But you've no need to tremble like that, miss. They found nothing here. You've nothing to be afraid of if you didn't take the brooch."

"But, Liza, it's vile . . . it's insulting," said Mashenka, breathless with indignation. "It's so mean, so low! What right had she to suspect me and to rummage in my things?"

"You are living with strangers, miss," sighed Liza. "Though you are a young lady, still you are . . . as it were . . . a servant. . . . It's not like living with your papa and mamma."

Mashenka threw herself on the bed and sobbed bitterly. Never in her life had she been subjected to such an outrage, never had she been so deeply insulted. . . . She, well-educated, refined, the daughter of a teacher, was suspected of theft; she could not imagine a greater insult.

"Dinner is ready," the servant summoned Mashenka.

Mashenka brushed her hair, wiped her face with a wet towel, and went into the dining-room. There they had already begun dinner. At one end of the table sat Madame Kushkin with a stupid, solemn, serious face; at the other end Nikolay Sergeitch. Everyone knew that there was an upset in the house, that Madame Kushkin was in trouble, and everyone was silent. Nothing was heard but the sound of munching and the rattle of spoons on the plates.

The lady of the house, herself, was the first to speak.

"It's not the two thousand I regret," said the lady, and a big tear rolled down her cheek. "It's the fact itself that revolts me! I cannot put up with thieves in my house. That's how they repay me for my kindness. . . ."

They all looked into their plates, but Mashenka fancied after the lady's words that everyone was looking at her. A lump rose in her throat; she began crying and put her handkerchief to her lips.

"*Pardon*," she muttered. "I can't help it. My head aches. I'll go away."

And she got up from the table, scraping her chair awkwardly, and went out quickly.

"It really was unsuitable, Fenya," said Nikolay Sergeitch, frowning. "Excuse me, Fenya, but you've no kind of legal right to make a search."

"I know nothing about your laws. All I know is that I've lost my brooch. And I will find the brooch!" She brought her fork down on the plate with a clatter, and her eyes flashed angrily. "And you eat your dinner, and don't interfere in what doesn't concern you!"

Nikolay Sergeitch dropped his eyes mildly and sighed. Meanwhile Mashenka, reaching her room, flung herself on her bed.

There was only one thing left to do—to get away as quickly as possible, not to stay another hour in this place. It was true it was terrible to lose her place, to go back to her parents, who had nothing; but what could she do? Mashenka could not bear the sight of the lady of the house nor of her little room; she felt stifled and wretched here. Mashenka jumped up from the bed and began packing.

"May I come in?" asked Nikolay Sergeitch at the door; he had come up noiselessly to the door, and spoke in a soft, subdued voice. "May I?"

"Come in."

He came in and stood still near the door. "What's this?" he asked, pointing to the basket.

"I am packing. Forgive me, Nikolay Sergeitch, but I cannot remain in your house. I feel deeply insulted by this search!"

"I understand, of course, but you must make allowances. You know my wife is nervous, headstrong; you mustn't judge her too harshly."

Mashenka did not speak.

"If you are so offended," Nikolay Sergeitch went on, "well, if you like, I'm ready to apologize. I ask your pardon."

"I know it's not your fault, Nikolay Sergeitch," said Mashenka, looking him full in the face with her big tear-stained eyes. "Why should you worry yourself?"

"I took my wife's brooch," Nikolay Sergeitch said quickly.

Mashenka, amazed and frightened, went on packing. "It's nothing to wonder at," Nikolay Sergeitch went on after a pause. "It's an everyday story! I need money, and she . . . won't give it to me. It was my father's money that bought this house and everything, you know! It's all mine, and the brooch belonged to my mother, and . . . it's all mine! And she took it, took possession of everything. . . . I beg you most earnestly, overlook it . . . stay on. Will you stay?"

"No!" said Mashenka resolutely, beginning to tremble. "Let me alone, I entreat you!"

"Then you won't stay?" asked Nikolay Sergeitch. "Stay! If you go, there won't be a human face left in the house. It's awful!"

Nikolay Sergeitch's pale, exhausted face besought her, but Mashenka shook her head, and with a wave of his hand he went out.

Half an hour later she was on her way.

—Anton Chekhov

Passage II

She was a small woman, old and wrinkled. When she started washing for us, she was already past seventy. Most women of her age were sickly, weak, broken in body. All the old women in our street had bent backs and leaned on sticks when they walked. But this washwoman, small and thin as she was, possessed a strength that came from generations
5 of peasant forebears. Mother would count out to her a bundle of laundry that had accumulated over several weeks. She would lift the unwieldy pack, load it on her narrow shoulders, and carry it the long way home. It must have been a walk of an hour and a half.

She would bring the laundry back about two weeks later. My mother had never been so pleased with any washwoman. Every piece of linen sparkled like polished silver.
10 Every piece was neatly ironed. Yet she charged no more than the others. She was a real find. Mother always had her money ready, because it was too far for the old woman to come a second time.

Laundering was not easy in those days. The old woman had no faucet where she lived but had to bring in the water from a pump. For the linens to come out so clean, they had
15 to be scrubbed thoroughly in a washtub, rinsed with washing soda, soaked, boiled in an enormous pot, starched, then ironed. Every piece was handled ten times or more. And the drying! It could not be done outside because thieves would steal the laundry. The wrung-out wash had to be carried up to the attic and hung on clotheslines. In the winter it would become as brittle as glass and almost break when touched. Only God knows all
20 the old woman had to endure each time she did a wash!

That winter was a harsh one. The streets were in the grip of a bitter cold. No matter how much we heated our stove, the windows were covered with frostwork and decorated with icicles. The newspapers reported that people were dying of the cold. Coal became dear. The winter had become so severe that even the schools were closed.

25 On one such day the washwoman, now nearly eighty years old, came to our house. A good deal of laundry had accumulated during the past weeks. Mother gave her a pot of tea to warm herself, as well as some bread. The old woman sat on a kitchen chair, trembling and shaking, and warmed her hands against the teapot. Her fingers were gnarled from work, and perhaps from arthritis too. These hands spoke of the
30 stubbornness of mankind, of the will to work not only as one's strength permits but beyond the limits of one's power. Mother counted and wrote down the list: men's undershirts, women's vests, long-legged drawers, bloomers, petticoats, shifts, featherbed covers, pillowcases, and sheets.

The bundle was big, bigger than usual. When the woman placed it on her shoulders,
35 it covered her completely. At first she swayed, as though she were about to fall under the load. But an inner obstinacy seemed to call out: No, you may not fall. A donkey may permit himself to fall under his burden, but not a human being, the crown of creation.

It was fearful to watch the old woman staggering out with the enormous pack, out into the frost, where the snow was dry as salt and the air was filled with dusty white
40 whirlwinds, like goblins dancing in the cold. Would the old woman ever reach home?

She disappeared, and Mother sighed and prayed for her.

Usually the woman brought back the wash after two or, at the most, three weeks. But three weeks passed, then four and five, and nothing was heard of the old woman.

One evening, while Mother was sitting near the kerosene lamp mending a shirt, the
45 door opened and a small puff of steam, followed by a gigantic bundle, entered. Under the bundle tottered the old woman, her face as white as a linen sheet. Mother uttered a half-choked cry. It was as though a corpse had entered the room. I ran toward the old woman and helped her unload her pack. She was even thinner now, more bent. Her face had become more gaunt, and her head shook from side to side as though she were saying
50 no. She could not utter a clear word, but mumbled something with her sunken mouth and pale lips.

After the old woman had recovered somewhat, she told us that she had been ill, very ill. She had been so sick that someone had called a doctor, and the doctor had sent for a priest. Someone had informed the son, and he had contributed money for a coffin and
55 for the funeral. But the Almighty had not yet wanted to take this pain-racked soul to himself. She began to feel better, she became well, and as soon as she was able to stand on her feet once more, she resumed her washing. Not just ours, but the wash of several other families too.

"I could not rest easy in my bed because of the wash," the old woman explained.
60 "The wash would not let me die."

"With the help of God you will live to be a hundred and twenty," said my mother, as a benediction.

"God forbid! What good would such a long life be? The work becomes harder and harder . . . my strength is leaving me . . . I do not want to be a burden on anyone!" The
65 old woman muttered and crossed herself and raised her eyes toward heaven. Then she left, promising to return in a few weeks for a new load of wash.

But she never came back. The wash she had returned was her last effort on this earth. She had been driven by an indomitable will to return the property to its rightful owners, to fulfill the task she had undertaken.

—Issac Singer

Multiple-Choice Questions

Directions (1–10): Select the best suggested answer to each question and write its number in the space provided on the answer sheet. The questions may help you think about the ideas and information you might want to use in your essay. You may return to these questions anytime you wish.

Passage I (the short story) — Questions 1–5 refer to Passage I.

1 The confusion Mashenka encounters upon returning to the Kushkin household was caused by the theft of
  (1) money
  (2) jewelry
  (3) a linen-basket
  (4) a portrait

2 From the events in the story, what feeling is Mashenka most likely referring to in lines 14 through 16?
  (1) guilt
  (2) gratitude
  (3) humiliation
  (4) fear

3 Which word best describes the character of Madame Kushkin?
  (1) domineering
  (2) dignified
  (3) courageous
  (4) independent

4 What reason did Nikolay Sergeitch give for stealing the brooch?
  (1) He wanted his wife to be blamed for the theft.
  (2) He wanted to give the brooch to Mashenka.
  (3) He felt the brooch had no real value.
  (4) He felt the brooch was rightfully his.

5 In choosing to leave the Kushkin household, Mashenka displays an attitude of
  (1) regret
  (2) apology
  (3) self-respect
  (4) ill humor

6 The author's description in lines 8 through 10 has the effect of emphasizing the
   (1) difficulty of pleasing his mother
   (2) washwoman's pride in her work
   (3) fee for the washwoman's services
   (4) author's status in the village

7 The author most likely describes the details of laundering (lines 13 through 20) in order to
   (1) highlight the difficulty of the task
   (2) reveal his own familiarity with laundering
   (3) contrast the washwoman's life with that of his family
   (4) identify the setting of the story

8 In lines 28 through 31, the author uses the washwoman's hands as a metaphor for
   (1) prayer
   (2) humility
   (3) forgiveness
   (4) endurance

9 In line 36, the word "obstinacy" most nearly means
   (1) stubbornness
   (2) honesty
   (3) warning
   (4) temptation

10 In lines 59 and 60, the washwoman implies that she refused to die because of her
   (1) need for money
   (2) sense of duty
   (3) longing for respect
   (4) love of work

After you have finished these questions, turn back to page 180. Review **Your Task** and the **Guidelines.** Use scrap paper to plan your response. Then write your response to Part A on separate sheets of paper. After you finish your response for Part A, go on to page 188 and complete Part B.

PART B

Your Task:

Write a critical essay in which you discuss *two* works of literature you have read from the particular perspective of the statement that is provided for you in the **Critical Lens.** In your essay, provide a valid interpretation of the statement, agree *or* disagree with the statement as you have interpreted it, and support your opinion using specific references to appropriate literary elements from the two works. You may use scrap paper to plan your response. Write your essay on separate sheets of paper.

Critical Lens:

> "All conflict in literature is, in its simplest form, a struggle between good and evil."

Guidelines:

Be sure to

- Provide a valid interpretation of the critical lens that clearly establishes the criteria for analysis

- Indicate whether you agree *or* disagree with the statement as you have interpreted it

- Choose *two* works you have read that you believe best support your opinion

- Use the criteria suggested by the critical lens to analyze the works you have chosen

- Avoid plot summary. Instead, use specific references to appropriate literary elements (for example: theme, characterization, setting, point of view) to develop your analysis

- Organize your ideas in a unified and coherent manner

- Specify the titles and authors of the literature you choose

- Follow the conventions of standard written English

COMPREHENSIVE EXAMINATION IN ENGLISH
SESSION TWO

Friday, June 15, 2001 — 9:15 a.m. to 12:15 p.m.

ANSWER SHEET

Student . . . .

School . . . . Grade . . . . Teacher . . . .

Write your answers to the multiple-choice questions for Part A on this answer sheet.

Part A

1	_____	6	_____
2	_____	7	_____
3	_____	8	_____
4	_____	9	_____
5	_____	10	_____

Your essay responses for Part A and Part B should be written on separate sheets of paper.

ANSWERS AND EXPLANATIONS FOR PRACTICE EXAM: JUNE 2001

SESSION ONE

Part A: Multiple-Choice Questions

1 (4) If you took good notes while listening to the passage, they will help you answer the question. The question asks about sequence, and the word *first* is the context clue that tells you this. Does the speaker think that talking about a book is the first step toward fully possessing it? No, so eliminate answer choice (1). Does he think that marking in a book is the first step toward fully possessing it? Most of his speech is about marking in books, so answer choice (2) may tempt you, but if you think about it logically, marking in a book is not the first step toward fully possessing it as explained by the speaker, so eliminate (2). Does the speaker think that reading a book is the first step toward fully possessing it? No, the speaker does not mention that reading is the first step toward possession of a book, so eliminate choice (3). What do you have to do before you can mark in a book? The speaker tells you not to mark up books you borrow, and he says explicitly in the beginning of his speech that you have to buy the book in order to mark it up. According to the speaker, buying a book is only the first step toward full possession. Answer choice (4) is correct.

2 (2) The question asks you about how something in the speech is best described. To answer the question correctly, you would have had to pay close attention to the language the speaker uses to describe "true" book owners and their books. Think about the speaker's idea of the "true book owner." Does the word *intact* best describe the condition of the books that belong to the true book owner? No; according the speaker, intact, untouched books belong to "deluded individual[s]," people who buy standard books that everyone has, but don't actually read them. You can eliminate answer choice (1). Does the word *worn* best describe the condition of the books that belong to the true book owner? Yes! Choice (2) is correct, as the word *worn* describes the "dog-eared and dilapidated" condition of books belonging to the true book owner.

3 (1) Think about the main idea of the speech in order to answer the question correctly. The speaker makes the argument that people should write in their books because they can learn more from them if they do so. According to the speaker, is active engagement required for reading to result in learning? Yes; active engagement refers to writing notes as the reader reads a book. The speaker says, "If reading is to accomplish anything more than passing time, it must be active." The activity of taking notes makes the reader question the author and helps the reader remember the author's ideas. The correct answer choice is (1). What about choice (2), "strong motivation" and choice (3), "a relaxed attitude"? The speaker does not focus on motivation or relaxed attitudes, so you can eliminate (2) and (3). Answer choice (4) may seem like a good answer because the speaker mentions that some books "should be read slowly and

even laboriously." However, the speaker does not suggest that reading at a slow pace is required for learning all the time—just some of the time. You can eliminate choice (4) because it's not as good as answer choice (1).

4 (3) When a question asks you about what the speaker *most likely* means, it is asking you to draw a conclusion based on the information in the passage. In these types of questions, the answer is not directly stated in the passage, so you have to use your logic and inference skills to come up with the correct answer choice. That might sound complicated, but if think about it in simple terms, the question is just asking you what makes sense in the context of the passage. When the speaker says that the empty space in a book is "not sacred," he's talking about writing marks and notes in the empty space. Of the answer choices given here, only (3), "usable," makes sense in this context. By saying that the empty space in a book is "not sacred," the speaker suggests that it is okay for you to use it to write.

5 (1) The question should be a snap to answer if you use Process of Elimination. Do the speaker's devices for marking a book serve as both a stimulus and a record? Yes, they do, so hold on to choice (1). You may feel certain that (1) is correct when you read it, but you should *always* read *all* the answer choices before selecting one because there may be an even better choice than the first one you think is correct. You can also compare the subsequent answer choices to see if they are as good as the first one you think is correct. Do the speaker's devices for marking a book serve as both a stimulus and a comfort? You might guess that they might be a comfort to the speaker, but he never mentions this, so you can eliminate choice (2). Do the speaker's devices for marking a book serve as both a stimulus and a distraction? No; there is no mention of the markings in a book as being distracting, so eliminate choice (3). Do the speaker's devices for marking a book serve as both a stimulus and a decoration? Although the scribbles in the margins and asterisks by key points may serve as decoration in the book, this is not the best answer choice. You can eliminate choice (4) as well. Using POE you see that your initial selection of choice (1) is correct. You know that the markings in a book serve as a record because they "stay there forever," according to the speaker.

6 (2) The question asks you to think about the effect of the speaker's language. Think about why he uses the word "you" throughout the speech and you will be able to determine its effect. By using the word "you," the speaker talks directly to the audience. Answer choice (1), "stressing the speaker's importance," contradicts the effect of using the word "you," so eliminate it. By using the word "you," the speaker stresses the importance of the audience throughout the speech. The word "you" as used throughout the speech has the effect of appealing directly to the audience, so answer choice (2) is correct. There is nothing humorous about the use of the word "you" in the speech, so you can eliminate choice (3). Parallel structure is a grammatical device in which an author uses similar patterns of words within a text. This is not the effect of using the word "you" throughout the speech, so you can eliminate choice (4) as well.

Part A: Essay

The people who grade your essay will be thinking about the following questions when they decide how to score it. You should think about these questions when you review your essay.

- Have you clearly stated the main idea of your essay in the introduction?

  - Your main idea should be specific to what your essay is about; don't just restate the Situation or Your Task.

  - The main idea of your essay should be to persuade your local Board of Education to provide personal copies of assigned novels for students to keep.

- Have you addressed each bullet point in the Guidelines in your essay?

  - The essay should tell your audience what they need to know in order to persuade them of the value of book ownership.

  - The essay should use relevant examples from Dr. Mortimer Adler's 1940 speech about the value of book ownership.

  - The essay should persuasively present your argument for why the Board should provide personal copies of assigned novels for students to keep.

- Have you supported the main idea of your essay with relevant opinions, examples, and details taken from Dr. Adler's speech, and properly indicated when you are quoting from the speech?

- Have you clearly and logically organized your essay?

  - The topic of each body paragraph should be clear and coherent.

  - The transitions from topic to topic should be clear.

- Have you written you essay in a tone that is appropriate for a presentation to the Board of Education?

- Have you concluded your essay with a summary of its main points?

- Have you used correct spelling, grammar, and punctuation?

Here's an example of top-score essay.

The proposal being considered by the Board of Education to provide personal copies of assigned novels for students to keep represents an exciting change in the way we think about learning and education. Owning a book can provide an entirely different learning experience to students than simply borrowing a book. It allows readers to engage with a text on a far deeper level. According to noted philosopher and educator Dr. Mortimer Adler, readers best engage with texts by having the freedom to write in books, an act which gives readers "full ownership" of a book by allowing them to engage in a conversation with the author. Providing students with their own copies of novels which they can keep will lead to more lasting learning.

In a 1940 speech whose ideas are still relevant today, Dr. Adler proclaims that you can make yourself a part of a book by writing in it. Dr. Adler goes on to list a variety of ways that writing in a book facilitates the reader's learning process, and I urge the Board of Education to bear these ideas in mind when considering the proposal. First of all, Adler states that marking up a book is is important while reading because it keeps the reader aware of what's being read. Writing in a book makes the act of reading more active, allowing readers to note thoughts, questions, and concerns as they read rather than just passively absorbing the text.

Second, Adler states that active reading is thinking, and jotting down notes as people read helps them think more deeply about what they are reading. As Adler puts it, "The marked book is usually the thought-through book." This is a very important point for the Board to consider. In my opinion, this point alone is sufficient argument in favor of the proposal, for it seems the Board would want to encourage anything that will help students think through books as they read them. Third and equally important, Adler points out that writing in a book facilitates recall. Marking up books actually helps readers remember both the thoughts they had while reading the book and the thoughts the author was expressing.

This third point is crucial because novels are usually full of layers of ideas and details, and it is often difficult for students to remember much of what they have read. For example, a student may want to recall a specific point that was particularly important to her from a *novel in order to discuss it in class. Having the freedom to mark up her book will make this much easier, and will ultimately contribute to a livelier, deeper class discussion of the text, a point which I think would make any teacher wholeheartedly support the proposal.*

Giving students their own copies of novels will grant them the opportunity to keep these books for a lifetime, and, according to Adler, allow them to resume their "conversations" with the author at any point in time just by opening a book and seeing their scribbled notes. As Adler points out, writing in books helps students be active readers and question what they are reading, leading them to question even themselves and their teachers, a step which is important to becoming a critical thinker. As the Board can see from the above points, the cost of providing students with their own copies of assigned novels is well worth the enormous benefits this will provide to students and teachers. Students who develop these active reading habits while in school will be much more likely to be lifelong readers, learners, and critical thinkers.

Here's an explanation of the top-score essay.

This essay receives full credit (6 points) because it provides a persuasive argument for why the Board of Education should provide personal copies of assigned novels for students to keep. The writing task requires test-takers to write a presentation persuading the Board of Education to provide personal copies of assigned novels for students to keep based on the information from Dr. Adler's speech about the importance of book ownership. The task is complete in this essay.

In this essay, the writer tells the audience what they need to know to persuade them of the value of book ownership. The writer discusses several examples taken from Dr. Adler's speech about the value of book ownership. The examples include the ideas that writing in a book (which is only possible if one owns the book) helps readers' minds stay active, helps readers think more deeply about what they are reading, and helps facilitate recall. The examples all support the assertion that book ownership empowers students to be more active readers, learners, and critical thinkers. Each example is clearly stated, coherent, and relevant to the task of convincing the Board of Education of the value of book ownership.

The writer summarizes the main points made in Dr. Adler's speech in a clear and well-written essay. The essay persuasively presents a solid argument for why the Board should provide personal copies of assigned novels for students to keep. The essay is highly organized, there are no grammatical errors, and the content is comprehensible.

Part B: Multiple-Choice Questions

7 (1) The question asks about the main purpose of "Roosevelt Renaissance 2000." When you answer questions that ask you about the main purpose of something, be careful not to get distracted by answer choices that mention a small detail from the passage. Try to look at the big picture when answering questions like this one. Choice (3), "encourage students to take paying jobs in the community," is an example of a small detail that may seem like a good answer choice. Although the passage does mention students and paying jobs, this is not the main purpose "Roosevelt Renaissance 2000." You can eliminate choice (3). Lines 4 and 5 of the passage state, "Determined to make school more relevant to the workplace, the faculty developed 'Roosevelt Renaissance 2000.'" So answer choice (1), "strengthen connections between school and work," best expresses the main purpose of "Roosevelt Renaissance 2000."

8 (2) The question asks about something the author *implies,* which means it may not be directly stated in the text. If you are unsure about which answer choice is correct, reread the part of the passage that uses the example of Eastman Kodak in Colorado. Line 17 states, "For many schools, the school-to-work initiative is built around a series of partnerships." The word "partnerships" is a good context clue. Does this imply that a school-to-work program depends partly on the diversity of the school population? No; it implies that the programs depend on schools and business, not the diversity of the school population. So you can eliminate choice (1). Does the word "partnerships" imply that a school-to-work program depends partly on the involvement of local businesses? Yes; partnerships between schools and business create an environment in which "everybody wins." Choice (2) is correct. You can eliminate choice (3) because the example of Eastman Kodak does not mention current technology. You can also eliminate choice (4) because Eastman Kodak is not a government agency; it's a privately owned business.

9 (4) If you look back at lines 45 through 46, answering this question will be a cinch. Nancy Ricker says, "We target middle school students because research shows that at age 12 kids start making choices that will affect them for the rest of their lives." Therefore, the middle school years are appropriate for career internships because middle school students begin to make significant decisions. Answer choice (4) is correct. None of the other answer choices refer back to the statement by Ricker that is mentioned in the question, so they cannot be correct.

10 (1) All the information you need to answer the question is right there in lines 55 through 57: "Vital Link students take harder courses, perform better on state-mandated tests, and have better attendance and discipline records than students who are not part of the project." Do the lines suggest a relationship between internships and a student's behavior at school? They certainly do! Answer choice (1) is correct because the lines suggest that students who have internships are well behaved in school. The lines of text do not suggest a relationship between internships and a student's salary at work, choice of college, or relationship with parents. None of these things are mentioned in lines 55 through 57, so you can eliminate choices (2), (3), and (4).

11 (3) You've already seen with the last two questions that it's simple to answer questions when they refer directly back to specific lines in the passage because the lines contain the information you need to select the correct answer choice. Reread lines 59 through 62. Eve Maria Hall says students learned "how math, science, writing, and communication skills relate to building new structures." Think about what the question is asking in relation to Hall's statement. Did students learn that city planning involves knowledge of economic systems? Math, science, writing, and communication skills aren't economic systems, so eliminate choice (1). Are they social structures? No, so eliminate choice (2). Are they academic subjects? Of course they are! Choice (3) is the correct answer.

12 (4) Read the line this phrase appears in to help you get a better sense of its context. If you already know what the word "transferable" means, answering the question may seem easy. But even if you aren't sure what the word means, the context of the sentence will give you clues to help you answer the question correctly. Lines 74–76 state that students "have to develop transferable skills, because it's predicted that they may have to change jobs six or seven times in their lifetime." If they need skills that they can use in different jobs, does the term "transferable skills" refer to skills that are easily learned by new workers? Answer choice (1) is a bit tricky. It may seem correct, because if people are changing jobs it would make it easier if the skills they need for a new job are easy to learn, but there is a better choice. If people need skills that they can use in different jobs, choice (4), "useful in different situations," makes more sense than choice (1). "Transferable skills" refers to skills that are useful in different situations. Choice (4) is the correct answer.

13 (3) Look back at lines 77–79, where Hoye's comment appears. Hoye states, "a majority of our kindergarten students will have jobs that don't even exist today." Does this comment imply that jobs will be scarce in the future? No; Hoye doesn't say anything about a lack of jobs, so you can eliminate choice (1). Does Hoye's comment imply that young children learn quickly? No; this is an irrelevant statement. It may be true, but it is not implied by Hoye's comment, so eliminate choice (2). Does the comment imply that society's needs change rapidly? Think about it. If today's kindergarten students will have jobs that don't even exist today, this does imply that society's needs change rapidly, doesn't it? Yes! New jobs are created to adapt to society's changing needs, which means that (3) is correct.

14 (1) Unlike most of the previous questions, which asked about specific details in the passage, this question requires you to think about the text as a whole. You have already answered seven questions about this particular text, so you should be familiar with it by now. The question asks how the author develops the text. That sounds more complicated than it is. The question is really asking what is primarily included in the text. Does the author primarily include illustrations of existing programs? Yes; the author mentions various school-to-work programs in Oregon, Colorado, Texas, Wisconsin, and Maryland. Answer choice (1) seems correct, but remember that it's always a good idea to read all the answer choices before you select one. Does the author primarily include advantages and disadvantages of programs, opinions of proponents and opponents, or ways to develop programs? No, she does not. So you can eliminate choices (2), (3), and (4). Now that you have read through and eliminated all of the other choices, you can be certain choice (1) is correct.

15 (2) It's time to shift gears, as this question asks about the graph, not the text. (You'd forgotten about the graph for a minute there, hadn't you?) What information is the graph representing? It is representing work-based activities offered by employers participating in school-to-work programs. The title above the graph tells you that. Can a reader determine from the graph which activities are most likely to be successful? No; the graph says nothing about success rates of the activities shown, so you can eliminate choice (1). Can a reader determine from the graph which activities are most likely to be available? The graph shows the percent of employers offering each of the activities, so a reader can determine from these percentages which activities are most likely to be available to students, making choice (2) the correct answer. The graph contains no information about how difficult or expensive the activities are, so you can eliminate choices (3) and (4).

16 (4) The question asks about the footnotes beneath the graph, which means you need to read them carefully. Sometimes it is tempting to just quickly scan a graph without carefully reading all the text, but this is a bad idea when you are taking a test! You can see from the graph that internships are defined in footnote 2. The question asks you to choose which example in the answer choices illustrates an internship. Does choice (1), "Tamika follows a physical therapist for a day," illustrate an internship? No; it illustrates job shadowing, which is another activity on the graph. Eliminate choice (1). Does choice (2), "José writes a research paper about law-related careers," illustrate an internship? No; an internship involves actually working at a job, not researching it, so you can eliminate choice (2). Does choice (3), "Sue alternates 3 hours in class with 3 hours at a restaurant job," illustrate an internship? No; it illustrates cooperative education, which is another activity on the graph. Eliminate choice (3). Does choice (4), "Tim works at a newspaper office for 2 weeks," illustrate an internship? Yes, it does. Choice (4) is correct because, according to footnote 2, the definition of an internship is that a student works for an employer for a specified period of time.

Part B: Essay

The people who grade your essay will be thinking about the following questions when they decide how to score it. You should think about these questions when you review your essay.

- Have you clearly stated the main idea of your essay in the introduction?
  - Your main idea should be specific to what your essay is about; don't just restate Your Task.
  - The main idea of your essay should describe the benefits of school-to-work programs and the conditions needed to make such programs successful.
- Have you addressed each bullet point in the Guidelines in the body paragraphs of your essay?
  - The body paragraphs should inform your audience about the benefits of school-to-work programs and the conditions needed to make such programs successful based on information in the text *and* the graph.
  - The body paragraphs should include use specific, accurate, and relevant information from the text *and* the graph to support your discussion.
- Have you supported the main idea of your essay with relevant facts, examples, and details from *both* the text and the graph, and properly indicated when you are quoting from the text or referring to statistics from the graph?
- Have you clearly and logically organized your essay?
  - The topic of each body paragraph should be clear and coherent.
  - The transitions from topic to topic should be clear.
- Have you written you essay in a tone that is appropriate for a letter to the school planning team?
- Have you remembered that "write only the body of the letter" means to leave off any addresses and greeting, but not the introduction?
- Have you concluded your essay with a summary of its main points?
- Have you used correct spelling, grammar, and punctuation?

Here's an example of a top-score essay.

I am writing this letter to share the benefits of school-to-work programs with the school planning team, and to let you know what conditions are necessary to make these programs successful. School-to-work programs have been successfully instituted at a number of schools and have proven to have great benefits for students and the business community. These programs help integrate school curriculum and the paying jobs students will move on to after graduation, better preparing students for their future work-lives. The programs also provide students with incentive to stay in school until graduation and help them perform better while in school.

School-to-work programs can include many different work-related activities that students can participate in. Two of the most common and most important such activities are job shadowing and internships. The U.S. Bureau of the Census's 1994 <u>National Employer Survey</u> provides helpful definitions of these activities and shows the percentage of employers offering them. Job shadowing, which is offered by eighteen percent of employers, allows a student to follow "an employee for a day or more to learn about a particular occupation or industry." One-on-one job shadowing has been successfully offered to Colorado students by Eastman Kodak, as have internships for high school juniors and seniors. According to the <u>National Employer Survey</u>, internships involve students working for an employer "for a specified period of time . . . to learn about a particular occupation or industry." Internships can be paid or unpaid, and they are offered by 14 percent of employers.

The involvement of Eastman Kodak with the Colorado students illustrates a fundamental principle of school-to-work programs: They rely on partnerships between businesses and schools. Fortunately, many businesses are eager to participate in these programs because they receive benefits along with the students. According to Harriett Webster, author of the article "School-to-Work Programs," this creates a "win-win" situation for both the participating businesses and the schools. Eastman Kodak's Lucille Mantelli states that school-to-work programs are "a way for us to work with the school systems to develop the type of workforce we'll need in future years."

Internships also play an important role in Texas's Vital Link program, in which nearly 300 companies participate. This program targets middle-school students, and the benefits of the program are proven. According to Webster, "Vital Link students take harder courses, perform better on state-mandated tests, and have better attendance and discipline records than students who are not part of the project." In addition to the weeklong internships, selected to match a student's interests, teachers work to "reinforce the link between skills they [students] have used in the workplace and those learned in the classroom." This allows students see how their academic skills can serve them in the real world, and how work skills can apply in the classroom as well, so neither school nor work seems to exist independently of each other.

Portland, Oregon's Roosevelt High created a successful school-to-work program in response to the realization that, according to Webster, "many of their students went directly from high school to low-paying, dead-end jobs." The school's dropout rate was 13 percent because school just didn't seem relevant to students with such dim prospects for the future. The "Roosevelt Renaissance 2000" program involved students from freshman year until graduation, and entailed first researching different professions, then job shadowing, and finally internships, empowering students to feel they have more work options open to them than just dead-end jobs.

Kathleen Floyd, director of the Baltimore National Academy of Finance, says that students "can learn as much outside the classroom as in. It helps them see how classes relate to what's happening in the real world." This is the key to successful school-to-work programs—an integration of academic and real-world skills that's supported by partnerships between businesses and schools. As you can see from the examples presented here, these programs offer numerous benefits to both students and the business community, and help students prepare to become successful members of that business community. Improved performance in school coupled with a better-prepared workforce truly is a "win-win" situation!

Here's an explanation of the top-score essay.

This essay receives full credit (6 points) because it provides a thorough explanation of the benefits of school-to-work programs and the conditions needed to make such programs successful. The writing task requires test-takers to discuss the benefits of school-to-work programs and the conditions needed to make such program successful using information from *both* documents. The task is complete in this essay.

In this essay, the writer explains many of the benefits of school-to-work programs as presented in the text, including benefits to students and the business community, as well as the conditions required to make these programs successful, focusing primarily on the partnerships between schools and businesses. The writer explains two of the main activities of school-to-work programs, job shadowing and internships, and provides specific examples of schools and businesses that have worked together to successfully institute these activities as part of school-to-work programs. The writer uses information from the graph as well as from the text in the explanations of these activities. Details and facts from the text and the graph substantiate the discussion of the benefits of school-to-work programs and explain the conditions needed to make such programs successful.

The writer summarizes the main points from the text in a clear and well-written essay and incorporates information from the graph as well. The essay clearly and persuasively explains the benefits of school-to-work programs and the conditions needed to make such programs successful. It is highly organized, there are no grammatical errors, it is written in a tone appropriate for a letter to a school planning team, and the content is comprehensible.

SESSION TWO

Part A: Multiple-Choice Questions

1 (2) Questions 1 through 5 refer to Passage I, the short story by Anton Chekhov. Think about what was stolen in the Kushkin household. It was Madame Kushkin's brooch. Do you know what a brooch is? If you do, you will know that it is a piece of jewelry worn as a pin, so choice (2) is correct. Even if you don't know what the word "brooch" means, POE can help you select the correct answer. Choice (1), "money," simply doesn't make sense, because if money were stolen the characters would have used the word "money" to describe what was stolen; Liza wouldn't have said that Madame Kushkin lost "a brooch worth two thousand." You can eliminate choice (1). Choice (3), "a linen-basket," is a distracting answer choice that may confuse you because the linen-basket is a detail that is mentioned in the story, but it is not the item that was stolen. You can eliminate choice (3). Even if you didn't know whether a brooch is a piece of jewelry or a "portrait," choice (4), you could use logic to figure out which choice is correct. Would a portrait be easy to hide in a workbag, or on the porter's person? Not unless it were a very small portrait! "Jewelry," choice (2), is the most logical answer.

2 (3) Look back at the lines the question asks about and think about them in the context of the story's events. Lines 14 through 16 tell the reader that Mashenka experiences "the feeling that is so familiar to persons in dependent positions, who eat the bread of the rich and powerful, and cannot speak their minds." If Mashenka were feeling "gratitude," choice (2), she would have no reason not to speak about it. You can eliminate (2). It's likely that she wouldn't speak about feelings of "guilt," choice (1); "humiliation," choice (3); or "fear," choice (4), but in the context of the story, it is most likely that Mashenka feels humiliation. She feels insulted because Madame Kushkin suspected her of stealing and searched her room for the brooch. Answer choice (3) is correct.

3 (1) Madame Kushkin is first described as "a stout, broad-shouldered, uncouth woman," and her character is revealed through her actions in the story. Her husband confides in Mashenka about how Madame Kushkin "took possession of everything" after they were married. The way Madame Kushkin searches the porter and Mashenka's room and makes a scene at dinner do not indicate that she is "dignified," choice (2), or "courageous," choice (3). She may be perceived as "independent," choice (4), but this is not the best answer choice. Madame Kushkin's actions certainly reveal her to be "domineering," choice (1). Her domineering, or controlling, nature is shown when she scolds her husband when tries to defend Mashenka at dinner. Madame Kushkin tells him, ". . . you eat your dinner, and don't interfere in what doesn't concern you!" The best answer choice is (1).

4 (4) Think about what Nikolay Sergeitch said to Mashenka when he confessed that he was the one who stole the brooch. Did he want his wife to blamed for the theft? No; he didn't mention this, and it doesn't make sense that Madame Kushkin would have stolen from herself, so eliminate choice (1). Nikolay didn't want to give the brooch to Mashenka, either, so eliminate answer choice (2). He obviously didn't think the brooch had no value, as it is clearly established in the story that the brooch is worth a lot of money, so eliminate choice (3). Nikolay did tell Mashenka that "the brooch belonged to my mother" and his wife "took possession of everything." He even exclaimed that "it's all mine!" so he did feel the brooch was rightfully his. Choice (4) is correct.

5 (3) When Nikolay Sergeitch begs Mashenka to stay, she replies "No! Let me alone, I entreat you!" and the author tells us that she said this "resolutely." Do Mashenka's words and tone display an attitude of regret or apology? No, quite the contrary, so eliminate answer choices (1) and (2). Do they display and attitude of self-respect? Yes! Mashenka feels compelled to leave the household of her wealthy employers to go back to her parents who "had nothing" because she feels her self-respect has been violated by the search of her room. Answer choice (3) is correct. Readers may think that Mashenka displays ill humor, or a bad mood by choosing to leave the Kushkin household. But choice (4) is clearly not the *best* answer choice, as her attitude of self-respect is supported by her comments and actions throughout the story.

6 (2) Questions 6 through 10 refer to Passage II, the excerpt from an autobiography by Issac Singer. Look back at lines 8 through 10. The lines read, in part, "My mother had never been so pleased. Every piece of linen sparkled like polished silver. Every piece was neatly ironed. Yet she charged no more than the others." Does this description have the effect of emphasizing the difficulty of pleasing the author's mother? No; this directly contradicts the passage, so eliminate (1). Does this description have the effect of emphasizing the washerwoman's pride in her work? It certainly does, because no one would bother to make linen "sparkle like polished silver" and not charge extra for it unless they took pride in their work. Choice (2) is the correct answer. The description does not have the effect of emphasizing the fee for the washerwoman's services. It states that her fee was "no more than the others," so you can eliminate choice (3). You can also eliminate choice (4) because the description has nothing to do with the author's status in the village.

7 (1) Take another look at lines 13 through 20. Why do you think the author describes the details of laundering? It sounds like very difficult work, especially for an older person. Think about these lines in the context of the whole story, keeping the story's end in mind, and it should be clear that the author most likely describes the details of laundering in order to highlight the difficulty of the task. The lines begin with the statement, "Laundering was not easy in those days," and they go on to describe all the hard work involved in washing clothes. Choice (1) is the best answer.

8 (4) The question asks you to interpret the author's use of metaphor. Look back at lines 28 through 31: "Her fingers were gnarled from work, and perhaps from arthritis too. These hands spoke of the stubbornness of mankind, of the will to work not only as one's strength permits, but beyond the limits of one's power." In these lines, does the author use the washerwoman's hands as a metaphor for prayer? No; these lines do not allude to prayer, so eliminate choice (1). Does the author use the washerwoman's hands as a metaphor for humility or forgiveness? No, so you can eliminate choices (2) and (3). The author does use her hands as a metaphor for endurance. Phrases such as "the stubbornness of mankind" and "the will to work . . . beyond the limits of one's power" indicate that choice (4) is correct.

9 (1) The question asks you to find a synonym for the word "obstinacy" in line 36. Look at the larger context surrounding this word. The washerwoman looks like she is about to fall down under the weight of her heavy load, but "an inner obstinacy seemed to call out: No, you may not fall." Does the word "obstinacy" most nearly mean "stubbornness" in this context? Yes, it does! When you try substituting answer choice (1) for the word "obstinacy" in the sentence, it makes sense: an inner stubbornness seemed to call out. She's stubborn because she refused to fall. Would it make sense to substitute any of the other answer choices for the word "obstinacy" in this sentence? No, it wouldn't. Choice (1) is the best answer.

10 (2) Look back at lines 59 and 60: "'I could not rest easy in my bed because of the wash,' the old woman explained. 'The wash would not let me die.'" Do these lines imply that she refused to die because of her need for money? No, so eliminate choice (1). Do they imply that she refused to die because of her sense of duty, choice (2)? Yes; she fights sickness in order to deliver the washed clothes to the narrator's family. Answer choice (2) is correct. Do these lines imply that the washerwoman refused to die because of her *longing for respect,* choice (3)? No, so eliminate (3). Do these lines imply that she refused to die because of her *love of work,* choice (4)? This may be a tempting answer, but it is not the *best* choice. In fact, lines 63 and 64 contradict this. Her sense of duty is implied far more than any love of her work, which means (2) is correct.

Part A: Essay

The people who grade your essay will be thinking about the following questions when they decide how to score it. You should think about these questions when you review your essay.

- Have you clearly stated the controlling idea, or main idea, of your essay in the introduction?

  - Your controlling idea should be specific to what your essay is about; don't just restate Your Task.

  - The controlling idea of your essay should discuss the meaning of human dignity as revealed in the two passages. You should have a controlling idea based on your interpretation of the two passages.

- Have you addressed each bullet point in the Guidelines in your essay?

  - The essay should discuss the meaning of human dignity as revealed in *both* passages in relation to your controlling idea.

  - The essay should use specific and relevant ideas and examples from *each* passage to develop your controlling idea.

  - The essay should incorporate discussion of specific literary elements used by the authors in relation to your controlling idea.

- Have you supported the controlling idea of your essay with relevant examples and quotations from *both* passages, with proper indication when you are quoting from the text?

- Have you clearly and logically organized your essay?

  - The topic of each body paragraph should be clear and coherent.

  - The transitions from topic to topic should be clear.

- Have you concluded your essay with a summary of its main points?

- Have you used correct spelling, grammar, and punctuation?

Here's an example of a top-score essay.

Human dignity is a large concept that is not easily defined by words and generalities. Where does one begin in exploring the meaning of human dignity? By looking at both reading passages, the first a short story by Anton Chekhov, and the second an excerpt from the autobiography of Issac Singer, readers are able to get an idea of the meaning of human dignity as specifically revealed through Chekhov's character of Mashenka and Singer's old washerwoman. An examination of these two characters' actions reveals that human dignity means self-respect and living in a manner that is true to one's code of ethics no matter what circumstances one must confront.

Both Mashenka and the washerwoman behave in ways that are dictated by their sense of self-respect and personal ethical codes in order to preserve their dignity as human beings. It is apparent in Chekhov's story that Mashenka would have an easier time financially if she were to stay in the household of her employers after the unwarranted search of her room for Madame Kushkin's stolen brooch, rather than go back to her parents who "had nothing." However, the psychological and emotional price Mashenka would have to pay is too high, as staying would ruin her sense of self-respect.

Upon first encountering Madame Kushkin in her room and seeing the search of her possessions that is still taking place, Mashenka has to swallow the words she longs to say. As Chekhov writes, she experiences for the first time in her life "the feeling that is so familiar to persons in dependent positions, who eat the bread of the rich and powerful, and cannot speak their minds." The search is a major affront to Mashenka's human dignity, and not being able to speak her mind is like rotten icing on the bitter cake she is forced to swallow. Chekhov characterizes Mashenka as an educated young girl who knows how to behave properly, as the reader can see when she does not confront her employer and is horrified that she may be "mixed up in something dreadful." However, the accusation of being a thief is too much of an affront to her dignity for her to tolerate, and her decision to leave the Kushkin household demonstrates that Mashenka's dignity is of the utmost importance to her. Breaking her earlier silence, Mashenka ultimately confronts Nikolay Sergeitch, saying, "I cannot remain in your house. I feel deeply insulted by this search!" The behavior of Madame Kushkin and Nikolay Sergeitch violated Mashenka's personal code of ethics and self-respect, and in order to preserve her dignity she feels forced to leave despite Nikolay Sergeitch's request to stay.

The old washerwoman embodies the principles of self-respect and living according to one's code of ethics as much as Mashenka does, though the circumstances of her story are very different. Singer uses descriptive details such as the woman's "gnarled" hands and vivid descriptions of the frigid winter conditions to give the reader a sense of what she endures to do her work. The pride she takes in her work and the hardships she endures to do the laundry demonstrate her sense of self-respect. Singer's use of simile and metaphor in descriptions like "Every piece of linen sparkled like polished silver" and "hands that spoke of the stubbornness of mankind" further impress the washerwoman's work ethic upon the reader.

The ultimate demonstration of the washerwoman's sense of self-respect and work ethic comes when she returns to the author's family's house after her long absence due to illness. Her statement, "I could not rest easy in my bed because of the wash. The wash would not let me die," makes it crystal clear just how important her work is to her. The reader gets the strong impression that her sense of dignity comes from her pride in her work and the responsibility to her customers that she fulfills above and beyond expectation. Her vehement reaction to the mother's "benediction" that the washerwoman "live to be a hundred and twenty" also reveals her sense of dignity, as she does not "want to be a burden on anyone" and would prefer to die before she becomes a burden. This is certainly the reason she has kept working to such an old age.

The characters of Mashenka and the washerwoman reveal that human dignity rests upon a foundation of self-respect and the ability to live according to one's personal ethical code. Both passages illustrate that human dignity is something that cannot be stolen from an individual no matter what circumstances she must deal with, as long as that individual does what is necessary to maintain her sense of self-respect. Both Mashenka and the washerwoman live in ways that are true to their own ethical codes, and thus they are both able to preserve their dignity in spite of extremely trying situations.

Here's an explanation of the top-score essay.

This essay receives full credit (6 points) because it presents a controlling idea about the meaning of human dignity as revealed in both passages. The writing task requires test-takers to write a unified essay with a controlling idea based on both passages. The task is complete in this essay.

In this essay, the writer's controlling idea is that human dignity is based on self-respect and living in a manner that is true to one's code of ethics. The writer substantiates this idea with a thorough discussion of Mashenka's actions and character in the passage by Chekhov, and the old washerwoman's actions and character in the passage by Singer. In separate paragraphs, the writer analyzes what human dignity meant to Mashenka and to the washerwoman. The writer uses a substantial amount of examples and details from each passage, and each example is clearly stated, coherent, and relevant to the controlling idea. The writer also shows how each author uses specific literary elements, such as characterization, simile, and metaphor, to reveal that human dignity is based on self-respect and living in a manner that is true to one's code of ethics.

The writer establishes and presents a controlling idea based on the two passages in a unified, clear, and well-written essay. The essay shows that human dignity is based on self-respect and living in a manner that is true to one's code of ethics, and therefore cannot be taken away from an individual by someone else as long as that individual confronts every circumstance she or he faces in a manner that is true to her or his sense of self-respect and personal ethical code. The essay makes good use of transitions; for example, after discussing Mashenka the writer begins the discussion of the washerwoman with the sentence, "The old washerwoman embodies the principles of self-respect and living according to one's code of ethics as much as Mashenka does, though the circumstances of her story are very different." This transitional sentence helps to make the essay writer's ideas flow smoothly. The essay is also highly organized, there are no grammatical errors, and the content is comprehensible.

Part B: Essay

This essay is different from the other essays on the Regents exam because you have to draw solely on your outside knowledge of literature in order to write it. No reading passages or other information will accompany the writing task for the critical essay.

The people who grade your essay will be thinking about the following questions when they decide how to score it. You should think about these questions when you review your essay.

- Have you clearly stated the main idea of your essay in the introduction?
  - Your main idea should be specific to your essay topic; don't just restate Your Task.
  - The main idea of your essay should present a valid interpretation of the statement in the Critical Lens and should agree or disagree with the statement as you have interpreted it.

- Have you discussed *two* works of literature that you believe best support your argument?

- Have you addressed each bullet point in the Guidelines in your essay?
  - Your essay should support your main idea with a detailed discussion of the works of literature you have chosen.
  - Your essay should also discuss specific literary elements of these works.

- Have you supported the main idea of your essay with specific examples and details from the works of literature you have chosen?

- Have you clearly and logically organized your essay?
  - The topic of each body paragraph should be clear and coherent.
  - The transitions from topic to topic should be clear.

- Have you concluded your essay with a summary of its main points?

- Have you used correct spelling, grammar, and punctuation?

Here's an example of a top-score essay.

The statement that "All conflict in literature is, in its simplest form, a struggle between good and evil" conveys the meaning that all themes and struggles in literature, when broken down to their most filtered form, come down to the conflict of good versus evil. I agree with this statement because good and evil are the purest forms of all emotion; all other emotions simply derive from these basic emotions. Two works of literature that best support this opinion are William Golding's Lord of the Flies and William Shakespeare's Othello.

In William Golding's Lord of the Flies, Golding uses the theme of power to show the conflict of good and evil. In this novel, the main characters are adolescent boys yearning to gain the acceptance and power of the group. All the young boys are free from adult rule to do as they please while they are stranded on an island. As the novel progresses, the true natures of the boys are revealed. Ralph, the leader of one group, is characterized as a pure, innocent, all-around good boy. He uses his reasoning and fairness to rule over the boys. Jack, on the other hand, is the leader of a separate group of boys. Golding depicts these boys as savage, constantly hunting to kill, and even creates the chant of "Kill the Beast" associated with Jack's group of boys. Jack rules maliciously with an iron fist. He is characterized as unjust, demanding, and basically ill-natured. Golding uses these sharp contrasts of good and evil to exemplify this contrast in our society. He states that once allowed total freedom in a society, our basic emotion of evil will be magnified. That is why a government with set rules and laws is imperative to the survival of our culture.

William Shakespeare also conveys a similar message in his play Othello. Shakespeare introduces the character of Othello as a brave, valiant, and honorable man. He also introduces the complete antithesis of Othello in the character of Iago. Iago is a two-faced manipulator, representing the evil element of this play. Shakespeare uses Iago to take advantage of Othello's trusting nature and prey on the good heart of Othello. Soon, Othello becomes consumed with hate and jealousy, which override all his other emotions. Shakespeare uses Othello to show how a character can cross the threshold of good and evil. He shows his readers the capacity of his characters to love through Othello and Desdemona's pure love. Shakespeare then shows the capacity of his characters to hate through Othello's murder of Desdemona. These emotions that Shakespeare conveys are also important in the themes of the play. The theme of love shows the good in all characters and the theme of jealousy shows the evil in all the characters.

In conclusion, the struggle of good and evil is a basic struggle that is prevalent in all literature. This struggle is exemplified in Shakespeare's Othello and Golding's Lord of the Flies through various themes and characterizations. Both Golding and Shakespeare discuss the effects of these emotions in society.

Here's an explanation of the top-score essay.

This essay receives full credit (6 points) because it provides a valid interpretation of the statement provided in the Critical Lens, agrees with the writer's interpretation of the statement in its discussion of two literary works, and supports the writer's opinion with specific references to the works. The writing task requires test-takers to discuss two literary works from the perspective of the statement provided in the Critical Lens. The task is complete in the essay.

In this essay, the writer provides an interpretation of the statement provided in the Critical Lens by stating that good and evil are the basis for all human emotion. The two literary works discussed are William Golding's *Lord of the Flies* and William Shakespeare's *Othello*. The writer argues that these works show that conflict is a result of the struggle between good and evil.

In the second paragraph, the writer discusses *Lord of the Flies* and relates the author's characterizations to the interpretation of the Critical Lens. In doing this, the writer develops an analysis by using specific references to the text. Mentioning the specific characterizations of Ralph and Jack supports the writer's interpretation of the Critical Lens. In the third paragraph, the writer discusses the characters of Othello and Iago in relation to the interpretation of the statement provided in the Critical Lens. The writer demonstrates with specific examples how Shakespeare's play supports this interpretation. The examples from each of the two literary works are clearly stated, coherent, and relevant to the writer's main idea. The writer neatly concludes the essay with restatement of the interpretation of the Critical Lens.

The writer provides an interpretation of the statement provided in the Critical Lens and intelligently supports the argument with lucid analysis of both literary works. The essay is well organized, the sentence structure is varied, there are no grammatical errors, and the content is comprehensible.

PRACTICE EXAM: AUGUST 2001

HOW TO TAKE THE PRACTICE REGENTS EXAM

Three of the most recent Regents Comprehensive Examinations in English are reprinted in this book: June 2001, August 2001, and January 2002. Each exam has two sessions, and each session should take no more than three hours to complete.

The August 2001 Regents Comprehensive Examination in English begins on the next page. Try to take this practice Regents exam as if it were the actual Comprehensive Examination in English that you will take. That means that you should complete one session of the practice exam at one time. For example, if you begin Session One, don't stop until you are finished with the session. You should limit yourself to three hours for each of the two sessions on the exam because that's exactly how much time you'll have on the testing days. It's recommended that you complete Session One on one day and Session Two on the following day. While taking the practice Regents Comprehensive Examination in English you should not have any books open. Also, you should not watch television, talk on the phone, or listen to music as you take this exam.

After you have taken the practice exam, check out the list of correct answer choices and explanations for each question. The answers and explanations for the August 2001 exam begin on page 239. Read the explanations for as many questions as you need to. Pay special attention to the explanations for questions that you answered incorrectly or had difficulty answering. If you take these steps, you should be prepared for anything the Regents can throw at you.

IMPORTANT NOTE:

The listening section, which starts the exam, requires you to listen to a passage read by someone else. It is essential that you have someone read this passage to you. The listening passage appears on pages 217–218. To best prepare for the Regents Comprehensive Examination in English, you should have someone read the passage aloud to you rather than reading it yourself. It's important to take the practice exams just as you'll take the actual exam. Listening skills are different from reading comprehension skills, so the best way to prepare for the listening section of the Regents Comprehensive Examination in English is to *listen* to the passage.

SESSION ONE

The University of the State of New York
REGENTS HIGH SCHOOL EXAMINATION

COMPREHENSIVE EXAMINATION

IN

ENGLISH
SESSION ONE

Thursday, August 16, 2001 — 8:30 a.m. to 11:30 a.m.

This session of the examination has two parts. Part A tests listening skills; you are to answer all six multiple-choice questions and write a response, as directed. For Part B, you are to answer all ten multiple-choice questions and write a response, as directed. The answer sheet for the multiple-choice questions in this session is on page 227. You will write your responses on separate sheets of paper.

PART A

Overview: For this part of the test, you will listen to a speech about the United Nations, answer some multiple-choice questions, and write a response based on the situation described below. You will hear the speech twice. You may take notes on a separate piece of paper anytime you wish during the readings. **Note: Have someone read the listening passage on pages 217–218 aloud to you.**

> **The Situation:** Your social studies class is learning about the United Nations (U.N.). Your teacher has asked you to write a report about the ways in which the U.N. functions in the United States. In preparation for writing your report, listen to a speech by Kofi Annan, Secretary-General of the United Nations, delivered in San Francisco in 1997. Then use relevant information from the speech to write your report.

Your Task: Write a report for your social studies class in which you discuss how the U.N. functions in the United States.

Guidelines:

Be sure to

- Tell your audience what they need to know to help them understand how the U.N. functions in the United States

- Use specific, accurate, and relevant information from the speech to support your discussion

- Use a tone and level of language appropriate for a report for a social studies class

- Organize your ideas in a logical and coherent manner

- Indicate any words taken directly from the speech by using quotation marks or referring to the speaker

- Follow the conventions of standard written English

Directions: Have someone read the listening passage on pages 217 and 218 to you now. Have the person read it to you a second time after you think about it for a few minutes. You may take notes on a separate piece of paper. When you have heard the passage twice, answer the multiple-choice questions that begin on page 219.

Listening Passage

I know that the San Francisco of song is a city of the heart, but for me it is also the city—the progressive, worldly city—where the soul of the United Nations was forged and made real. At this crucial juncture in world affairs, I am pleased to have this opportunity to hear what Californians have to say about the state of the world: where we have been, and more importantly where we are going.

What is this crucial juncture to which I have just referred? It is a moment of promise and peril, an era of complexities and contradictions. Peace spreads in one region as hatred rages in another. Unprecedented wealth coexists with terrible deprivation. Globalization presents new opportunities and knits us closer together while intolerance keeps us apart.

My mind cannot help but turn to other challenges as well: the fight against drug trafficking, for example, or the struggle to uphold human rights, or the negotiations to establish an International Criminal Court. We need only summon the political will. I say "only" because I believe that political will is not finite, as some would argue; like the California sun, it is a renewable resource.

So this seems an appropriate time, and certainly the right place, to dwell on the meaning and presence of the United Nations in our daily lives.

Here in San Francisco and around the world, the big picture is familiar: the U.N. as an advocate of universal values such as equality and tolerance, justice and progress, democracy and peace, harmony among peoples and nations.

Most people also know a fair amount about our work on the ground: our blue-helmeted peacekeepers, our programs of disaster relief, refugee protection, and electoral monitoring; our immunization of children against deadly diseases: efforts which have brought the U.N. system seven Nobel peace prizes.

As familiar as we are, however, I know that sometimes the United Nations can seem very remote, especially in the developed world. Our activities take place in conflict zones you will rarely if ever visit; in impoverished areas far from major tourist sites; or behind the scenes, in clinics and classrooms, where progress occurs without bells and whistles and is measured steadily but slowly.

Media reports can bring you closer. Sometimes they generate concern and prompt people to get involved. But they also do the opposite, accentuating the distance between *your* lives, in one of the world's richest nations, and *their* lives somewhere else, somewhere poorer and less secure. A sense of common humanity is our saving grace; it is why the United Nations was created and why polls show such strong American support for the organization at the grass roots level.

But I would also like to suggest that even here, in the United States, Americans need look no further than your own lives to experience the United Nations system at work.

Consider the last 24 hours of my own life. I flew to San Francisco yesterday afternoon, enjoying a smooth flight while reading and watching an in-flight movie, *As Good As It Gets*—an appropriate title! After settling into my hotel, I made a few telephone calls. Dinner last night featured some fine California seafood. Before going to sleep I watched the news on television. And prior to joining you here today I ate a light California breakfast of fresh fruit and whole-grain bread.

Where is the U.N. family to be found in such ordinary scenes of day-to-day life? Let us examine this picture again, this time in slow motion. I said that I had had a smooth flight. Thanks to the International Civil Aviation Organization, there are global standards for airplane and airport safety; a common language, English, for aviation communications; and standards for the performance of pilots, flight crews, air traffic controllers, and ground and maintenance crews.

And let us not forget the in-flight entertainment, and the fact that the World Intellectual Property Organization helps protect copyrights for one of California's major exports: movies.

Next, I said I made a few telephone calls. Since taking office, I have rarely been more than a few feet from a telephone. This is sometimes an intrusion on my privacy, but more often it is quite convenient: I can enjoy a walk in the woods while doing business. So I am grateful for the International Telecommunication Union, which helps connect national communications infrastructures into global networks, and which manages the sharing of radio frequencies and satellite orbital positions. The news I watched last night, including reports from abroad, also owes no small debt to the ITU.

As for my meals, Californians need no lessons from anyone about growing high-quality produce; your Central Valley is one of the wonders of the world. Even here the United Nations plays a part.

The Food and Agricultural Organization and the World Health Organization set international norms for food additives and limits for pesticide residues. The International Labor Organization promotes safe working conditions for migrant farmworkers. The United Nations Convention on the Law of the Sea, meanwhile, stipulates that coastal states have sovereign rights over natural resources and certain other economic activities in a 200-nautical mile exclusive economic zone, meaning that California's waters are protected from fishing armadas from other countries.

This is not world government; it is sovereign nations such as the United States coming together in common use. Nor is this intrusive; it is pragmatic problem solving. The United Nations is your tool, your vehicle, your instrument; it exists to help nations navigate the new landscapes of international life.

So let us not think in terms of your lives and their lives, but of our lives. If you thought that the United Nations was something of a charity, existing only for the poor and less fortunate on Earth, think again: for Americans are not only giving to the United Nations, you are living the United Nations.

Multiple-Choice Questions

Directions (1–6): Use your notes to answer the following questions about the passage read to you. Select the best suggested answer and write its number in the space provided on the answer sheet. The questions may help you think about ideas and information you might use in your writing. You may return to these questions anytime you wish.

1 The speaker describes the "crucial juncture" as a time of
   (1) changing priorities
   (2) contrasting conditions
   (3) shrinking resources
   (4) fading traditions

2 In referring to American support for the United Nations (U.N.), the speaker probably uses the expression "a sense of common humanity" to indicate America's feeling of
   (1) superiority
   (2) isolation
   (3) frustration
   (4) responsibility

3 The speaker implies that one purpose of the International Civil Aviation Organization is to
   (1) reduce dependency on airline travel
   (2) preserve artifacts from historical flights
   (3) establish standards for airplane safety
   (4) provide information about aviation careers

4 The speaker mentions California-made movies in order to emphasize the importance of
   (1) copyright protection
   (2) industry standardization
   (3) geographic location
   (4) audience expectation

5 According to the speaker, the United Nations Convention on the Law of the Sea gives a coastal state the right to
   (1) impose travel restrictions on its citizens
   (2) prohibit other countries from fishing nearby
   (3) dump industrial waste into the sea
   (4) seize cargo from foreign ships

6 How are the organizations mentioned in the speech connected to the U.N.?
   (1) They are part of the U.N.
   (2) They oppose the U.N.
   (3) They were replaced by the U.N.
   (4) They were a model for the U.N.

After you have finished these questions, turn back to page 216. Review **The Situation** and read **Your Task** and the **Guidelines.** Use scrap paper to plan your response. Then write your response for Part A on separate sheets of paper. After you finish your response for Part A, go to page 220 and complete Part B.

Directions: Read the text and study the table on the following pages, answer the multiple-choice questions, and write a response based on the situation described below. You may use the margins to take notes as you read and scrap paper to plan your response.

> **The Situation:** The director of after-school programs wants to offer a physical fitness program. You have decided to write a letter to the director in which you discuss components of physical fitness and recommend activities that should be included in the after-school physical fitness program.

Your Task: Using relevant information from **both** documents, write a letter to the director of after-school programs discussing the components of physical fitness and recommending activities that should be included in the new after-school physical fitness program. ***Write only the body of the letter.***

Guidelines:

Be sure to

- Tell your audience what they need to know about the components of physical fitness

- Recommend activities that should be included in the after-school physical fitness program

- Use specific, accurate, and relevant information from the text **and** the table to develop your recommendations

- Use a tone and level of language appropriate for a letter to the director of after-school programs

- Organize your ideas in a logical and coherent manner

- Indicate any words taken directly from the text by using quotation marks or referring to the source

- Follow the conventions of standard written English

Physical Fitness

Regular exercise is a vital component of overall health. Fitness is not simply a matter of good genes; it requires taking responsibility for your health. A sensible exercise program will help promote overall well-being—not only physical health, but mental and emotional health as well. In addition to conditioning your body, exercise can also help

5 relieve the effects of stress, provide a sense of personal accomplishment, and improve self-esteem. Regular exercise can help you look and feel your best.

No single definition of physical fitness satisfies everyone. To an Olympic athlete, fitness might mean the ability to break a world record in the 440-yard dash. To a more sedentary person, fitness might mean nothing more than the ability to perform the

10 routine chores of everyday life.

Although performance standards vary, most exercise experts recognize five basic components of physical fitness:

    1. Aerobic fitness or cardiorespiratory endurance. The ability to do moderately strenuous activity over a period of time. It reflects how well your

15   heart and lungs work to supply your body with oxygen during exercise.

    2. Body composition. The proportion of fat to bone and muscle.

    3. Muscular strength. The ability to exert maximum force. Lifting the heaviest weight you can in a single exertion is an example of muscular strength.

20   **4. Muscular endurance.** The ability to repeat a movement many times, or to hold a particular position for a prolonged period, for example, the work required to lift a weight 20 times or to hold it up for five minutes.

    5. Flexibility. The ability to move a joint through its full range of motion and elasticity of the muscle.

25 A well-rounded exercise program should develop each fitness component. The human body has an amazing ability to adapt to physical demands. If you follow a sensible exercise program, your body will respond to the increased demands you make on it, and you will become more fit.

Aerobic Fitness

The term *aerobic* means "using oxygen." During aerobic exercise, your heart and

30 lungs work harder than normal to provide your muscles with the oxygen they need. You work at a slow and steady pace—hard enough to get you breathing heavily, but not hard enough to leave you gasping for breath. Aerobic exercise is the most important component of a fitness program.

Sudden bursts of activity, such as sprinting for the bus or spiking a volleyball, are
35 *anaerobic,* which means you are exercising so hard that your muscles demand more
oxygen than your body can provide. This is why sprinters gasp for breath at the end of
a race. No one can do anaerobic exercise for more than a couple of minutes, but
everyone can and should do aerobic exercise for extended periods.

To improve aerobic fitness and strengthen your heart and lungs, you need to choose
40 an aerobic exercise program that uses your large muscle groups steadily and
rhythmically.

To determine whether or not you are working hard enough, you should monitor your
heart rate. You can take your pulse at your radial artery (in your wrist, just inside your
wristbone). Hold your fingers firmly in place to feel the artery pulsating. Each pulsation
45 indicates a single heartbeat.

To find your pulse rate, use a stopwatch or a watch with a sweep second hand to time
yourself as you count the number of heartbeats in ten seconds, then multiply the number
by six.

To build and maintain aerobic fitness and strengthen your cardiovascular system you
50 need to exercise 20 to 30 minutes at 60 to 85 percent of your maximum heart rate at least
three times a week. If you exercise less often or less intensely, your cardiovascular
fitness will not improve and you will lose conditioning.

Body Composition

Your body is made up of muscle, bone, and fat. Do not be afraid of some fat. Your
body needs a certain amount of stored fat to function properly; acceptable rates are
55 about 15 to 20 percent body fat for men and about 20 to 25 percent for women. You
should be concerned with *excess* fat, which has been linked to heart disease, diabetes,
gallbladder disease, and high blood pressure.

The best way to lose fat is to eat less and exercise more. Dieting alone can make you
lose muscle as well as fat, but a combination of diet and exercise will help you tone
60 muscle while you lose fat. Strengthening muscle actually helps you lose weight more
quickly because it takes more energy for your body to work muscle than to burn fat.
About 90 percent of the calories you use each day are consumed by muscle, even when
you are not exercising.

Do not assume you will use more calories by doing a high-intensity exercise. If you
65 do a low-intensity exercise for a longer time, you may burn more calories than by doing
a high-intensity exercise for a shorter time. For example, you may actually use more
calories in walking an hour than you would by jogging for 20 minutes.

Remember, the best way to lose fat is through a combination of balanced diet and
aerobic exercise.

Muscular Strength and Endurance

70 The only way to increase strength and endurance is to overload your muscles *gradually*. The best way to do this is to follow a weight-training program. You can use free weights or weight machines for resistance, or you can do calisthenics and work against your own body weight.

You can adjust the amount of weight you lift to build either muscular strength, muscular endurance, or both. To build strength, lift the heaviest weight you can for six

75 to eight repetitions of an exercise, doing two or three sets of each exercise. When you can do two or three sets of eight repetitions, increase the weight and return to six repetitions. To build endurance, follow the same overload principle, but use a lighter weight that allows you to do one set of 10 to 20 repetitions. To build both strength and endurance, do one set of 8 to 15 repetitions with moderate weight before increasing the

80 weight. When you start out, begin with less weight and *gradually* increase it to increase your workload.

Flexibility

Your flexibility depends on the condition of your bones, tendons, ligaments, and muscles. Joints that are regularly moved through their full range of motion retain their normal mobility, while those that are not become less supple. Flexibility not only

85 permits freedom of movement, but it also makes you less prone to many injuries such as muscle pulls, strains, and tears.

To improve flexibility, you must stretch regularly. This is especially important if your fitness program includes an exercise that does not take a joint through its full range of motion. Jogging, for example, can tighten the hamstrings, the hip flexors that bring your

90 leg forward, the Achilles tendons in the calves, and the quadriceps in the upper thigh. Joggers can maintain—and even gain—flexibility in these muscles if they stretch them regularly. Just as with aerobic fitness activities, every fitness routine should include some stretching.

Every well-rounded exercise program includes some form of regular aerobic exercise to

95 strengthen the cardiovascular system. When it comes to fitness, it does not matter how slim or muscular you are; you are not really in shape until your heart and lungs are in shape.

If you try one type of exercise and find, after a reasonable time, that you do not like it, switch to another. Find two or more kinds of exercise you enjoy, and vary your routine.

—Consumers Union

TABLE

Fitness Ratings for Popular Activities

Key: Excellent—1   Very Good—2   Good—3   Fair—4   Poor—5

Activity	Aerobic Fitness	Body Composition	Muscle Strength	Muscle Endurance	Flexibility
Aerobic exercise routines					
Low-impact	1	2	4	3	2
High-impact	1	1	2	1	2
Aqua stretching	5	4	4	4	1
Ballet	3	3	2	1	1
Ballroom dancing	3	4	2	1	1
Basketball	2	2	4	2	3
Bicycling					
13-mph	1	2	3	1	2
20-mph	1	1	2	1	2
Bowling	5	5	4	5	4
Calisthenic circuit training	1	1	3	1	3
Canoeing, kayaking	3	3	3	2	3
Cheerleading	3	3	3	3	2
Cross-country skiing	1	1	3	1	2
Dancing: folk, square	2	3	4	3	3
Dancing: rock and roll	3	4	5	3	4
Field hockey	1	1	3	1	3
Football (touch)	4	4	4	4	4
Golf (carrying bag)	3	4	4	3	3
Handball (singles)	2	2	4	2	2
Hiking	1	2	3	2	5
Hockey (ice)	1	2	3	2	4
Horseback riding	4	4	4	4	5
Jogging/running					
12 min/mile	1	1	3	2	5
7 min/mile	1	1	2	1	5
Sprinting	4	3	2	3	4
Karate	2	2	3	1	1
Racquetball	2	2	4	3	3
Rope jumping	1	2	4	2	4
Rowing	1	2	1	1	2
Sailing	5	5	5	4	5
Skateboarding	3	4	4	3	4
Skating (ice, roller)	2	3	3	2	3
Skiing (downhill)	3	3	2	2	4
Soccer	1	1	3	1	3
Swimming					
20 yd/min	2	2	3	1	2
55 yd/min	1	1	2	1	2
Tennis (singles)	3	3	4	3	3
Volleyball	3	3	5	4	3
Walking					
Brisk walking	1	2	3	4	3
Racewalking	1	1	2	2	4
Waterskiing	4	5	3	2	4
Weightlifting	5	3	1	2	2
Windsurfing	3	4	3	2	3
Yoga	5	4	5	3	1

Multiple-Choice Questions

Directions (7–16): Select the best suggested answer to each question and write its number in the space provided on the answer sheet. The questions may help you think about ideas and information you might want to use in your writing. You may return to these questions anytime you wish.

7 The first paragraph of the text explains some
   (1) components of an exercise program
   (2) benefits of regular exercise
   (3) alternatives to traditional exercise
   (4) types of effective exercise

8 Lines 13 through 24 contain a list of
   (1) explanations
   (2) reasons
   (3) suggestions
   (4) definitions

9 According to the text, the primary purpose of aerobic exercise is to
   (1) strengthen the lungs and the heart
   (2) decrease body weight
   (3) improve rhythm and balance
   (4) increase range of motion

10 The author implies that people who are trying to lose excess fat should develop more muscle because
   (1) fat weighs more than muscle
   (2) fat can gradually turn into muscle
   (3) muscle uses more energy than fat
   (4) muscle is more attractive than fat

11 According to the text, lifting a moderately heavy weight 20 times will help improve
   (1) muscular endurance
   (2) flexibility
   (3) body composition
   (4) muscular strength

12 According to the table, which activity offers the same overall fitness results as high-impact aerobic exercise routines?
   (1) jogging/running 7-minute miles
   (2) swimming 55 yards per minute
   (3) racewalking
   (4) weight lifting

13 According to the table, which sport is *least* effective for overall fitness?

   (1) basketball

   (2) field hockey

   (3) football (touch)

   (4) tennis (singles)

14 According to the table, which activity results in the best aerobic fitness?

   (1) dancing: rock and roll

   (2) rope jumping

   (3) skateboarding

   (4) skating (ice, roller)

15 According to the table, which activity is most useful in building muscle strength?

   (1) ballroom dancing

   (2) bowling

   (3) cheerleading

   (4) rowing

16 The table implies that a personal fitness routine consisting only of handball and volleyball would be most lacking in the component of

   (1) muscle strength

   (2) body composition

   (3) aerobic fitness

   (4) flexibility

After you have finished these questions, turn back to page 220. Review **The Situation** and read **Your Task** and the **Guidelines.** Use scrap paper to plan your response. Then write your response to Part B on separate sheets of paper.

The University of the State of New York

REGENTS HIGH SCHOOL EXAMINATION

COMPREHENSIVE EXAMINATION IN ENGLISH
SESSION ONE

Thursday, August 16, 2001 — 8:30 a.m. to 11:30 a.m.

ANSWER SHEET

Student . . . .

School . . . . Grade . . . . Teacher . . . .

Write your answers to the multiple-choice questions for Part A and Part B on this answer sheet.

Part A	Part B
1 _____	7 _____
2 _____	8 _____
3 _____	9 _____
4 _____	10 _____
5 _____	11 _____
6 _____	12 _____
	13 _____
	14 _____
	15 _____
	16 _____

Your essay responses for Part A and Part B should be written on separate sheets of paper.

SESSION TWO

The University of the State of New York
REGENTS HIGH SCHOOL EXAMINATION

COMPREHENSIVE EXAMINATION

IN

ENGLISH
SESSION TWO

Friday, August 17, 2001 — 8:30 to 11:30 a.m.

This session of the examination has two parts. For Part A, you are to answer all ten multiple-choice questions and write a response, as directed. For Part B, you are to write a response, as directed. The answer sheet for the multiple-choice questions in this session is on page 237. You will write your responses on separate sheets of paper.

PART A

Directions: Read the passages on the following pages (a memoir and a poem). Write the number of the answer to each multiple-choice question on your answer sheet. Then write the essay on separate sheets of paper as described in **Your Task.** You may use the margins to take notes as you read and scrap paper to plan your response.

Your Task:

> After you have read the passages and answered the multiple-choice questions, write a unified essay about the experience of visiting libraries as revealed in the passages. In your essay, use ideas from *both* passages to establish a controlling idea about the experience of visiting libraries. Using evidence from *each* passage, develop your controlling idea and show how the author uses specific literary elements or techniques to convey that idea.

Guidelines:

Be sure to

* Use ideas from *both* passages to establish a controlling idea about the experience of visiting libraries

* Use specific and relevant evidence from *each* passage to develop your controlling idea

* Show how each author uses specific literary elements (for example: thcmc, characterization, structure, point of view) or techniques (for example: symbolism, irony, figurative language) to convey the controlling idea

* Organize your ideas in a logical and coherent manner

* Use language that communicates ideas effectively

* Follow the conventions of standard written English

Passage I

From the nearest library I learned every sort of surprising thing—some of it, though not much of it, from the books themselves.

The Homewood Library had graven across its enormous stone facade: FREE TO THE PEOPLE. In the evenings, neighborhood people—the men and women of Homewood—
5   browsed in the library and brought their children. By day, the two vaulted rooms, the adults' and children's sections, were almost empty. The kind Homewood librarians, after a trial period, had given me a card to the adult section. This was an enormous silent room with marble floors. Nonfiction was on the left.

Beside the farthest wall, and under leaded windows set ten feet from the floor, so that
10 no human being could ever see anything from them—next to the wall, and at the farthest remove from the idle librarians at their curved wooden counter, and from the oak bench where my mother waited in her camel's-hair coat chatting with the librarians or reading—stood the last and darkest and most obscure of the tall nonfiction stacks: NATURAL HISTORY. It was here, in the cool darkness of a bottom shelf, that I found
15 *The Field Book of Ponds and Streams.*

The Field Book of Ponds and Streams was a small, blue-bound book printed in fine type on thin paper. Its third chapter explained how to make sweep nets, plankton nets, glass-bottomed buckets, and killing jars. It specified how to mount slides, how to label insects on their pins, and how to set up a freshwater aquarium.

20 One was to go into "the field" wearing hip boots and perhaps a head net for mosquitoes. One carried in a "ruck-sack" half a dozen corked test tubes, a smattering of screwtop baby-food jars, a white enamel tray, assorted pipettes and eyedroppers, an artillery of cheesecloth nets, a notebook, a hand lens, perhaps a map, and *The Field Book of Ponds and Streams*. This field—unlike the fields I had seen, such as the field where
25 Walter Milligan played football—was evidently very well watered, for there one could find, and distinguish among, daphniae, planaria, water pennies, stonefly larvae, dragonfly nymphs, salamander larvae, tadpoles, snakes, and turtles, all of which one could carry home.

That anyone had lived the fine life described in Chapter 3 astonished me. Although the
30 title page indicated quite plainly that one Ann Haven Morgan had written *The Field Book of Ponds and Streams,* I nevertheless imagined, perhaps from the authority and freedom of it, that its author was a man. It would be good to write him and assure him that someone had found his book, in the dark near the marble floor at the Homewood Library. I would, in the same letter or in a subsequent one, ask him a question outside the scope
35 of his book, which was where I personally might find a pond, or a stream. But I did not know how to address such a letter, of course, or how to learn if he was still alive.

I was afraid, too, that my letter would disappoint him by betraying my ignorance, which was just beginning to attract my own notice. What, for example, was this substance called cheesecloth, and what do scientists do with it? What, when you really got down to it, was enamel? If candy could, notoriously, "eat through enamel," why would anyone make trays out of it? Where—short of robbing a museum—might a fifth-grade student at the Ellis School on Fifth Avenue obtain such a legendary item as a wooden bucket?

The Field Book of Ponds and Streams was a shocker from beginning to end. The greatest shock came at the end.

When you checked out a book from the Homewood Library, the librarian wrote your number on the book's card and stamped the due date on the sheet glued to the book's last page. When I checked out *The Field Book of Ponds and Streams* for the second time, I noticed the book's card. It was almost full. There were numbers on both sides. My hearty author and I were not alone in the world, after all. With us, and sharing our enthusiasm for dragonfly larvae and single-celled plants, were, apparently, many adults.

Who were these people? Had they, in Pittsburgh's Homewood section, found ponds? Had they found streams?

Every year, I read again *The Field Book of Ponds and Streams*. Often, when I was in the library, I simply visited it. I sat on the marble floor and studied the book's card. There we all were. There was my number. There was the number of someone else who had checked it out more than once. Might I contact this person and cheer him up?

For I assumed that, like me, he had found pickings pretty slim in Pittsburgh.

The people of Homewood, some of whom lived in visible poverty, on crowded streets among burned-out houses—they dreamed of ponds and streams. They were saving to buy microscopes. In their bedrooms they fashioned plankton nets. But their hopes were even more vain than mine, for I was a child, and anything might happen; they were adults, living in Homewood. There was neither pond nor stream on the streetcar routes. The Homewood residents whom I knew had little money and little free time. The marble floor was beginning to chill me. It was not fair.

—Annie Dillard

Passage II

Maple Valley Branch Library, 1967

1 For a fifteen-year-old there was plenty
2 to do: browse the magazines,
3 slip into the Adult section to see
4 what vast *tristesse*[1] was born of
   rush-hour traffic,
5 décolletés[2], and the plague of too
   much money.
6 There was so much to discover—how to
7 lay out a road, the language of flowers,
8 and the place of women in the tribe
   of Moost.
9 There were equations elegant as a
   French twist,
10 fractal geometry's unwinding maple leaf;

11 I could follow, step-by-step, the slow
    disclosure
12 of a pineapple Jell-O mold—or take
13 the path of Harold's purple crayon through
14 the bedroom window and onto a lavender
15 spill of stars. Oh, I could walk any aisle
16 and smell wisdom, put a hand out to touch
17 the rough curve of bound leather,
18 the harsh parchment of dreams.

19 As for the improbable librarian
20 with her salt and paprika upsweep,
21 her British accent and sweater clip
22 (mom of a kid I knew from school)—
23 I'd go up to her desk and ask for help
24 on bareback rodeo or binary codes,
25 phonics, Gestalt theory,
26 lead poisoning in the Late Roman Empire;
27 the play of light in Dutch Renaissance
    painting;
28 I would claim to be researching
29 pre-Columbian pottery or Chinese
    foot-binding,

30 but all I wanted to know was:
31 *Tell me what you've read that keeps*
32 *that half smile afloat*
33 *above the collar of your impeccable blouse.*

34 So I read *Gone with the Wind* because
35 it was big, and haiku because they
    were small.
36 I studied history for its rhapsody of dates,
37 lingered over Cubist art for the way
38 it showed all sides of a guitar at once.
39 All the time in the world was there,
    and sometimes
40 all the world on a single page.
41 As much as I could hold
42 on my plastic card's imprint I took,

43 greedily: six books, six volumes of bliss,
44 the stuff we humans are made of:
45 words and sighs and silence,
46 ink and whips, Brahma and cosine,
47 corsets and poetry and blood sugar levels—
48 I carried it home, five blocks of
    aluminum siding
49 and past the old garage where, on its
    boarded-up doors,
50 someone had scrawled:
51   I CAN EAT AN ELEPHANT
52   IF I TAKE SMALL BITES.

53 *Yes*, I said to no one in particular: *That's*
54 *what I'm gonna do!*

—Rita Dove

---

[1] sadness

[2] low-cut necklines

Multiple-Choice Questions

Directions (1–10): Select the best suggested answer to each question and write its number in the space provided on the answer sheet. The questions may help you think about the ideas and information you might want to use in your essay. You may return to these questions anytime you wish.

Passage I (the memoir) — Questions 1–5 refer to Passage I.

1 The author's repeated references to *The Field Book of Ponds and Streams* has the effect of emphasizing the book's
  (1) age
  (2) significance
  (3) unpopularity
  (4) size

2 Lines 20 through 27 are developed primarily through the use of
  (1) listing
  (2) definition
  (3) metaphor
  (4) analogy

3 The narrator implies that *The Field Book of Ponds and Streams* was a "shocker" partly because it revealed to her the
  (1) cruelty of nature
  (2) capabilities of women
  (3) existence of a different way of life
  (4) importance of preserving the environment

4 In lines 51 through 54, the narrator implies that studying the book's card gave her a sense of
  (1) commitment
  (2) order
  (3) privacy
  (4) community

5 At the end of the passage, the narrator implies that she is chilled by both the coldness of the floor and her awareness of
  (1) dishonest people
  (2) unequal opportunities
  (3) unworthy goals
  (4) irresponsible behavior

6 In lines 9 and 10, equations and geometry
   are depicted as being
   (1) difficult
   (2) beautiful
   (3) ancient
   (4) useful

7 The images in lines 11 through 15 are used
   to suggest two different
   (1) historical eras
   (2) character types
   (3) book genres
   (4) architectural elements

8 According to the narrator, the list of topics
   in lines 24 through 29 was
   (1) an excuse
   (2) an assignment
   (3) a symbol
   (4) an apology

9 The expression "my plastic card's imprint"
   (line 42) refers to
   (1) copying books
   (2) buying books
   (3) signing out books
   (4) writing in books

10 In line 51, the narrator most likely uses the
   expression "eat an elephant" to mean
   (1) gain knowledge
   (2) achieve fame
   (3) be patient
   (4) banish fear

After you have finished these questions, turn back to page 230. Review **Your Task** and the **Guidelines.** Use scrap paper to plan your response. Then write your response to Part A on separate sheets of paper. After you finish your response for Part A, go on to page 236 and complete Part B.

PART B

Your Task:

Write a critical essay in which you discuss *two* works of literature you have read from the particular perspective of the statement that is provided for you in the **Critical Lens.** In your essay, provide a valid interpretation of the statement, agree *or* disagree with the statement as you have interpreted it, and support your opinion using specific references to appropriate literary elements from the two works. You may use scrap paper to plan your response. Write your essay on separate sheets of paper.

Critical Lens:

> "What lasts is what is written. We look to literature to find the essence of an age."
>
> —Peter Brodie (adapted)

Guidelines:

Be sure to

- Provide a valid interpretation of the critical lens that clearly establishes the criteria for analysis

- Indicate whether you agree *or* disagree with the statement as you have interpreted it

- Choose *two* works you have read that you believe best support your opinion

- Use the criteria suggested by the critical lens to analyze the works you have chosen

- Avoid plot summary. Instead, use specific references to appropriate literary elements (for example: theme, characterization, setting, point of view) to develop your analysis

- Organize your ideas in a unified and coherent manner

- Specify the titles and authors of the literature you choose

- Follow the conventions of standard written English

COMPREHENSIVE EXAMINATION IN ENGLISH
SESSION TWO

Friday, August 17, 2001 — 8:30 to 11:30 a.m.

ANSWER SHEET

Student . . . .

School . . . . Grade . . . . Teacher . . . .

Write your answers to the multiple-choice questions for Part A on this answer sheet.

Part A

1 _____		6 _____
2 _____		7 _____
3 _____		8 _____
4 _____		9 _____
5 _____		10 _____

Your essay responses for Part A and Part B should be written on separate sheets of paper.

ANSWERS AND EXPLANATIONS FOR PRACTICE EXAM: AUGUST 2001

SESSION ONE

Part A: Multiple-Choice Questions

1 (2) Think carefully about what you heard in the passage, and the context surrounding the phrase "crucial juncture." Did the speaker suggest that it was a time of changing priorities? No; there is no mention of the U.N. changing priorities, so you can eliminate answer choice (1). Did the speaker suggest that it was a time of contrasting conditions? He said that it was an era of "complexities and contradictions," and spoke of peace and hatred as well as "unprecedented wealth" coexisting with "terrible deprivation." Because peace is the opposite of hatred and wealth is the opposite of deprivation, or poverty, you should know that the speaker thinks that these are contrasting conditions. Answer choice (2) is correct. The speaker does not suggest that the "crucial juncture" is a time of shrinking resources or fading traditions, so you can also eliminate answer choices (3) and (4).

2 (4) The speaker discusses conflict zones and poor nations that the United Nations helps when he mentions "a sense of common humanity." Also, he mentions that the United Sates is one of the "world's richest nations" and that it supports the efforts of the United Nations. Is the speaker trying to indicate America's feeling of superiority by using the expression "a sense of common humanity"? No; a sense of common humanity and a feeling of superiority do not go together, so eliminate answer choice (1). Is the speaker trying to indicate America's sense of isolation or frustration? Neither of these words accurately relates to the idea of "common humanity," so eliminate choices (2) and (3). Is the speaker trying to indicate America's feeling of responsibility? Yes! A sense of common humanity refers to the fact that America, as a rich nation with many resources, should feel responsible for helping poorer, less fortunate nations. Answer choice (4) is correct.

3 (3) The question asks you to identify a specific detail from the speech that was read to you. If you listened closely to the speech, you should have answered the question correctly. The speaker says, "Thanks to the International Civil Aviation Organization, there are global standards for airplane and airport safety." It is clear that the purpose of the organization is to establish standards for airplane safety. Answer choice (3) is correct. The speaker does not mention reduced dependency on airline travel, artifacts from historical flights, or information about aviation careers, so it should be pretty easy for you to eliminate choices (1), (2), and (4).

4 (1) Again, if you listened closely to the passage it should have been easy to select the correct answer choice. The speaker mentions a series of United Nations organizations and the positive effects they have on the world. California-made movies are mentioned along with the World

Intellectual Property Organization. Does the speaker mention California movies in order to emphasize the importance of copyright protection? Yes; he says that "The World Intellectual Property Organization helps protect copyrights for one of California's major exports: movies." The correct answer choice is (1). Even if you don't remember the exact words the speaker used, you should know that choice (2), "industry standardization," and choice (4), "audience expectation," are not mentioned in reference to California-made movies, so you can eliminate those choices. Answer choice (3), "geographic location," may seem correct because the speaker is talking specifically about California-made movies, but in the context of the speech this answer choice does not make sense. The World Intellectual Property Organization does not have anything to do with geographic location; it protects copyrights.

5 (2) The question asks about another specific detail within the speech. The notes you took while listening to the speech should have helped you answer the question correctly. In your notes you may have kept a list of the organizations mentioned in the speech and the work that each one does. The United Nations Convention on the Law of the Sea was mentioned toward the end of the speech. The speaker mentions that coastal states have rights over resources and economic activities within the sea. Even if you didn't write down any of that information in your notes, you may have remembered the speaker explaining that "California's waters are protected from fishing armadas from other countries." So, the convention gives coastal states the right to prohibit other countries from fishing nearby. The correct answer choice is (2). Because the United Nations works to preserve the rights of individuals and promote international relations, you can assume that the convention would not grant coastal states the right to impose travel restrictions on citizens, dump industrial waste, or seize foreign cargo. So you can eliminate answer choices (1), (3), and (4) rather easily.

6 (1) Rather than asking you to recall a specific detail from the speech, the question tests your understanding of an important idea in the speech. The list of organizations and their purposes is preceded by the speaker's statement, "Americans need look no further than your own lives to experience the United Nations system at work." Before mentioning the organizations, the speaker goes on to say that the "U.N. family" has great influence over our day-to-day lives. Using the information provided in the speech, it should be obvious that all of the organizations mentioned are part of the U.N. Answer choice (1) is correct.

Part A: Essay

The people who grade your essay will be thinking about the following questions when they decide how to score it. You should think about these questions when you review your essay.

- Have you clearly stated the main idea of your essay in the introduction?
  - Your main idea should be specific to what your essay is about; don't just restate the Situation or Your Task.
  - The main idea of your essay should be the ways in which the U.N. functions in the United States.

- Have you addressed each bullet point in the Guidelines throughout your essay?
  - The essay should present examples of how the U.N. functions in the United States.
  - The essay should include relevant examples from Kofi Annan's 1997 speech to explain how the U.N. functions in the United States.
  - The body paragraphs (or your conclusion) may consider the significance of the U.N.'s role in the United States.

- Have you supported the main idea of your essay with relevant facts, examples, and details taken from Annan's speech, and properly indicated when you are quoting from the speech?

- Have you clearly and logically organized your essay?
  - The topic of each body paragraph should be clear and coherent.

- The transitions from topic to topic should be clear.

- Have you concluded your essay with a summary of its main points?

- Have you used correct spelling, grammar, and punctuation?

Here's an example of a top-score essay.

Although usually thought of in terms of international affairs, the United Nations (U.N.) plays a very important role right here in the United States. The U.N. was not only founded in the United States, but every day it is playing a big—though largely unseen—part in many aspects of our lives. We often don't think about how different U.N. agencies are functioning behind the scenes in a wide variety of ways that benefit our country. They do everything from helping to protect our safety when flying to helping our phone systems function, and so much more.

The U.N. is not a single entity, but is made up of many diverse organizations that it runs. Though these organizations are global in scope, they directly affect our lives in the U.S., while also linking certain systems in place in the U.S. to international frameworks. The International Civil Aviation Organization, International Telecommunication Union, Food and Agricultural Organization, World Health Organization, and World Intellectual Property Organization are just some examples of U.N. organizations that play vital roles in U.S. life.

U.N. Secretary-General Kofi Annan, in a 1997 speech in San Francisco, illustrated many of the ways U.N. agencies and organizations function in the U.S. He credited the International Civil Aviation Organization as being responsible for "global standards for airplane and airport safety" as well as for establishment of English as the common language used in aviation communications. Annan credited the World Intellectual Property Organization for helping to protect copyrights of American movies. He spoke of California-made movies in particular, but the intellectual property/copyright issue applies to any American-made entertainment or invention, including books, music, and even things like medicines. In addition, the communications systems we depend so dearly on, such as telephones, wireless communications, radios, and satellites, are facilitated by the International Telecommunications Union (ITU). Annan says that this organization connects national communications structures with global networks. It makes sense that an international body such as the ITU is in a better position to do this global work than an organization that is merely national in scope.

U.N. agencies even have an effect on the food we eat every day. The Food and Agricultural Organization and the World Health Organization create international standards for processing and growing food. These standards are important because they serve as a reference point for dealing with serious dietary and health issues.

It's not only U.N. organizations that are significant to life in the U.S. U.N. conventions, or laws, are also crucial in protecting our rights. Annan mentioned the United Nations Convention on the Law of the Sea as protecting U.S. waters from the fishing industries of other countries, thus preserving the natural resources of U.S. waters. We tend to think of international law more in reference to foreign countries than our own, but these laws protect our country, too.

As is apparent from just the small list of ways the U.N. functions in the United States mentioned here, the U.N. is making a large contribution to our lives every day, though we may never realize it unless we're aware of these U.N. organizations and conventions. As Annan put it so well, "Americans are not only giving to the United Nations, you are living the United Nations."

Here's an explanation of the top-score essay.

This essay receives full credit (6 points) because it provides a detailed and comprehensive explanation of how the U.N. functions in the United States. The writing task requires test-takers to discuss how the U.N. functions in the United States based on information in the speech by U.N. Secretary-General Kofi Annan. This task is complete in the essay provided.

In the essay, the writer discusses numerous examples of how the U.N. functions in the United States. The examples include U.N. agencies such as the International Civil Aviation Organization, the International Telecommunication Union, the Food and Agricultural Organization, the World Health Organization, and the World Intellectual Property Organization. The examples also include U.N. conventions, specifically the United Nations Convention on the Law of the Sea. In separate paragraphs, the writer accurately describes each organization and its relevance to life in the United States. The writer uses as many examples from Annan's speech as possible and properly indicates when she or he is quoting Annan. Each example is clearly stated, coherent, and relevant to how the U.N. functions in the United States.

The writer summarizes all the main points about the U.N. functioning in the United States in a clear and well-written essay. The essay shows how the U.N. functions in the United States, and concludes with a statement that summarizes and restates exactly how important the U.N. is to life in the United States. The essay is highly organized, there are no grammatical errors, and the content is comprehensible.

Part B: Multiple-Choice Questions

7 (2) The question should be easy for you to answer as long as you pay attention to what it is asking you about specifically—the *first paragraph* of the text. If you don't pay attention to this, you may be confused by the incorrect answer choices because they are mentioned in the text, just not in the first paragraph. The first paragraph explains why exercise is important to physical, mental, and emotional health. It states that exercise can relieve stress and improve self-esteem. Based on the information in the first paragraph, it's clear that it explains some benefits of regular exercise. Answer choice (2) is correct. Questions like this one illustrate why it is important to read every word of every question thoroughly so that you avoid making careless mistakes.

8 (4) When a question asks you about specific lines in the text, go back to those lines and reread them. You are allowed to do this, and it makes finding the correct answer choice a piece of cake! Do lines 13 through 24 contain a list of explanations? The lines are explaining specific terms related to exercise, so choice (1) seems like it could be correct. Remember that it's always best to read *all* of the answer choices before you select one. Do the lines contain a list of reasons or suggestions? No, they don't, so eliminate answer choices (2) and (3). Do the lines contain a list of definitions? Yes, they do. There are words and terms in boldface type followed by definitions of the terms. The list looks much like something you'd see in the glossary at the back of a textbook. Answer choice (4), "definitions" is a much better term to describe the contents of lines 13 through 24 than choice (1), "explanations," so get rid of choice (1). Answer choice (4) is your best bet.

9 (1) Pay attention to the wording of the question; it asks about the *primary* purpose of aerobic exercise *according to the text.* While you may know that aerobic exercise can help *decrease body weight,* answer choice (2), the section of the text entitled "Aerobic Fitness" focuses on strengthening your heart and lungs, making (1) the correct choice. Lines 39 through 40 contain the information you'd need in order to answer this question correctly. The lines state, "To improve aerobic fitness and strengthen your heart and lungs, you need to choose an aerobic exercise program . . . ." You can eliminate answer choice (3) because there is no mention of improved rhythm and balance in the section of the text that addresses aerobic fitness. You can eliminate choice (4) because an increased range of motion relates to flexibility, not aerobic fitness.

10 (3) If you read the section of the text entitled "Body Composition" carefully, you will see that answer choice (1), "fat weighs more than muscle," is not mentioned, and you may already know that this statement is actually the opposite of the truth. Even if you didn't know that, you can eliminate choice (1) because it is not mentioned in the text. Does the author suggest that people who want to lose excess fat should develop more muscle because fat can gradually turn into muscle? That doesn't make sense, so you may eliminate answer choice (2). Does the author suggest that people who want to lose excess fat should develop more muscle because muscle uses more energy than fat? Yes! Lines 59 through 60 state, "Strengthening muscle actually helps you lose weight more quickly because it takes more energy for your body to work muscle than to burn fat." Therefore, choice (3) is correct. You can eliminate answer choice (4) because the author does not suggest that muscle is more attractive than fat.

11 (1) The question requires you to recall a specific detail from the text, but that shouldn't be hard because you are allowed to look back at the text. You shouldn't have to remember every small detail from a passage that you read; it's usually a good idea to look back at the text to find evidence that supports the answer choice you select. The section entitled "Muscular Strength and Endurance" contains the information you'd need to answer this question. The text states, "To build endurance . . . use a lighter weight that allows you to do one set of 10 to 20 repetitions." Lifting a weight 20 times helps to improve muscular endurance, so answer choice (1) is correct. The definition of *muscular endurance* toward the beginning of the text mentions that it requires lifting a weight 20 times. Answer choice (4), "muscular strength," may be distracting because it is similar to the correct answer choice, but you know from reading the definitions that muscular strength and muscular endurance are not the same.

12 (2) All the information you need to answer the question is provided in the table, so you should have read the table very carefully. You are being asked to find which activity offers the same overall fitness results as high-impact aerobic exercise routines. The first thing you should have done is to look up high-impact aerobic exercise on the table and read the fitness ratings. Then you'd compare those ratings to the ratings for each of the answer choices. Only choice (2), "swimming 55 yards per minute," has the same fitness ratings as high-impact aerobic exercise, which means it will offer the same overall fitness results. Therefore answer choice (2) is correct.

13 (3) The question requires you to do the exact same thing you did to answer the previous question: compare information about various activities provided in the table. Note that the key at the top of the table indicates that low numbers represent good fitness ratings and that high numbers represent bad fitness ratings. The question asks which activity of the ones listed in the answer choices has the worst fitness ratings. The correct answer choice is the activity with the highest numbers. You can see from the fitness ratings provided in the table that touch football has fitness ratings of 4 for each of the five categories in the table. Basketball, field hockey, and singles tennis all have ratings with numbers lower than 4, so you can conclude that they are all more effective for overall fitness than touch football. Answer choice (3) is correct.

14 (2) Again, simply compare the information provided in the table in order to find the correct answer choice. This time you only have to look at the fitness ratings in one column, "Aerobic Fitness," rather than all the columns. No sweat, right? Of the four activities listed in the answer choices, the best one for aerobic fitness would be the one that has a rating with the lowest number. Rope jumping has a rating of 1, which is better than dancing: rock and roll (which has a rating of 3), skateboarding (3), and skating (4). The correct answer choice is (2), "rope jumping," because it results in the best aerobic fitness according to the table.

15 (4) To answer the question correctly you just have to look at the column entitled "Muscle Strength" and compare the ratings for the activities listed in the answer choices. If you read the table carefully and remember that a rating of 1 is excellent and a rating of 5 is poor, you should have answered this question without a problem. The table indicates that rowing has a rating of 1 for muscle strength, ballroom dancing has a rating of 2, cheerleading has a rating of 3, and bowling has a rating of 4. Because rowing is most useful in building muscle strength, answer choice (4) is correct.

16 (1) The question requires you to make an inference from information in the table. You should have looked at the fitness ratings for handball and volleyball before you selected an answer choice. When you look over the ratings, you will see that handball receives a 4 and volleyball receives a 5 in the category of muscle strength. Both activities receive better ratings in body composition, aerobic fitness, and flexibility. Because they receive the poorest ratings in the category of muscle strength, you can infer that they are most lacking in this component of fitness. Answer choice (1) is correct.

Part B: Essay

The people who grade your essay will be thinking about the following questions when they decide how to score it. You should think about these questions when you review your essay.

- Have you clearly stated the main idea of your essay in the introduction?
    - Your main idea should be specific to what your essay is about; don't just restate Your Task.
    - The main idea of your essay should discuss components of physical fitness and recommend activities that you think should be included in a new after-school fitness program.

- Have you addressed each bullet point in the Guidelines in the body paragraphs of your essay?
    - The body paragraphs should inform your audience about physical fitness, using information in the text *and* the table.
    - The body paragraphs should include recommendations for activities you think the new after-school fitness program should include.
    - The body paragraphs should explain why you are recommending the specific activities you choose.

- Have you supported the main idea of your essay with relevant facts, examples, and details from *both* the text and the table?

- Have you clearly and logically organized your essay?
    - The topic of each body paragraph should be clear and coherent.
    - The transitions from topic to topic should be clear.

- Have you written you essay in a tone that is appropriate for a letter to the director of after-school programs?

- Have you remembered that "write only the body of the letter" means to leave out the addresses and greeting, but not the introduction?

- Have you concluded your essay with a summary of its main points?

- Have you used correct spelling, grammar, and punctuation?

Here's an example of a top-score essay.

I am writing this letter in regard to the new physical fitness program you are developing for our school. I am very glad this program is being developed, as physical fitness is extremely important to health and happiness, and can even help control stress and boost self-esteem. We are always hearing about how self-esteem levels of American youth are low, and how poor self-esteem is the cause of countless problems including underachievement, so I can think of nothing better than to improve one's self-esteem and stay healthy, or get healthier, at the same time. I have lots of ideas for the program that I would like to share with you.

A thorough program for overall physical fitness involves five different components, including aerobic exercise, strength-building exercises, endurance training, exercises that improve flexibility, and exercises that improve body composition. There is some form of aerobic exercise to suit every taste, and it's a good thing because everyone should participate in aerobic exercise a minimum of three times a week for 20 to 30 minutes. This kind of exercise strengthens the lungs and heart and, according to the article "Physical Fitness" published by the Consumers Union, it is the single most important part of any exercise program.

The activities I recommend to start our program are karate, soccer, and swimming, and we should organize a competitive rope-jumping team like they have at one of my friend's schools. The activities I am suggesting are all excellent for aerobic fitness, and they also offer multiple fitness benefits, and are fun to do. Rope jumping is very cool and so much fun you hardly feel like you are doing an exercise that is not only highly aerobic but also is recommended for improving your body composition, which is defined in the "Physical Fitness" article as "the proportion of fat to bone and muscle." When you improve your body composition, your body functions more efficiently, and you help prevent health problems associated with being overweight like high blood pressure, heart disease, and diabetes.

Karate is a great all-around exercise and is excellent for improving muscle endurance and flexibility, which is defined as "the ability to move a joint through its full range of motion and elasticity of the muscle." Flexibility is so important because if you are strong but not flexible, you will be much more likely to get injured while exercising.

Karate is also good for increasing muscle strength and improving body composition. Muscle strength is defined in the article as "the ability to exert maximum force," but we all know what it means to be strong, and how much easier many daily tasks are when we feel strong. Muscular endurance is defined as "the ability to repeat a movement many times, or to hold a particular position for a prolonged period," and it goes hand in hand with muscle strength. If you are strong but have no endurance, you are not really physically fit, and your activities will be limited. It is important that our new program offers a variety of activities like these that provide the best range of fitness benefits so participants can attain all-around fitness.

Soccer is excellent for aerobic fitness, muscle endurance, and improving body composition, and is good for muscle strength and flexibility. Swimming, like karate, is a really great all-around exercise that is rated excellent or very good for each of the five physical fitness components by the Consumers Union. By offering karate, soccer, swimming, and rope jumping, our new program will give participants the opportunity to try different activities and discover which ones are right for them. They will have fun while working towards achieving their fitness goals and attaining all-around fitness, helping them lead healthier, happier lives.

Here's an explanation of the top-score essay.

This essay receives full credit (6 points) because it provides a thorough explanation of the components of physical fitness and detailed and comprehensive recommendations for what activities the new after-school program should offer, and why. The writing task requires test-takers to discuss the components of physical fitness and recommend activities that they think should be included in a new after-school fitness program. The task is complete in this essay.

In the essay, the writer explains the five basic components of physical fitness as stated in the text. In separate paragraphs, the writer recommends different activities for the program and incorporates the explanations of the five components with the recommendations, which makes the essay more interesting. The writer clearly uses a substantial amount of information from the table as well as from the text in explaining the benefits of each recommended activity. Details and facts from the text and the table make the recommendations valid. The writer also discusses the overall importance of physical fitness in one's life.

The writer summarizes all the main points from the text in a clear and well-written essay while incorporating information from the table as well. The essay explains why physical fitness is important and what the five components of physical fitness are, and recommends a good variety of activities to create a balanced fitness program. It is highly organized, there are no grammatical errors, it is written in a tone appropriate for a letter to the director of after-school programs, and the content is comprehensible.

SESSION TWO

Part A: Multiple-Choice Questions

1 (2) Questions 1 through 5 refer to Passage I, the memoir by Annie Dilliard. Do the author's repeated references to *The Field Book of Ponds and Streams* have the effect of emphasizing the book's age? No; the age of the book is not mentioned and is irrelevant to the author's point, so eliminate answer choice (1). Do the repeated references emphasize the book's significance? Yes; by repeating the title of the book, the author wants to highlight it because it is important or significant in some way. Answer choice (2) is correct. The repeated references to the book do not emphasize the book's unpopularity. You can eliminate choice (3) because you learn near the end of the essay that the book was popular; the author was surprised to discover that so many people had checked out the book before her. The repeated references have nothing to do with the book's size, so you can eliminate choice (4) as well.

2 (1) You should have done a close reading of lines 20 through 27 in order to answer this question correctly. What literary technique does the author use here? The lines begin with a list of equipment that *The Field Book of Ponds and Streams* recommends people to have when exploring bodies of water (test tubes, baby-food jars, white-enamel tray, etc.). The lines conclude with a list of things that one could find in a pond or stream (daphniae, planaria, water pennies, etc.). These lines are primarily comprised of lists, so choice (1), "listing," is correct. The lines do not contain definitions, metaphors, or analogies, so you can eliminate choices (2), (3), and (4).

3 (3) Think about what was revealed to the author in reading *The Field Book of Ponds and Streams*. The author mentions nothing about the cruelty of nature, so you can get rid of choice (1). Answer choice (2), "capabilities of women," may distract you, because the author does mention that the tone of the book made her feel like it was written by a man even though she knew the author was a woman, but this is not the best answer choice. In the sixth paragraph, the author states, "That anyone had lived the fine life described in Chapter 3 astonished me." The author emphasizes how foreign and unknown nature was to a young person in Pittsburgh, so choice (3), the "existence of a different way of life," is the best answer.

4 (4) Look for context clues in lines 52 through 55 to answer the question. The question asks about the effect that the card for *The Field Book of Ponds and Streams* has on the author. Phrases such as "There we all were" and "Might I contact this person and cheer him up?" suggest that the card made the narrator feel like that she was connected to the other people who borrowed the book. The book's card gave her a sense of community, choice (4).

5 (2) Answer choice (2), "unequal opportunities," stands out as the correct answer choice because the last line of the passage reads "It was not fair," and you can immediately associate unfairness with inequality. The narrator mentions that people she knew would not have the opportunity to explore ponds or streams because they did not have money or free time. Choice (1), "dishonest people," is never mentioned in the passage, nor is choice (4), "irresponsible behavior," so eliminate (1) and (4). The author does say that the people of Homewood "dreamed of ponds and streams" and "were saving to buy microscopes," but she never implies that she thinks these goals are unworthy; they were just unattainable for the people she knew. So you can also eliminate choice (3).

6 (2) Questions 6 through 10 refer to Passage II, the poem entitled "Maple Valley Branch Library, 1967." In lines 9 and 10 the poet describes "equations elegant as a French twist" and uses the metaphor of fractal geometry as an "unwinding maple leaf." Do the descriptions depict equations and geometry as difficult? No, they don't. Although you may think that geometry is difficult, the author of the poem is not suggesting that in the poem. You can eliminate answer choice (1). Do the descriptions depict equations and geometry as beautiful? Yes; the word *elegant* and the comparison to an unwinding leaf suggest the author thinks that equations and geometry are beautiful. Answer choice (2) is correct. The author does not indicate that equations and geometry are ancient or useful, so you can eliminate choices (3) and (4).

7 (3) Think about what the images in lines 11 through 15 are suggesting. The lines mention a Jell-O mold being made step-by-step and a boy who seems to have a fantastic adventure with a crayon. The images in the lines do not suggest two different historical eras, so you can eliminate choice (1). Because there's only on character mentioned in the lines, not two, you can eliminate choice (2), "character types," as well. The images in the lines seem to suggest a cookbook (the making of a Jell-O mold) and a children's book (Harold and his purple crayon). Therefore, choice (3), "book genres" is correct. Cookbooks and children's books are each a type of book genre. Another hint could be that the poem is about a library, and you should know that there are many genres, or types, of books in a library. The lines do not suggest anything about architecture, so you can eliminate choice (4).

8 (1) The question asks how the narrator uses the list of topics in lines 24 through 29. You should have thought about the context of the lines when answering this question. Based on the context, you know that the narrator is asking a librarian for books on the various topics listed. The word *claim* in line 28 provides a big hint here. The narrator "would claim to be researching" the topics listed in order to find out what the librarian had *read that keeps / that half smile afloat.* So the list of topics in lines 24 through 29 was an excuse the narrator used to find out what the librarian liked to read. Choice (1) is the correct answer.

9 (3) Look back at line 42, the line referenced in the question, and the lines immediately following it. What action is the narrator performing here? You know that she's in a library and that she leaves with "six books, six volumes of bliss." The lines in the poem make it clear that she is borrowing, or signing out, books from the library. Choice (3) is the correct answer. The plastic card that the question asks about is the narrator's library card.

10 (1) Which answer choice makes sense in the context of the poem? The author is very excited by all types of books in the library, so she obviously wants to gain knowledge. Choice (1) is the correct answer. The idea of being able to eat an elephant by taking small bites gives the narrator a metaphor with which to think about acquiring and digesting all the knowledge contained in the books that are in the library. Like the elephant, the library is large, and it contains many books, which represent knowledge. By "eating in small bites," the poet suggests that she could gain a large amount of knowledge by reading one book at a time.

Part A: Essay

The people who grade your essay will be thinking about the following questions when they decide how to score it. You should think about these questions when you review your essay.

- Have you clearly stated the controlling idea, or main idea, of your essay in the introduction?

  - Your controlling idea should be specific to what your essay is about; don't just restate Your Task.

  - Your essay should discuss the experience of visiting libraries as revealed in the two passages. You should have a controlling idea about visiting libraries based on your interpretation of the two passages.

- Have you addressed each bullet point in the Guidelines in your essay?

  - The essay should discuss the experience of visiting libraries as revealed in *both* passages in relation to your controlling idea.

  - The essay should incorporate discussion of specific literary elements used in the two passages in relation to your controlling idea.

- Have you supported the controlling idea of your essay with relevant examples and quotations from *both* passages?

- Have you clearly and logically organized your essay?

  - The topic of each body paragraph should be clear and coherent.

- The transitions from topic to topic should be clear.

- Have you concluded your essay with a summary of its main points?

- Have you used correct spelling, grammar, and punctuation?

Here's an example of a top-score essay.

Rita Dove's poem "Maple Valley Branch Library, 1967" and Annie Dillard's essay about the Homewood Library both express the significance of libraries as places of discovery in the lives of young people. Both passages are written from the perspective of an adult narrator describing her experiences visiting the library when she was younger. In Dove's poem, she was fifteen years old, and in Dillard's essay, she was a fifth-grader. Both young women are characterized as being curious and intelligent with a desire for knowledge and an appetite for discovering new things. Visiting the library gives the young women in both passages major opportunities for discovery, although the results of those discoveries sharply contrast each other.

In Dove's poem, she initially focuses on the amazing variety of subjects and information a fifteen-year-old could discover in the library. She uses lush language, including similes, metaphors and strong visual images, to evoke the feeling of wonder she got visiting the library, describing "equations elegant as a French twist." She describes the atmosphere as being filled with knowledge, stating, "Oh, I could walk any aisle and smell wisdom." Her tone throughout the poem illustrates her sense of discovery and enjoyment, which is made clear in the lines, "All the time in the world was there, and sometimes all the world on a single page."

In Dillard's essay there is as great a sense of discovery as in Dove's poem, although Dillard focuses on the discoveries initiated by one particular book, The Field Book of Ponds and Streams. This book revealed a way of life and existence of nature that were completely unknown to her, as is expressed in the line, "That anyone had lived the fine life described in Chapter 3 astonished me." This "fine life" is so foreign to her that she wants to write the author to learn "where I might personally find a pond, or a stream." Dillard also uses strong descriptive language to establish the atmosphere where she discovers this book, stringing together superlative adjectives in the phrase "the last and darkest and most obscure of the tall nonfiction stacks" so the reader perceives the library's atmosphere as the author did.

The fifteen-year-old Dove gets great pleasure from the books she is able to check out from the library, as is illustrated with the metaphorical phrase "six volumes of bliss." The inspiration she takes from the scrawled graffiti she sees on her way home, "I CAN EAT AN ELEPHANT IF I TAKE SMALL BITES" and her reaction "Yes...That's what I'm gonna do!" clearly illustrate the sense of empowerment she gets from all the knowledge she feels capable of acquiring through books. This feeling builds throughout the poem and the tone does not change much from beginning to end.

On the other hand, Dillard's tone changes dramatically near the end of her essay. Her fifth-grader has the bitter realization that the people in her town are impoverished and won't have the opportunities to explore and enjoy the ponds and streams she reads about and imagines the people of Homewood dream about. Her tone becomes less positive as she begins to question her own lack of knowledge in lines 41-47. Though Dove ends her poem on a note of triumph, Dillard conveys a sense of disappointment and sadness in the essay's concluding sentences, "The marble floor was beginning to chill me. It was not fair." In describing this chill, she gives the reader the sense that not only was she physically chilled, but that even the contrast between the library's expensive marble floor and the "burned-out houses" on the "crowded streets" of Homewood chilled her soul. These things remind her just how far out of reach the discovery of nature is for Homewood residents.

Both passages explicitly reveal that visiting libraries is an experience of discovery for young people, and both authors rely on metaphor and the use of lots of descriptive adjectives and details to convey both the atmosphere of the library and the subject matter they are discovering. While Dillard's sudden change in tone at the end of the essay has the effect of surprising the reader and causing the reader to feel the narrator's sense of disappointment and injustice, Dove's consistent tone of excitement builds to the narrator's realization at the end of the poem. The reader can see from these two passages that while the discoveries made visiting the library may be uplifting or upsetting, there is no doubt that a visit to the library will entail discovery.

Here's an explanation of the top-score essay.

This essay receives full credit (6 points) because it presents a controlling idea about visiting libraries as revealed in both passages. The writing task requires test-takers to write a unified essay with one controlling idea based on both passages. The task is complete in this essay.

In the essay, the writer's controlling idea is that libraries are revealed in both passages as places of discovery for young people. The writer contrasts the discoveries made by both authors and the tone of the two passages, discussing how the tone changes or remains the same from the beginning to the end of each passage. In separate paragraphs, the writer analyzes what visiting the library meant to a young Rita Dove and Annie Dillard. The writer uses many examples from each passage, and each example is clearly stated, coherent, and relevant to controlling idea. The writer also shows how each author uses specific literary elements, such as metaphor and characterization, to reveal that libraries are places of discovery.

The writer establishes and presents a controlling idea based on the two passages in a unified, clear, and well-written essay. The essay shows that visiting the library entails a great deal of discovery for young people, although those discoveries may not always be positive. The essay is highly organized, there are no grammatical errors, and the content is comprehensible.

Part B: Essay

This essay is different from the other essays on the Regents exam because you have to draw solely on your outside knowledge of literature in order to write it. No reading passages or other information will accompany the writing task for the critical essay.

The people who grade your essay will be thinking about the following questions when they decide how to score it. You should think about these questions when you review your essay.

- Have you clearly stated the main idea of your essay in the introduction?
  - Your main idea should be specific to your essay topic; don't just restate Your Task.
  - The main idea of your essay should present a valid interpretation of the statement in the Critical Lens and should agree or disagree with the statement as you have interpreted it.
- Have you discussed *two* works of literature that you believe best support your argument?
- Have you addressed each bullet point in the Guidelines in your essay?
  - Your essay should support your main idea with a detailed discussion of the works of literature you have chosen.
  - Your essay should also discuss specific literary elements of these works.
- Have you supported the main idea of your essay with specific examples and details from the works of literature you have chosen?
- Have you clearly and logically organized your essay?
  - The topic of each body paragraph should be clear and coherent.
  - The transitions from topic to topic should be clear.
- Have you concluded your essay with a summary of its main points?
- Have you used correct spelling, grammar, and punctuation?

Here's an example of a top-score essay.

Literature can hold up a mirror to the times in which we live, allowing us to see a clear reflection of our society and ourselves. The literary mirror can also reflect the times that preceded our own lives, offering us not simply a glimpse of the past, but the ability to actually grasp something almost indefinable yet apparent when we feel it, the essence of the era the work represents. The collective consciousness of a generation is often revealed in great literature through specific, individual characters, as are the generational conflicts that arise with particular severity in changing times. This can be seen in Flannery O'Connor's "Everything That Rises Must Converge" and J. D. Salinger's The Catcher in the Rye.

O'Connor's story captures the essence of a period of conflict in American history, the era of desegregation in the South. The interactions between Julian and his mother (who is not given a name other than "Julian's mother") represent the huge tensions in this time of change and the inability of the older and younger generations to identify with or even try to understand each other. Julian's mother's patronizing attitude towards African Americans and her feeling of superiority over them disgust Julian, who considers himself a liberal, "enlightened" white person. O'Connor expertly develops the conflict between mother and son by using pitch-perfect dialogue.

The complexity in the story arises from the fact that as unsympathetic as Julian's mother may be to the reader, Julian's harsh, disrespectful, even mocking attitude toward his mother makes him equally unsympathetic. O'Connor reveals that as enlightened as Julian considers himself to be, he is actually just as ignorant as his mother, lacking compassion and respect for her as she does for African Americans. Julian's so-called liberal mentality effectively makes him see African Americans as objects, rather than as human beings. O'Connor employs irony to great effect. For example, an African American woman wearing the same gaudy hat Julian's mother has just purchased and has been obsessing about whether or not to return gets on the bus Julian and his mother are riding. Because this is the newly desegregated South, the woman with the identical hat can sit anywhere she pleases on the bus, and she sits down next to Julian and his mother. Julian is at first ecstatic, then incredibly uncomfortable as his mother wants to give the African American woman's young son a nickel, and he tries to prevent her from doing so.

O'Connor presents Julian's mother as being ignorant but well-meaning in her own limited way, and in the story's climactic final scene she is revealed to be less harmful than Julian. Both mother-and-son couples get off the bus at the same stop, and when Julian's mother can't find a nickel and offers the little boy a penny, the African American woman gets incredibly insulted and hits Julian's mother. When Julian directs his anger towards his mother, as though this is just punishment for her attitude, the reader sees a portrait of two people who are lost in the changing times. At story's end both mother and son are helpless, with Julian literally shouting into the dark night for help that the reader knows won't come. This one short story conveys more about the emotions and reality of living in the newly desegregated South than perhaps an entire textbook could.

Holden Caulfield, the teenage protagonist of J. D. Salinger's novel _The Catcher in the Rye_, also feels lost in the rarefied East Coast prep school world of the 1940s, just before the end of World War II. His feeling that everything and everyone around him is "phony" reveals the disaffected attitude of a generation of privileged American youth. Holden's inability to connect with anyone other than his nine-year-old sister, Phoebe, and his desire for something genuine—though he doesn't know what that might be—reflect his generation's search for authenticity. The only authentic thing Holden is able to find is African American music, in the form of a piano player in a smoky jazz bar and a record he buys for Phoebe. Though New York is a far different environment than the South, wealthy white culture and black culture are still different worlds, especially in the 1940s, and Holden is drawn to the authenticity he finds lacking in his prep school world of fencing teams and snobbery about who has the most expensive luggage.

The generational conflict in _The Catcher in the Rye_ is less obvious than in "Everything That Rises Must Converge," but it is evident nonetheless. The fact that Holden's parents barely exist as characters in the novel and he does all he can to avoid them is evidence of the generational conflict in the novel. His interactions with his teachers and ultimate departure from school demonstrate the inability of the generations to relate to each other. Tone is everything in Salinger's *novel, and Holden's voice very strong and unique. The originality of this novel is demonstrated in Holden's vocabulary and conversational style of relating his story; his tone truly captures the essence of the age the novel portrays from the perspective of its disaffected narrator.*

Both "Everything That Rises Must Converge" and The Catcher in the Rye wonderfully illustrate the way a work of literature can serve as a mirror, reflecting back a particular age and providing the reader with insight into that time. Both O'Connor and Salinger present that insight through detailed characterization and revealing dialogue. The specific characters of Julian and his mother and Holden Caulfield become bigger than themselves through these works. They embody the struggles each particular generation faces within its time.

Here's an explanation of the top-score essay.

The essay receives full credit (6 points) because it provides a valid interpretation of the statement provided in the Critical Lens, agrees with the statement as interpreted by the writer in its discussion of two literary works, and supports the writer's opinion with specific references to the works. The writing task requires test-takers to discuss two literary works from the perspective of the statement provided in the Critical Lens. The task is complete in this essay.

In the essay, the writer provides an interpretation of the statement provided in the Critical Lens relating to generational conflict and the way a specific literary character can reveal the collective consciousness of a generation. The two literary works discussed are Flannery O'Connor's "Everything That Rises Must Converge" and J. D. Salinger's The Catcher in the Rye. In the second, third, and fourth paragraphs, the writer analyzes the characters of Julian and his mother in relation the interpretation of the statement provided in the Critical Lens, and demonstrates with specific examples how O'Connor's story supports the interpretation of the statement. In the fifth and sixth paragraphs, the writer analyzes the character of Holden Caulfield in relation to the interpretation of the statement provided in the Critical Lens, and demonstrates with specific examples how Salinger's novel supports the writer's interpretation of the statement. The examples from each work are clearly stated, coherent, and relevant to the writer's main idea.

The writer provides an interpretation of the statement provided in the Critical Lens and intelligently supports the arguments in the essay with clear analysis of both literary works. The essay is well organized—the first paragraph provides an interpretation of the Critical Lens and introduces the two literary works the writer intends to discuss; the second, third, and fourth paragraphs discuss one of the literary works in detail; the fifth and sixth paragraphs discuss the other literary work; and the final paragraph brings the essay together by making connections between the two literary works. Also, the sentence structure is varied, the language is interesting and sometimes complex, there are no grammatical errors, and the content is comprehensible.

PRACTICE EXAM: JANUARY 2002

HOW TO TAKE THE PRACTICE REGENTS EXAM

Three of the most recent Regents Comprehensive Examinations in English are reprinted in this book: June 2001, August 2001, and January 2002. Each exam has two sessions, and each session should take no more than three hours to complete.

The January 2002 Regents Comprehensive Examination in English begins on the next page. Try to take this practice Regents exam as if it were the actual Regents Comprehensive Examination in English that you will take. That means that you should complete one session of the practice exam in one sitting. For example, if you begin Session One, don't stop until you are finished with the session. You should limit yourself to three hours for each of the two sessions on the exam because that's exactly how much time you'll have on the testing days. It's recommended that you complete Session One on one day and Session Two on the following day. While taking the practice Regents Comprehensive Examination in English you should not have any books open. Also, you should not watch television, talk on the phone, or listen to music as you take this exam.

After you have taken the practice exam, check out the list of correct answer choices and explanations for each question. The answers and explanations for the January 2002 exam begin on page 287. Read the explanations for as many questions as you need to. Pay special attention to the explanations for questions that you answered incorrectly and had difficulty answering. If you take these steps, you should be prepared for anything the Regents can throw at you.

IMPORTANT NOTE:

The listening section, which starts the exam, requires you to listen to a passage read by someone else. It is essential that you have someone read this passage to you. The listening passage appears on page 265–266. To best prepare for the Regents Comprehensive Examination in English, you should have someone read the passage aloud to you rather than reading it yourself. It's important to take the practice exams just as you'll take the actual exam. Listening skills are different from reading comprehension skills, so the best way to prepare for the listening section of the Regents Comprehensive Examination in English is to *listen* to the passage.

SESSION ONE

The University of the State of New York
REGENTS HIGH SCHOOL EXAMINATION

COMPREHENSIVE EXAMINATION
IN
ENGLISH
SESSION ONE

Wednesday, January 23, 2002 — 9:15 a.m. to 12:15 p.m.

This session of the examination has two parts. Part A tests listening skills; you are to answer all six multiple-choice questions and write a response, as directed. For Part B, you are to answer all ten multiple-choice questions and write a response, as directed. The answer sheet for the multiple-choice questions in this session is on page 275. You will write your responses on separate sheets of paper.

PART A

Overview: For this part of the test, you will listen to a speech about the use of technology in studying leatherback turtles, answer some multiple-choice questions, and write a response based on the situation described below. You will hear the speech twice. You may take notes on a separate sheet of paper anytime you wish during the readings. **Note: Have someone read the listening passage on pages 265–266 aloud to you.**

> **The Situation:** Your science teacher has asked each student in the class to select a special project that could benefit endangered animals. You have decided to write a letter to the Research and Exploration Committee of the National Geographic Society. The purpose of your letter is to persuade the Committee to provide funding for the use of technology in saving endangered animals. In preparation for writing your letter, listen to a speech by Peter Tyson, a science writer. Then use relevant information from the speech to write your letter.

Your Task: Write a letter to the Research and Exploration Committee of the National Geographic Society in which you persuade the Committee to provide funding for the use of technology in saving endangered animals. *Write only the body of the letter.*

Guidelines:

Be sure to

- Tell your audience what they need to know to help them understand why funding for technology is important in the preservation of endangered animals

- Use specific, accurate, and relevant information from the speech to support your argument

- Use a tone and level of language appropriate for a letter to the Research and Exploration Committee of the National Geographic Society

- Organize your ideas in a logical and coherent manner

- Indicate any words taken directly from the speech by using quotation marks or referring to the speaker

- Follow the conventions of standard written English

Directions: Have someone read the listening passage on pages 265–266 to you now. Have the person read it to you a second time after you think about it for a few minutes. You may take notes on a separate piece of paper. When you have heard the passage twice, answer the multiple-choice questions that begin on page 267.

Listening Passage

I was kneeling on a sandy beach called Playa Grande in Costa Rica on a balmy January night helping biologists administer an ultrasound to a leatherback sea turtle. The turtle had come ashore to lay her eggs. I watched as she hauled her enormous bulk up the beach, pivoted slowly around to face the ocean, and began scooping out an oval pit in the sand with her hind flippers. She soon entered an egg-laying trance.

In her reverie, she took no notice of us as we got to work. We unpacked the equipment, which looked like a desktop computer, and set it down in the sand just behind her. We waited while she dropped about 100 moist, white eggs into the nest. When she finished, David Rostal, a biologist, carefully moved the ultrasound probe across her skin. It would reveal whether or not she would return later in the season to lay another batch of eggs.

I found it truly incongruous to witness one of the most modern of medical tests being used on one of the most ancient animals. Yet such scenes are becoming increasingly common. In many cases, advanced technologies are allowing scientists to investigate aspects of ecology, physiology, and behavior that they were never able to investigate before.

The work taking place with leatherbacks on this beach—Playa Grande on Costa Rica's Pacific coast—is a case in point. For on that half-mile-long stretch of sand, biologists are making use of perhaps more high-tech gadgets than any other biologists working on any other animal. And with these tools they are answering a sea of previously unanswerable questions about the turtles—and so learning how remarkable they are and what kinds of conservation measures may help them.

The leathery turtle is unique among sea turtles. It is the most ancient living reptile, around in its current form for at least 20 million years and possibly over 100 million years. It is also the biggest, having watched its rivals for size, the dinosaurs, go extinct some 65 million years ago.

Despite its uniqueness, the leatherback is also on the road to extinction. Frank Paladino, a biologist, recently estimated that the global population has dropped by two-thirds since 1980 alone, from 115,000 to 34,500 nesting females.

Though the leatherback spends most of its life far out to sea, its chief threats, ironically, lie ashore. On leatherback nesting beaches throughout the tropical world, people raid the turtles' nests for their delectable eggs, build over their habitat with houses and hotels, and occasionally kill nesting females for their meat. Increasingly, though, leatherbacks are also losing their lives on the high seas, where fishermen harpoon them for food or for the thick, yellow oil contained in their flesh. The turtles also perish at sea when scattered longline fishing gear snags and drowns them, and floating plastic garbage chokes them when the turtles mistake it for jellyfish.

In their efforts to gather as much information as they can about each turtle, nest, egg, and hatchling on Playa Grande and elsewhere, biologists rely on a wide range of techniques. Certain methods remain low-tech, such as recording each mother's length and width with a measuring tape to determine average sizes. But other methods rely on some of the most advanced technologies available.

Arguably the most valuable technology is also the smallest. About the size of a grain of rice, a microchip identification tag is injected into the shoulder muscle of every nester that crawls onto Playa Grande. As each turtle comes ashore, project staff members pass a hand-held scanner, like those used in supermarket checkout lines, across the reptile's shoulder to read the I.D. code.

By identifying individuals, researchers can answer a bevy of questions. Over the years, Paladino and his colleagues have proven, for instance, that Playa Grande is one of the largest leatherback nesting colonies in the Pacific Ocean. They have also shown that females tend to lay eggs, on average, five times during the October-to-February nesting season. This finding may have conservation implications. For example, if females hang around relatively close to the beach, boating and fishing near nesting beaches may need to be restricted during these months.

Researchers soon hope to inject microchips into hatchlings to identify turtles when they return to nest. Scientists can also examine nesting females by taking blood samples, measurements, and ultrasound tests of their ovaries to understand the species' egg-laying cycles and determine when to protect its shoreline habitat.

Some questions, such as where baby turtles go when they disappear into the waves, may have to await breakthroughs in available technologies, such as miniaturized satellite transmitters perhaps, or even new technologies altogether. "We have to get a better understanding of where leatherbacks go, what they're doing out there, and what habitats they need to survive, or we're wasting all our efforts everywhere else," says Scott Eckert, a biologist, referring to attempts to safeguard nesting beaches. "That's my crusade of perhaps the next 50 years."

Another crusade of Eckert's is informing the general public about leatherbacks and their plight. "It's your long-term insurance," he notes. One of the best ways to educate people, he says, is with yet another burgeoning technology—the Internet. There are now a number of popular sea-turtle-oriented Web pages. "The Internet is an inexpensive way to distribute information to a very wide readership," Eckert says, "and any time you do that you are benefiting conservation of the species."

Meanwhile, until wider scientific understanding of leatherbacks exists, researchers agree that the most promising way of preserving the species remains protecting its nesting grounds. Toward that end, there is good news at Playa Grande. In July 1995, the Costa Rican government declared Playa Grande and two neighboring nesting beaches a national park. Beyond a strong national conservation ethic, the Costa Rican authorities granted protection largely based on the cutting-edge research of Paladino and his colleagues.

Multiple-Choice Questions

Directions (1–6): Use your notes to answer the following questions about the passage read to you. Select the best suggested answer and write its number in the space provided on the answer sheet. The questions may help you think about ideas and information you might use in your writing. You may return to these questions anytime you wish.

1 The speaker implies that ultrasound tests on sea turtles are becoming
   (1) dangerous
   (2) lucrative
   (3) controversial
   (4) commonplace

2 The principal purpose of the research at Playa Grande is to determine the most effective
   (1) conservation measures
   (2) technological procedures
   (3) medical tests
   (4) feeding patterns

3 According to the speaker, what characteristics make the leatherbacks unique among sea turtles?
   (1) behavior and personality
   (2) speed and energy
   (3) size and age
   (4) color and patterning

4 According to the speaker, leatherback products used by humans include
   (1) leather
   (2) oil
   (3) shell
   (4) bone

5 The primary purpose of the speech is most likely to
   (1) protest current practice
   (2) challenge a point of view
   (3) evaluate multiple perspectives
   (4) educate the public

6 At the end of the speech the speaker indicates that declaring Playa Grande as a national park is a direct result of
   (1) media exposure
   (2) Internet communication
   (3) scientific research
   (4) economic need

After you have finished these questions, turn back to page 264. Review **The Situation** and read **Your Task** and the **Guidelines.** Use scrap paper to plan your response. Then write your response for Part A on separate sheets of paper. After you finish your response for Part A, go to page 268 and complete Part B.

PART B

Directions: Read the text and study the table on the following pages, answer the multiple-choice questions, and write a response based on the situation described below. You may use the margins to take notes as you read and scrap paper to plan your response.

> **The Situation:** Several local teenagers have been injured while working in part-time jobs. As part of a project for your health class, you have decided to write a feature article for the school newspaper in which you discuss teenagers' work-related injuries and suggest some ways employers can help to reduce these injuries.

Your Task: Using relevant information from *both* documents, write a feature article for the school newspaper in which you discuss teenagers' work-related injuries and suggest ways employers can help reduce these injuries.

Guidelines:

Be sure to

- Tell the readers of the school newspaper what they need to know about teenagers' work-related injuries

- Suggest some ways employers can help to reduce these injuries

- Use specific, accurate, and relevant information from the text *and* the table to develop your discussion

- Use a tone and level of language appropriate for a feature article for the school newspaper

- Organize your ideas in a logical and coherent manner

- Indicate any words taken directly from the text by using quotation marks or referring to the source

- Follow the conventions of standard written English

Workplace Injuries

A 16-year-old crew cook in a fast-food restaurant was pushing a container of hot grease from the kitchen to the outside for filtration. When he reached to open the door, his foot slipped, the lid fell off, and hot grease spilled over much of his body. He sustained second- and third-degree burns to his ankles, arms, chest, and face and was hospitalized for two weeks. Scarring occurred on all the burned areas.

Work may be an integral part of the lives of many children and adolescents, but how safe is the workplace for children? Despite child labor laws that are intended to protect children from hazardous working conditions, many young workers face health and safety hazards on the job. In general, typical "teen jobs" cannot be assumed to be safe. Such factors as inexperience, developmental characteristics, and the need to balance school and work may place younger workers at greater risk than adults confronted with similar hazards.

The National Center for Health Statistics reports an occupational injury rate for 15- to 17-year-olds of 4.9 per 100 full-time-equivalent workers in 1996. The injury rate for all workers 16 years old and older in 1996, based on the same sample, was 2.8 per 100 full-time-equivalent workers.

The injury rates alone do not provide a sense of the consequences of occupational injuries for the injured adolescents or for the adolescent population in general. Adolescents who are injured seriously enough to miss work may also miss days of school.

Studies show remarkably consistent patterns of nonfatal occupational injuries by age. In general, studies at both the national and state levels find older adolescents to have more injuries than younger adolescents. The reasons behind this pattern are not entirely clear. Federal child labor laws and many state laws have stronger restrictions on the work that may be performed by those under the age of 16. Therefore, younger workers may be in less hazardous jobs. Or, because of limits on their hours of employment, they may simply have less exposure to situations in which they could be injured. Employers also may give older teens more responsibility and more hazardous tasks to perform than their younger counterparts are given. And older teens may be more likely to perceive themselves as mature and therefore attempt tasks for which they are unprepared.

Interviews with young workers demonstrate the prevalence of exposure to potential hazards at work. Of 300 Massachusetts high-school students who reported that they were currently working or had previously worked, 50 percent reported using cleaning chemicals at work, nearly 50 percent used case cutters, 37 percent used ladders, 19 percent used food slicers, and 13 percent used box crushers—despite the fact that child labor laws prohibit individuals under the age of 18 from operating either food slicers or box crushers. Twelve percent reported working alone at night.

It seems clear that work may pose substantial safety risks for young workers. Identification of the factors that place children and adolescents at risk in the workplace is essential for developing effective preventive efforts.

The Work: Types of Jobs

40   Many of the industries that employ large numbers of children and adolescents—grocery stores, hospitals and nursing homes, and agriculture—have higher-than-average injury rates for workers of all ages. Children and adolescents face the same workplace hazards faced by adults in similar occupations, ranging from hot grease, large machinery, and unstable ladders to pesticides and other toxic chemicals.

45   Young workers are congregated in jobs that are characterized by the absence of opportunities for significant promotion within the firm, high turnover, little on-the-job training, limited scope for worker discretion or application of skill, heightened job insecurity, wide variation and uncertainty in hours, low pay, and few benefits. Jobs with these characteristics are, in general, more dangerous than those without them. For
50   example, one study found that incidence of occupational injuries and illnesses positively associated with authoritarian work structures and negatively associated with on-the-job training, promotion opportunity, and job security.

The Work Environment

        Health and safety training for workers is considered an essential component of comprehensive occupational health-and-safety programs. Studies of adult workers
55   suggest that safety training may reduce injuries and acute illness among young or inexperienced workers. It is reasonable to assume that lack of training could affect working children and adolescents, who are by definition inexperienced, to a greater extent than adults. Recent, consistent evidence shows that young workers do not receive adequate health and safety training at work. General surveys of working youth find that
60   about half of the young workers surveyed report no such training. Of 180 students interviewed in California, few had received any information about job safety from anyone at their workplaces or schools.

        In one survey of 14- to 16-year-olds who were treated in hospital emergency rooms for occupational injuries, 54 percent of the respondents reported no safety training at all.
65   These youngsters were much more likely to have serious injuries—involving eight or more days of restricted activity—than were those who had received such training.

        The structure of some work settings may be inappropriate for teens. One study noted a lack of adult supervision of young people on the job: The average young worker spent only 12 percent of his or her time in the presence of a supervisor.

70   One survey found that 80 percent of work-related injuries suffered by adolescents occurred when no supervisor was present. Some work schedules, such as those involving long or unusually late or early hours, may contribute to fatigue in adolescents, and fatigue is associated with an increased likelihood of injury. Working alone or late at night may also be a risk factor for work-related assaults associated with robberies.

75   Another issue that is just beginning to be recognized is the assignment of youths to jobs other than the ones they were hired to perform. For example, a cashier in a fast-food restaurant may also regularly be asked to cook or clean. Anecdotal reports indicate that when there is a shortage of staff, young workers are often assigned to fill in on a variety of tasks for which they have had no preparation. Even if all the tasks are age-

80   appropriate and performing them provides opportunities to explore new responsibilities, the assignment of a multiplicity of tasks has important implications for job-skills training and health and safety training.

— National Academy Press

TABLE

Work injuries and illnesses involving days away from work for children under 18—New York and neighboring states

State	Estimated frequency	Median days away from work	Frequent industries (% total cases)	Frequent events and exposure (% total cases)
Connecticut	220	4	Grocery stores (33%) Eating and drinking places (28%)	Fall on same level (24%) Overexertion in lifting (11%)
Massachusetts	519	4	Eating and drinking places (32%) Grocery stores (22%) Department stores (10%)	Overexertion in lifting (20%) Struck by slipping handheld object (10%)
New Jersey	248	3	Grocery stores (27%)	Fall on same level (28%) Overexertion in lifting (16%) Caught in running equipment or machinery (13%)
New York	1,060	6	Eating and drinking places (34%) Grocery stores (32%) Hospitals (10%)	Caught in or compressed by equipment or objects (15%) Contact with hot objects or substances (13%) Fall on same level (13%)
Pennsylvania	719	3	Eating and drinking places (27%) Grocery stores (16%)	Fall on same level to floor, walkway, etc. (25%) Overexertion in lifting (13%) Struck by slipping handheld object (10%)
Vermont	24	1	Hotels and motels (27%)	Fall on same level to floor, walkway, etc. (27%) Exposure to sun (22%) Struck by slipping handheld object (21%)

Roadmap to the Regents: Comprehensive English

Multiple-Choice Questions

Directions (7–16): Select the best suggested answer to each question and write its number in the space provided on the answer sheet. The questions may help you think about ideas and information you might want to use in your writing. You may return to these questions anytime you wish.

7 The story of the 16-year-old at the beginning of the text is used to illustrate the
   (1) reasons teens work
   (2) inexperience of teen workers
   (3) dangers teen workers face
   (4) need for more teen workers

8 The text implies that, compared to adults, teenagers are more likely to
   (1) recover quickly from injuries
   (2) report injuries to officials
   (3) exaggerate the seriousness of injuries
   (4) become injured at work

9 According to the text, one serious consequence of teen work-related injuries is
   (1) absence from school
   (2) loss of jobs
   (3) a shortage of workers
   (4) an increase in hospital costs

10 The text implies that one reason that younger adolescents have fewer workplace injuries than older adolescents is because younger adolescents
   (1) work more slowly
   (2) work fewer hours
   (3) receive better training
   (4) take fewer breaks

11 The text cites the use of food slicers as an example of the
   (1) limits of technology
   (2) carelessness of young workers
   (3) violation of child labor laws
   (4) lack of special training programs

12 In line 46, the term "high turnover" refers to the number of
   (1) products or services sold
   (2) raises and bonuses given
   (3) accidents that occur
   (4) employees that leave

13 The example of the cashier who is asked to cook (lines 76 and 77) is used to illustrate a problem with

(1) customer relations
(2) hygiene regulations
(3) job assignments
(4) working hours

14 According to the table, most work-related injuries to workers under 18 occur in grocery stores and

(1) eating and drinking places
(2) hotels and motels
(3) factories
(4) hospitals

15 In most of the states shown on the table, the most common injuries to young workers are caused by

(1) falls
(2) burns
(3) machinery
(4) glass

16 The differences in "Median days away from work," as shown on the table, are probably due to the

(1) workplace in which the injury occurred
(2) seriousness of the injury
(3) cause of the injury
(4) year in which the injury occurred

After you have finished these questions, turn back to page 268. Review **The Situation** and read **Your Task** and the **Guidelines.** Use scrap paper to plan your response. Then write your response to Part B on separate sheets of paper.

COMPREHENSIVE EXAMINATION IN ENGLISH
SESSION ONE

Wednesday, January 23, 2002 — 9:15 a.m. to 12:15 p.m.

ANSWER SHEET

Student . . . .

School . . . . Grade . . . . Teacher . . . .

Write your answers to the multiple-choice questions for Part A and Part B on this answer sheet.

Part A	Part B
1 _____	7 _____
2 _____	8 _____
3 _____	9 _____
4 _____	10 _____
5 _____	11 _____
6 _____	12 _____
	13 _____
	14 _____
	15 _____
	16 _____

Your essay responses for Part A and Part B should be written on separate sheets of paper.

SESSION TWO

The University of the State of New York
REGENTS HIGH SCHOOL EXAMINATION

COMPREHENSIVE EXAMINATION

IN

ENGLISH

SESSION TWO

Thursday, January 24, 2002 — 9:15 a.m. to 12:15 p.m.

This session of the examination has two parts. For Part A, you are to answer all ten multiple-choice questions and write a response, as directed. For Part B, you are to write a response, as directed. The answer sheet for the multiple-choice questions in this session is on page 285. You will write your responses on separate sheets of paper.

PART A

Directions: Read the passages on the following pages (a poem and an excerpt from a short story). Write the number of the answer to each multiple-choice question on your answer sheet. Then write the essay on separate sheets of paper as described in **Your Task.** You may use the margins to take notes as you read and scrap paper to plan your response.

Your Task:

> After you have read the passages and answered the multiple-choice questions, write a unified essay about the meaning of play as revealed in the passages. In your essay, use ideas from *both* passages to establish a controlling idea about the meaning of play. Using evidence from *each* passage, develop your controlling idea and show how the author uses specific literary elements or techniques to convey that idea.

Guidelines:

Be sure to

• Use ideas from *both* passages to establish a controlling idea about the meaning of play

• Use specific and relevant evidence from *each* passage to develop your controlling idea

• Show how each author uses specific literary elements (for example: theme, characterization, structure, point of view) or techniques (for example: symbolism, irony, figurative language) to convey the controlling idea

• Organize your ideas in a logical and coherent manner

• Use language that communicates ideas effectively

• Follow the conventions of standard written English

Passage I

The Centaur[1]

The summer that I was ten—
Can it be there was only one
summer that I was ten? It must

have been a long one then—
5   each day I'd go out to choose
a fresh horse from my stable

which was a willow grove
down by the old canal.
I'd go on my two bare feet.

10   But when, with my brother's jack-knife,
I had cut me a long limber horse
with a good thick knob for a head,

and peeled him slick and clean
except a few leaves for the tail,
15   and cinched my brother's belt

around his head for a rein,
I'd straddle and canter him fast
up the grass bank to the path,

trot along in the lovely dust
20   that talcumed over his hoofs,
hiding my toes, and turning

his feet to swift half-moons.
The willow knob with the strap
jouncing between my thighs

25   was the pommel and yet the poll
of my nickering pony's head.
My head and my neck were mine,

yet they were shaped like a horse.
My hair flopped to the side
30   like the mane of a horse in the wind.

My forelock swung in my eyes,
my neck arched and I snorted.
I shied and skittered and reared,

stopped and raised my knees,
35   pawed at the ground and quivered.
My teeth bared as we wheeled

and swished through the dust again.
I was the horse and the rider,
and the leather I slapped to his rump

40   spanked my own behind.
Doubled, my two hoofs beat
a gallop along the bank,

the wind twanged in my mane,
my mouth squared to the bit.
45   And yet I sat on my steed

quiet, negligent riding,
my toes standing the stirrups,
my thighs hugging his ribs.

At a walk we drew up to the porch.
50   I tethered him to a paling.
Dismounting, I smoothed my skirt

and entered the dusky hall.
My feet on the clean linoleum
left ghostly toes in the hall.

55   *Where have you been?* said my mother.
Been riding, I said from the sink,
and filled me a glass of water.

What's that in your pocket? she said.
Just my knife. It weighted my pocket
60   and stretched my dress awry.

Go tie back your hair, said my mother,
and *Why is your mouth all green?*
*Rob Roy, he pulled some clover
as we crossed the field,* I told her.

—May Swenson

---

[1] a mythological creature that was part horse and part human

Passage II

The Pebble People

Ben Adam sat outside his grandparents' weathered old loghouse. He liked to sit outside and listen to the sounds of the forest. Especially after one of his grandma's famous chicken-and-dumpling dinners. And he liked to play one of his favorite games—making rocks war dance. So he started looking for different colored pebbles. Some were
5 easily scraped off the surface of the well-worn path to the grandparents' loghouse, others he had to dig and scratch out of the earth.

Finally, he found the ones he wanted—black ones, white ones, red ones, yellow ones, and blue ones. Holding the pebbles on an open palm, Ben Adam talked to them. He spoke to the pebbles for a long time about the respect and discipline they should have
10 while wearing the traditional clothing the Creator had given them. He talked of the symbols the old people said were in their dress. He spoke of how they should all try to conduct themselves with dignity. Ben Adam repeated the words of an uncle who had helped him dress for a war dance many times before.

After several moments of serious meditation, he placed the pebbles on the bottom of
15 an overturned tin bucket, each according to its own size and color. He carefully placed the red, yellow, blue, white, and black pebbles into the circular grooves of the bucket in the formation of a bustle, the middlemost circle being the drum. Under his breath, he sang the ancient words of his favorite war dance song, but he did not drum yet because he did not want the dancers moved.

20 Ben Adam finished his silent song and again spoke to the pebbles. His message contained a prayer of thanksgiving that his people were alive to see another day and that they had chosen this day to come together in celebration of tribal customs. He thanked all the dancers, drummers, and spectators. He asked the Creator to bestow special blessings upon them throughout the evening and as they traveled back to their homes.

25 Ben Adam asked for blessings on behalf of people who were sick and could not attend the dance. He prayed for those imprisoned by steel bars and by personal weaknesses. And he asked the people to remember those people who had died since the last time they had gathered. Ben Adam's words were very well selected and delivered for an eight-year-old.

Following a moment of silence, he started singing a warm-up song. He drummed
30 slowly on the bottom ridge of the battered old bucket and watched proudly as the pebbles began to dance. At first they moved slowly about the grooves of the bucket according to the rhythm of the song. "For this slow beat, the traditional dancers should be thankful," Ben Adam said.

The pace quickened. Ben Adam sang louder and drummed faster. The dancers hopped
35 about fervently, like fancy dancers, their thunderous hoofbeats in tune with the
drumming and their blurred colors lighting the air. Some of the pebbles began falling off
the edge of the bucket to the ground. Ben Adam drummed and sang as long as there were
some pebble dancers left.

After only a few were left, Ben Adam announced to them, "This will be a contest
40 song!" He drummed faster and faster, harder and harder, until all the pebbles fell off the
bucket. Then, carefully, he picked up those that were the last to fall. "Gee, that was a
good contest," he said.

He thanked the dancers and said, "One day there will be a big, big contest. Only those
who are really good can come and participate in it." Ben Adam put the winning pebbles
45 into marked jars to save. "The winners of the contest and my favorite dancers, I will take
into the house and put away in my fishtank for the winter," he said to the pebble people.

—Roger Jack

Multiple-Choice Questions

Directions (1–10): Select the best suggested answer to each question and write its number in the space provided on the answer sheet. The questions may help you think about the ideas and information you might want to use in your essay. You may return to these questions anytime you wish.

Passage I (the poem) — Questions 1–5 refer to Passage I.

1 Lines 2 through 4 suggest that the narrator found her tenth summer to be
  (1) tedious
  (2) lonely
  (3) refreshing
  (4) memorable

2 In line 19, the narrator implies that the dust is "lovely" because it
  (1) makes her feet resemble hoofs
  (2) covers her tracks
  (3) lets her trot faster
  (4) keeps her toes from hurting

3 The verbs used in lines 29 through 44 help establish a feeling of
  (1) apprehension
  (2) regret
  (3) exhilaration
  (4) relief

4 In the last stanza, the poet implies that the narrator had
  (1) hidden in the field
  (2) buried her face in clover
  (3) fought with her brother
  (4) picked wildflowers

5 The title is best reinforced by which line?
  (1) "I'd go on my two bare feet" (line 9)
  (2) "I'd straddle and canter him fast" (line 17)
  (3) "I shied and skittered and reared" (line 33)
  (4) "I was the horse and the rider" (line 38)

6 Lines 20 through 24 suggest that one purpose of Ben's play is to

(1) challenge traditional roles

(2) solve personal problems

(3) practice social traditions

(4) develop survival skills

7 In lines 25 through 28, Ben's prayers reveal a sense of

(1) duty

(2) compassion

(3) courage

(4) humility

8 Ben selected as winners of the contest those pebble people who had

(1) drummed the loudest

(2) danced the fastest

(3) lasted the longest

(4) jumped the highest

9 Ben's attitude toward play can best be described as

(1) mischievous

(2) courageous

(3) innocent

(4) thoughtful

Question 10 refers to both passages.

10 Ben's action of digging the pebbles from the earth parallels which action in the poem?

(1) "cut me a long limber horse" (line 11)

(2) "cinched my brother's belt" (line 15)

(3) "tethered him to a paling" (line 50)

(4) "filled me a glass of water" (line 57)

After you have finished these questions, turn back to page 278. Review **Your Task** and the **Guidelines.** Use scrap paper to plan your response. Then write your response to Part A on separate sheets of paper. After you finish your response for Part A, go on to page 284 and complete Part B.

PART B

Your Task:

Write a critical essay in which you discuss *two* works of literature you have read from the particular perspective of the statement that is provided for you in the **Critical Lens.** In your essay, provide a valid interpretation of the statement, agree *or* disagree with the statement as you have interpreted it, and support your opinion using specific references to appropriate literary elements from the two works. You may use scrap paper to plan your response. Write your essay on separate sheets of paper.

Critical Lens:

> "All literature is protest. You can't name a single literary work that isn't protest."
>
> —Richard Wright (adapted)

Guidelines:

Be sure to

- Provide a valid interpretation of the critical lens that clearly establishes the criteria for analysis

- Indicate whether you agree *or* disagree with the statement as you have interpreted it

- Choose *two* works you have read that you believe best support your opinion

- Use the criteria suggested by the critical lens to analyze the works you have chosen

- Avoid plot summary. Instead, use specific references to appropriate literary elements (for example: theme, characterization, setting, point of view) to develop your analysis

- Organize your ideas in a unified and coherent manner

- Specify the titles and authors of the literature you choose

- Follow the conventions of standard written English

The University of the State of New York

REGENTS HIGH SCHOOL EXAMINATION

COMPREHENSIVE EXAMINATION IN ENGLISH
SESSION TWO

Thursday, January 24, 2002 — 9:15 a.m. to 12:15 p.m.

ANSWER SHEET

Student . . . .

School . . . . Grade . . . . Teacher . . . .

Write your answers to the multiple-choice questions for Part A on this answer sheet.

Part A

1 _____	6 _____
2 _____	7 _____
3 _____	8 _____
4 _____	9 _____
5 _____	10 _____

Your essay responses for Part A and Part B should be written on separate sheets of paper.

ANSWERS AND EXPLANATIONS FOR
PRACTICE EXAM: JANUARY 2002

SESSION ONE

Part A: Multiple-Choice Questions

1 (4) Although you may not remember the exact words of the passage, if you listened closely and took good notes you should have a general idea about what this question is asking. The passage states, "I found it truly incongruous to witness one of the most modern medical tests being used on one of the most ancient animals. Yet such scenes are becoming increasingly common." Think about what the phrase "increasingly common" tells you about ultrasound tests on sea turtles. Are they becoming dangerous? No, so eliminate choice (1). Are they becoming lucrative, which means profitable, or controversial? No; "increasingly common" does not imply either of those things, so eliminate choices (2) and (3). Are they becoming commonplace? Yes, they are! Choice (4) is correct.

2 (1) This question is asking about the *principal* purpose of the research at Playa Grande. When answering this kind of question, be careful you don't select an answer choice that mentions a detail from the passage but does not convey the main idea. Is the principal purpose, or main purpose, of the research at Playa Grande to determine the most effective conservation methods? That sounds true, so hold onto choice (1) while you read the other answer choices to make sure there is not an even better answer. Is the principal purpose of the research at Playa Grande to determine the most effective technological procedures, medical tests, or feeding patterns? Be careful! These are all details mentioned in the passage, but none of them are the *principal* purpose of the research at Playa Grande. The passage mentions that researchers is able to use technology to learn things about leatherback turtles that were previously unknown. The passage also mentions that the turtles are in danger of becoming extinct. The findings of the researchers help them determine what conservation measures will prevent the turtles from becoming extinct. Choice (1) is the best answer.

3 (3) This question is asking you about a detail from the passage. If you took good notes while listening to the passage, they should help you select the correct answer choice. Did the speaker state that behavior and personality are the characteristics that make leatherbacks unique among sea turtles? No; the speaker did not mention these characteristics, so you can get rid of choice (1). Did the speaker suggest that speed and energy are the characteristics that make leatherbacks unique among sea turtles? No, so get rid of choice (2) as well. What about size and age? The speaker said that the leatherback turtle "is the most ancient living reptile" and "is also the biggest," making (3) the correct answer choice.

4 (2) Your notes will help you answer this question, too, as it is asking you to recall a specific detail from the passage about a product of leatherback turtles used by humans. Did the

---

speaker mention leather as a leatherback product used by humans? This is a tricky answer choice because the turtles themselves are called *leather*backs, so you might think leather is a product of the turtles that humans use. But don't be fooled! Leather as a product was not mentioned in the passage, so you can eliminate answer choice (1). Did the speaker mention oil as a leatherback product used by humans? Yes; the passage said that fisherman harpoon leatherbacks "for the thick, yellow oil contained in their flesh," which means (2) is the correct answer choice.

5 (4) This is a main idea question, as it is asking you about the *primary* purpose of the speech. Process of Elimination will help you find the correct answer choice. Does it seem like the speaker is trying to protest current practice? No; the speaker is not protesting anything. In fact, he supports the technological methods that are being used to help preserve leatherbacks, so eliminate choice (1). Is the speaker trying to challenge a point of view? No, so throw out answer choice (2). Is the speaker trying to evaluate multiple perspectives? No, he does not examine multiple perspectives in the speech; instead, he focuses on the ways in which a group of researchers studies leatherback turtles. You can eliminate answer choice (3). Is the speaker trying to educate the public? Yes! The primary purpose of the speech is to teach people about the preservation efforts of biologists on behalf of leatherbacks, making (4) the correct answer choice. Near the end of the speech, the speaker mentions that one of the researchers is on a crusade to inform people about leatherback turtles. This is a clue that could have helped you select answer choice (4).

6 (3) Think about what the speaker indicates at the end of the speech about Playa Grande being declared a national park. Does he indicate that it is a direct result of media exposure? No; media exposure is not mentioned in the speech, so eliminate answer choice (1). Does he indicate that Playa Grande was declared a national park as a direct result of Internet communication? Be careful with answer choice (2)! The Internet is mentioned in the speech as "one of the best ways to educate people," but it is not the reason why Playa Grande was declared a national park, so you can safely eliminate choice (2). Does the speaker indicate that Playa Grande was declared a national park as a direct result of scientific research? Yes; he says that "the Costa Rican authorities granted protection largely based on the cutting-edge research of Paladino and his colleagues," making answer choice (3) correct.

Roadmap to the Regents: Comprehensive English

Part A: Essay

The people who grade your essay will be thinking about the following questions when they decide how to score it. You should think about these questions when you review your essay.

- Have you clearly stated the main idea of your essay in the introduction?
  - Your main idea should be specific to what your essay is about; don't just restate the Situation or Your Task.
  - The main idea of your essay should be to persuade the Research and Exploration Committee of the National Geographic Society to provide funding for the use of technology in saving endangered animals.

- Have you addressed each bullet point in the Guidelines in your essay?
  - The essay should inform your audience about how funding for technology is important in the preservation of endangered animals.
  - The essay should use relevant examples from the speech about leatherback turtles at Playa Grande in Costa Rica.
  - The essay should persuasively present your argument for why the National Geographic Society should provide funding for the use of technology in saving endangered animals.

- Have you supported the main idea of your essay with relevant facts, examples, and details taken from the speech, and properly indicated when you are quoting from the speech?

- Have you clearly and logically organized your essay?
  - The topic of each body paragraph should be clear and coherent.
  - The transitions from topic to topic should be clear.

- Have you written your essay in a tone that is appropriate for a letter to the Research and Exploration Committee of the National Geographic Society?

- Have you remembered that "write only the body of the letter" means to leave out the addresses and greeting, but not the introduction?

- Have you concluded your essay with a summary of its main points?

- Have you used correct spelling, grammar, and punctuation?

Here's an example of a top-score essay.

Advances in technology are greatly benefiting scientific research on endangered animals. New technology is being used to investigate physiological and behavioral aspects of endangered animals so scientists and conservationists can help prevent the extinction of many threatened species.

The leatherback turtle, one of the oldest living reptiles on Earth, is in grave danger of extinction. Since 1980, its population has plummeted by nearly two thirds. Recent studies in Playa Grande, Costa Rica, involving newly emerging technology, have helped to identify the mating season of the turtle, and are allowing scientists to encourage policies which will help the turtles avoid extinction.

Playa Grande, Costa Rica, is one of the largest leatherback nesting grounds in the world. Scientists there have been using ultrasound imaging to discover whether or not a pregnant turtle laying eggs will come back later in the year to nest again. These findings are made possible by combining new technology with scientific procedures. One of the most advanced pieces of technology at the researchers' disposal is the new microchip identification tag, which allows researchers to identify individual turtles they have marked previously. This kind of information is crucial to learning new conservation methods.

On Playa Grande and other nesting grounds, leatherback turtles and their nests have long been targets of raids for their meat and eggs, considered a delicacy in some areas. In the sea, the turtles are killed off by fishermen, both for their meat and their thick yellow oil. Leatherbacks also die from being caught in large fishing nets, which ensnare and drown them. They also ingest plastic garbage, which they mistake for jellyfish, and this causes them to choke. Researchers reported their findings to the Costa Rican Government, causing laws to be passed in 1995 that recognized Playa Grande and two other leatherback nesting grounds as national parks and granting protection to the turtles under law. These measures were made possible by information gathered using new technology.

Although current technology is helping scientists with their research, there is still much to be done, and funding for new technology must continue. If a breakthrough in technology were to allow researchers to discover what happens to baby leatherbacks when they disappear into the ocean, better ways to safeguard the species would undoubtedly develop. Currently, the Internet is being used to educate the public about endangered animals and what can be done to preserve them, providing an inexpensive way of reaching thousands of people. These steps are only the beginning, though. If funding for emerging technologies used in research can continue, the possibilities are endless.

Here's an explanation of the top-score essay.

This essay receives full credit (6 points) because it provides a persuasive argument for why the National Geographic Society should provide funding for the use of technology in saving endangered animals. The writing task requires you write a letter persuading the National Geographic Society to provide funding for the use of technology in saving endangered animals based on the speech about leatherback turtles, and in this essay, the task is complete.

In this essay, the writer makes it clear to the audience why funding for technology is important in the preservation of endangered animals. The writer discusses several facts and examples taken from the speech about leatherback turtles in Costa Rica. These include important background about the leatherback turtles, threats to the leatherbacks, and measures taken to protect the turtles. The writer includes specific examples of technological advances that researchers in Costa Rica used to preserve the population of leatherback turtles, such as ultrasound imaging and the microchip identification tag. These examples are persuasive because they show specific ways in which the leatherback turtle population can be preserved. The inclusion of such examples from the speech is likely to convince the National Geographic Society that the funding it provides for technological advancements in research would actually be put to good use. Each fact and example in the essay is clearly stated, coherent, and relevant to the task of persuading the National Geographic Society to provide funding for the use of technology in saving endangered animals. The writer goes on to discuss a possible breakthrough in technology that could further help save the leatherbacks, which is also a very persuasive point.

The writer summarizes the main points made in the speech in a clear and well-written essay. It persuasively presents a solid argument for why the National Geographic Society should provide funding for the use of technology in saving endangered animals. The essay is highly organized, there are no grammatical errors, and the ideas are well communicated.

Part B: Multiple-Choice Questions

7 (3) Think about why the story of the 16-year-old appears at the beginning of the text. The story is about a teenager who experienced severe burns while working at a fast-food restaurant. Would the author use the story to illustrate the reasons teens work? No, so toss out choice (1). Is the story used to illustrate the inexperience of teen workers? Be careful with answer choice (2)! The story may very well illustrate the inexperience of teen workers, but that is probably not the purpose of putting this story at the beginning of the article. Look at the other answer choices. Is the story used to illustrate the dangers teen workers face? Yes, it is! This is a better answer than choice (2) because the focus of the article is workplace injuries, and the point of the story was that the teenager was badly injured, not that he was inexperienced. Choice (3) is the correct answer.

8 (4) The question is asking you to draw a comparison between teens and adults based on what the text suggests. Does the text suggest that, compared to adults, teenagers are more likely to recover quickly from injuries? This is not mentioned in the text, so eliminate choice (1). Does the text suggest that, compared to adults, teenagers are more likely to report injuries to officials? This comparison is not suggested in the text, so get rid of choice (2) as well. Does the text suggest that, compared to adults, teenagers are more likely to exaggerate the seriousness of injuries? Again, this idea is not mentioned in the text, so you can toss out answer choice (3). Does the text suggest that teenagers are more likely than adults to become injured at work? Yes, it does! At the end of the second paragraph of the text (lines 10–12), the author states that there are many factors that "place younger workers at greater risk than adults confronted with similar hazards." Of all the answer choices provided, this is the only comparison you can make based on the information in the text.

9 (1) You should have looked back at the text to help you select the correct answer choice for the question. The fourth paragraph of the text states: "The injury rates alone do not provide a sense of the consequences of occupational injuries for the injured adolescents or for the adolescent population in general. Adolescents who are injured seriously enough to miss work may also miss days of school." Rereading this statement, you can see that according to the text, one serious consequence of teen work-related injuries is absence from school. This makes answer choice (1) correct. None of the other answer choices are mentioned as results of teen work-related injuries.

10 (2) The text addresses the fact that younger adolescents have fewer workplace injuries than older adolescents in the fifth paragraph. The question may seem difficult because the text states that the reasons for younger adolescents having fewer injuries "are not entirely clear." Even so, don't be intimidated by the question; there will not be any questions on the Regents that you can't answer based on the information you are given. If you were to reread the whole fifth paragraph, you'd find the information you need to pick the correct answer choice just sitting there, waiting for you to spot it. Based on the information you are given in the paragraph, why do younger adolescents have fewer workplace injuries than older adolescents? Is it

because younger adolescents work more slowly? The fifth paragraph does not mention this idea, so eliminate answer choice (1). Is it because younger adolescents work fewer hours? Based on the statement that child labor laws limit the number of hours of employment for workers under sixteen, answer choice (2) makes sense. Choice (2) is the best answer, as the text does not suggest that younger adolescents receive better training or take fewer breaks. So you can eliminate choices (3) and (4).

11 (3)   The question asks about a specific detail from the text, and because you are allowed to look back at the text, answering it should be a piece of cake. The sixth paragraph states that some Massachusetts high school students used food slicers "despite the fact that child labor laws prohibit individuals under the age of 18 from operating . . . food slicers." So the text cites the use of food slicers as an example of the violation of child labor laws, making (3) the correct answer choice.

12 (4)   Whenever a question asks you about a specific line in the text, look back at that line and a few lines before and after it to help you answer the question. This question is asking about the term "high turnover" in line 46, and the context surrounding this term will give you clues to help you select the correct answer choice. The lines surrounding this term describe the poor conditions of the jobs most young workers do. Does the term "high turnover" refer to the number of products or services sold? No; this does not relate to the context, so eliminate answer choice (1). Does it refer to the number of raises and bonuses given? No; raises and bonuses are not mentioned, but "low pay" is, so eliminate choice (2). Does the term "high turnover" refer to the number of accidents that occur? The passage does focus on the number of accidents that occur, but not in these lines, so you can eliminate choice (3) as well. Does the term "high turnover" refer to the number of employees that leave? Yes, it does! "High turnover" means that employees frequently leave jobs and get replaced with other young employees. Choice (4) is correct.

13 (3)   Think about what problem the example of the cashier who is asked to cook is illustrating. Is this example used to illustrate a problem with customer relations? No; an employee performing multiple tasks has little to do with customer relations, so you can eliminate answer choice (1). Is the example used to illustrate a problem with hygiene regulations? No; the paragraph in which the example appears does not mention problems with hygiene, so you can eliminate choice (2). Is the example used to illustrate a problem with job assignments? Yes; the example comes after the sentence, "Another issue that is just beginning to be recognized is the assignment of youths to jobs other than the ones they were hired to perform." Choice (3) is the correct answer because this sentence suggests multiple job assignments are a problem for youths in the workplace.

14 (1) You'd have to take another look at the table to help you answer the question. Find the industry other than grocery stores has the highest percentage of work-related injuries and is most frequently listed. The column labeled "frequent industries" contains the information you need to answer the question correctly. Choice (1), "eating and drinking places," has a higher percentage of work-related injuries and is listed in the column more frequently than "hotels and motels," choice (2), or "hospitals," choice (4). "Factories," choice (3), are not even mentioned in the table. You can eliminate choices (2), (3), and (4). Based on the information in the table, most work-related injuries to workers under 18 occur in grocery stores and eating and drinking places, so answer choice (1) is correct.

15 (1) Look at the fifth column in the table, which is labeled "Frequent events and exposure," to find the correct answer to the question. In most of the states shown on the table, the most common injuries to young workers are caused by falls, as you can see by the percentage of accidents caused by falls in the states of Connecticut, New Jersey, New York, Pennsylvania, and Vermont. Although falls are not the number one cause of accidents in New York, they are in all the other states except Massachusetts, making answer choice (1) correct.

16 (2) The question requires you to make an inference based on common sense and your reasoning ability. "Median days away from work" refers to the average number of days of work that children missed due to injuries or illnesses. Basically, the question asks why some people missed more days of work than others. To what do you think the differences in "Median days away from work" are most likely due? Are they probably due to the workplace in which the injury occurred? The workplace probably doesn't have much of an effect on why some people missed more days of work than others, so you can eliminate choice (1). Are they probably due to "the seriousness of the injury," choice (2)? That makes a lot more sense than choice (1), because the seriousness of an injury would be directly related to how many days a person would be away from work. Are the differences in days away from work probably due to the cause of the injury or the year in which the injury occurred? Neither of these answer choices is likely, so you can eliminate (3) and (4). Choice (2) is a more logical answer than either of these choices. It makes the most sense as an explanation for the differences in "Median days away from work" and is therefore correct.

Part B: Essay

The people who grade your essay will be thinking about the following questions when they decide how to score it. You should think about these questions when you review your essay.

- Have you clearly stated the main idea of your essay in the introduction?
  - Your main idea should be specific to what your essay is about; don't just restate Your Task.
  - The main idea of your essay should discuss teenagers' work-related injuries and suggest ways employers can help reduce these injuries.

- Have you addressed each bullet point in the Guidelines in the body paragraphs of your essay?
  - The body paragraphs should inform your audience about teenagers' work-related injuries and suggest ways employers can help reduce these injuries based on information in the article "Workplace Injuries" *and* the table.
  - The body paragraphs should include specific, accurate, and relevant information from the article *and* the table to support your discussion.

- Have you supported the main idea of your essay with relevant facts, examples, and details from *both* the text and the table, and properly indicated when you are quoting from the text or referring to statistics from the table?

- Have you clearly and logically organized your essay?
  - The topic of each body paragraph should be clear and coherent.
  - The transitions from topic to topic should be clear.

- Have you written your essay in a tone that is appropriate for a feature article for the school newspaper?

- Have you concluded your essay with a summary of its main points?

- Have you used correct spelling, grammar, and punctuation?

Here's an example of a top-score essay.

Recently, a number of local teenagers have suffered on-the-job injuries. Fortunately, their injuries were not life threatening. However, these incidents raise an interesting question: Are our teenagers especially accident-prone, or are teenagers in general likely to be injured at work?

According to the National Center for Health Statistics, in 1996 the injury rate for 15-to-17-year-olds was 4.9 per 100 full-time-equivalent workers, compared to all workers over 16, for whom the rate was 2.8. Interestingly enough, workers under 16 had fewer injuries than teens over 16. Therefore, kids from 16 to 18 have more injuries than their younger counterparts, but far fewer than adults. What's going on here?

Authorities aren't sure, but it's likely that the sharp federal limits placed on workers under 16 (in terms of hours and types of work) result in less exposure to dangerous situations. Older teens, however, may work longer hours, increasing the opportunity for accidents to happen. Furthermore, both the teens and their employees may consider the teens mature and able to handle situations which, in fact, they are not prepared for.

Interviews with young workers reveal some startling facts. Many young workers are exposed to dangerous situations such as working with chemicals, case cutters, food slicers, box crushers, or ladders. Some reported working alone at night. Clearly, all of these situations are dangerous; some of them are illegal.

Another factor in workplace injuries for teenagers is simply the kinds of jobs they hold. Adolescents tend to be hired by grocery stores, hospitals, and nursing homes. These places have higher injury rates for all workers—they are simply more dangerous places in which to work. Adolescents generally work in low-level jobs that offer little in the way of benefits, promotion, or skill-building. These jobs offer little security, erratic hours, and low pay. These are some characteristics associated with jobs that are more dangerous than those with more positive characteristics.

A key factor in the high rate of workplace injuries among teenagers can be found in a survey of teenagers being treated in emergency rooms for job-related injuries. A majority of those injured reported that they had received no safety training at all. That revelation makes sense when you examine the types of injuries that occur.

In New York and five neighboring states, two of the most common causes of injuries were "fall on some level" and "overexertion in lifting." If you connect that information with an understanding of where kids work, you can begin to see a pattern. In New York, for example, 34% of the injuries took place in "eating and drinking places," and 32% of the injuries took place in "grocery stores." These are places where employees are likely to be lifting heavy trays, boxes, and equipment. These are also places where spills occur, making floors treacherous. If workers had training in how to lift heavy objects and how to avoid spills, they could prevent many injuries.

Employers can take measures to prevent injury to their young workers. It is important for employers to provide appropriate supervision for all young workers. Although teenagers are reliable and eager workers, they are still inexperienced and need guidance. Teenagers are often over-confident and reluctant to ask for help. Supervisors must see to it that young workers are trained in the safe use of equipment and shown how to follow procedures that will prevent accidents such as falls. Supervisors should also constantly check to see if the young employees are actually following those procedures. They should make it clear that failure to follow all the safety rules may result in the loss of a job.

Here's an explanation of the top-score essay.

The essay receives full credit (6 points) because it provides a thorough explanation of teenagers' work-related injuries and suggests ways employers can help reduce these injuries. The writing task requires test-takers to write a feature article for the school newspaper discussing teenagers' work-related injuries and suggesting ways employers can help reduce these injuries using information from *both* documents. The task is complete in the sample essay provided.

In this essay, the writer explains the serious problem of work-related injuries sustained by teenagers and suggests some theories as to why older teens have higher on-the-job injury rates than younger teens. The writer discusses the factors often involved in teenagers' work-related injuries, such as being exposed to "dangerous situations" and the types of jobs teenagers tend to have. The writer makes these points clear by providing specific examples of equipment that makes on-the-job situations dangerous for teens, including chemicals, food slicers, and ladders. Details and facts from the text and the table substantiate the writer's discussion of teenagers' work-related injuries and inform his or her suggestions about ways employers can help reduce these injuries.

The writer summarized the main points from the text in a clear and well-written essay and also incorporated information from the table. The questions posed within the essay make its tone very engaging, which is appropriate for a feature article for the school newspaper. The essay is highly organized because each paragraph concentrates on one major idea and the transitions from paragraph to paragraph are smooth. Also, there are no major grammatical errors in the essay, and the content is comprehensible.

SESSION TWO

Part A: Multiple-Choice Questions

1 (4) Questions 1 through 5 refer to Passage I, the poem entitled "The Centaur." Look back at lines 2 through 4 in the poem: "Can it be there was only one / summer that I was ten? It must / have been a long one then." Do these lines suggest that the narrator found her tenth summer to be tedious, meaning difficult to get through? The line "it must have been a long one then" may suggest it was tedious, but if you think about the fun, playful tone of the poem, you'd figure out that the narrator would not describe the summer as "tedious." So you can eliminate answer choice (1). Do lines 2 through 4 suggest that the narrator found her tenth summer to be lonely or refreshing? No, neither description is suggested by the lines, so eliminate answer choices (2) and (3). Do lines 2 through 4 suggest that the narrator found her tenth summer to be memorable? Yes, they do! The fact that she thinks that it seemed long suggests that the narrator had many memories from that summer. Choice (4) is the best answer choice.

2 (1) Look at the answer choices and consider which of them is suggested by the context surrounding line 19. According to lines 20 through 21, the dust covered the narrator's feet and made them look like a horse's hoofs. Does the narrator imply that the dust is "lovely" because it makes her feet resemble hoofs? She certainly does, so answer choice (1) is correct. The narrator does not imply that the dust is "lovely" because it covers her tracks or lets her trot faster. These choices are both related to her imaginary horse, but they are not as good as choice (1). So you can eliminate choices (2) and (3). The narrator does not imply that the dust is "lovely" because it keeps her toes from hurting. This is not suggested at all and does relate to the content of the poem, so you can eliminate choice (4) as well.

3 (3) Think about the verbs used in lines 29 through 44. Some of these verbs are *flopped, swung, arched, skittered, reared, wheeled,* and *swished.* These are all action verbs that are meant to convey the feeling of riding and being part of the imaginary horse. Do the action verbs help establish a feeling of apprehension? Do they help establish a feeling of regret? No; the feeling conveyed in the poem is not apprehensive or regretful at all, so you can eliminate answer choices (1) and (2). Do the action verbs help establish a feeling of exhilaration, or excitement and liveliness? Yes, they most certainly do! This is the perfect word to describe the feeling expressed by the action verbs, so answer choice (3) is correct. Most of the action verbs refer to dramatic movements that the child makes as she plays.

4 (2) The question is asking you about something *implied* in the last stanza, which means you have to make an inference in order to select the correct answer choice. Although the answer to this question is not directly stated in the passage, you can still figure out which answer choice is best. Does the poet imply that the narrator had hidden in the field? This seems possible because the stanza does mention a field, but there is no indication that the narrator had hidden in the field. You can eliminate answer choice (1). Does the poet imply that the narrator had

buried her face in clover? Yes; there is a direct reference to clover in the last stanza, so answer choice (2) is clearly better than choice (1). Also, the narrator's mother asks her why her mouth is green in the last stanza. This is another indication that the narrator had buried her face in clover. The correct answer choice is (2). The poet's brother has nothing to do with the poem at all, so you can eliminate choice (3). You can also eliminate choice (4) because the last stanza mentions clover, not wildflowers.

5 (4) The title of this poem is "The Centaur." The footnote at the bottom of the first page of the poem tells you exactly what a centaur is. It defines a centaur as a "creature that was part horse and part human." If you read the footnote, answering the question should have been pretty easy. Line 38, "I was the horse and the rider," reinforces the title because the narrator uses the line to express than she is both horse and human as she was playing outdoors. The correct answer choice is (4).

6 (3) Questions 6 through 10 refer to Passage II, the short story excerpt entitled "The Pebble People." Look back at lines 20 through 24. Do theses lines suggest that one purpose of Ben's play is to challenge traditional roles? No. These lines mention "thanksgiving that his people were alive to see another day and that they had chosen this day to come together in celebration of tribal customs." This does not suggest challenging traditional roles, so eliminate choice (1). Do the lines suggest that one purpose of Ben's play is to solve personal problems? No; the lines do not suggest that Ben is trying to solve anyone's problems, so eliminate choice (2). Do the lines suggest that one purpose of Ben's play is to practice social traditions? Yes; the way Ben is reenacting a war dance celebration with the pebbles suggests that he is practicing social traditions. The lines mention practicing tribal customs; customs are the same thing as traditions, so choice (3) is correct.

7 (2) Look back at lines 25 through 28. Ben "asked for blessings on behalf of people who were sick and could not attend the dance . . . for those imprisoned by steel bars and by personal weakness. And he asked the people to remember those who had died since last time they had gathered." The prayers are for people who are experiencing misfortune. Do Ben's prayers reveal a sense of duty? They do not really convey a sense of duty because they do not mention that anyone actually has to do anything for the unfortunate people mentioned. Eliminate choice (1). Do the prayers reveal a sense of compassion, or sympathy? Yes, they do, because Ben's prayers show that he is thinking about those who are less fortunate. Answer choice (2) is correct. The prayers do not necessarily reveal a sense of courage or humility (showing that one is humble), so you can eliminate choices (3) and (4).

8 (3) The question asks you about a specific detail from the passage. Because you can look back at the passage whenever you want, answering this question should not be difficult. Which pebbles does Ben put into a jar at the end of the passage? "Those that were last to fall" (line 41), which means that Ben selected as winners of the contest those pebble people who had lasted the longest, choice (3). None of the other answer choices are accurate based on the information in the passage.

Roadmap to the Regents: Comprehensive English

9 (4) To answer the question correctly, you'd have to think about Ben's attitude toward play throughout the passage. Think about everything he does and says while he plays. The question asks you how to describe what he does and says. Can he best be described as "mischievous," or causing trouble? No; there is nothing mischievous about Ben as he plays, so you can eliminate answer choice (1). Can he best be described as "courageous"? No; neither he nor the pebble people are performing acts that show courage, so you can eliminate answer choice (2). Can Ben be best described as "innocent"? He is aware of people in prison and those who are limited by their own weaknesses, so it seems that he is more sophisticated than innocent. This is not a good description, so you can eliminate choice (3) as well. Can Ben be best described as "thoughtful," choice (4)? Yes; this is the best description out of the four possible answer choices. Ben shows that his play is thoughtful because it includes many details to make it seem as realistic as possible. The correct answer choice is (4).

10 (1) The question requires you to think about both passages and decide which action in the poem is similar to Ben's action of digging the pebbles from the earth. In the story, digging the pebbles from the earth is Ben's first action before beginning to play his war dance game. In the poem, the narrator has to cut down her "horse" from the willows before she can ride it. Therefore, line 11 of the poem, "cut me a long limber horse," is most similar to Ben's action of digging the pebbles from the earth, because both actions are the first things the children do before they are able to engage in their imaginary play. The correct answer choice is (1).

Part A: Essay

The people who grade your essay will be thinking about the following questions when they decide how to score it. You should think about these questions when you review your essay.

- Have you clearly stated the controlling idea, or main idea, of your essay in the introduction?

  - Your controlling idea should be specific to what your essay is about; don't just restate Your Task.

  - The controlling idea of your essay should discuss the meaning of play as revealed in the two passages. Your essay should include your own ideas about play based on your interpretation of the two passages.

- Have you addressed each bullet point in the Guidelines in your essay?

  - The essay should discuss the meaning of play as revealed in *both* passages in relation to your controlling idea.

  - The essay should use specific and relevant ideas and examples from *each* passage to develop your controlling idea.

  - The essay should incorporate discussion of specific literary elements used by the authors in relation to your controlling idea.

- Have you supported the controlling idea of your essay with relevant examples and quotations from *both* passages, with proper indication when you are quoting from the text?

- Have you clearly and logically organized your essay?

  - The topic of each body paragraph should be clear and coherent.

  - The transitions from topic to topic should be clear.

- Have you concluded your essay with a summary of its main points?

- Have you used correct spelling, grammar, and punctuation?

Here's an example of a top-score essay.

Each child creates his or her own definition of play. The meaning of play is similar in many ways for the 10-year-old girl in "The Centaur" and 8-year-old Ben from "The Pebble People." They both play outdoors with nature, and both spin a whole new reality from thoughts alone. The meaning of play for these two children can best be defined as using imagination to recreate something they truly loved.

The girl and Ben Adam each turned to nature for their objects of play. The girl whittles and peels a "horse" from willow wood; the boy searches out pebbles of the right type from the ground. Their intentions were clearly the same, although each imagined a different fantasy. The girl imagined she was a horse, and a rider as well, because she truly loved how horses behave. Ben Adam imagined dancers performing the ancient dances of his people because he truly loved the philosophy and culture they represented.

The author of "The Centaur" uses literary elements to convey the girl's experience. In style, the poem most resembles a memoir. The first-person point of view brings emotions directly to the reader, and the lively figurative language of the verbs "snorted," "shied," "skittered," and "quivered" convey the girl's complete involvement. The poem and title are an extended metaphor: the centaur, and the girl also, are horse and rider in one creature.

The author of "The Pebble People" places the boy's solitary play on his grandparents' land, symbolically connecting the past and present. Though their differing colors, the pebbles become individual. In the driveway of an old house, a battered tin becomes an arena and a sacred drum in the mind's eye of Ben Adam. He uses his memory of past events to enact an imaginary scene, and his reverence is obvious to the reader.

In his playing, Ben is in control. He prays, meditates, and directs the dancers. In fantasy he is ageless. The author then lets us see, through the use of dialogue and detail, that Ben is after all a young boy. "Gee, that was a good contest," he says, and the dancers become mere stones again, to be kept in a "fishtank."

"The Centaur" and "The Pebble People," through each author's choice of language and literary elements, illustrate that play is based on ideas and objects that arouse love in those who play.

Here's an explanation of the top-score essay.

This essay receives full credit (6 points) because it presents a controlling idea, or main idea, about the meaning of play as revealed in both passages. The writing task requires test-takers to write a unified essay with a controlling idea based on both passages. The task is complete in the essay provided here.

In this essay, the writer's controlling idea is that the meaning of play "can best be defined as using imagination to recreate something they [Ben Adam and the poem's narrator] truly loved." The writer supports this idea with an intelligent discussion of the girl's creation of and transformation into an imaginary horse in the poem, and Ben Adam's creation of and interaction with his pebble people dancers in his imaginary dance arena in the short story. In separate paragraphs, the writer analyzes what play meant to the girl and to Ben Adam. The writer uses specific examples and details from each passage, and each example is clearly stated, coherent, and relevant to the controlling idea. The writer also shows how each author uses specific literary elements, such as point of view, figurative language, and symbolism, to reveal that play is about using imagination to recreate something one feels deeply about.

The writer establishes and presents a controlling idea based on the two passages in a unified, clear, and well-written essay. The writer's analysis of the literary techniques is thoughtful ("The poem and the title are an extended metaphor"). The essay is highly organized, there are no major grammatical errors, and the content is comprehensible.

Part B: Essay

This essay is different from the other essays on the Regents exam because you have to draw solely on your outside knowledge of literature in order to write it. No reading passages or other information will accompany the writing task for the critical essay.

The people who grade your essay will be thinking about the following questions when they decide how to score it. You should think about these questions when you review your essay.

- Have you clearly stated the main idea of your essay in the introduction?
  - Your main idea should be specific to your essay topic; don't just restate Your Task.
  - The main idea of your essay should present a valid interpretation of the statement in the Critical Lens and should agree or disagree with the statement as you have interpreted it.
- Have you discussed *two* works of literature that you believe best support your argument?
- Have you addressed each bullet point in the Guidelines in your essay?
  - Your essay should support your main idea with a detailed discussion of the works of literature you have chosen.
  - Your essay should also discuss specific literary elements of these works.
- Have you supported the main idea of your essay with specific examples and details from the works of literature you have chosen?
- Have you clearly and logically organized your essay?
  - The topic of each body paragraph should be clear and coherent.
  - The transitions from topic to topic should be clear.
- Have you concluded your essay with a summary of its main points?
- Have you used correct spelling, grammar, and punctuation?

Here's an example of a top-score essay.

Author Richard Wright once stated that "All literature is protest. You can't name a single literary work that isn't protest." In the history of American literature, there is evidence that supports Wright's claim. American authors often have served as agents of change in their societies. Their protests against evils that threaten society have had major effects on American attitudes at times. Two authors who have influenced Americans to evaluate their beliefs are Arthur Miller and Ray Bradbury. Through his play <u>The Crucible</u>, Miller protested the mass hysteria that accompanied the Communist scare during the McCarthy era. Through his short story "The Other Foot," Bradbury was able to take a stand against racism during a period of extreme racial prejudice in America.

At the time of the McCarthy hearings, American society was permeated by the fear that Communists would take over the country. Miller, himself, became the target of such fear. He was called to testify before Senator Joseph McCarthy's committee, which was in charge of finding Communists. Realizing that those who were called to testify were presumed guilty simply because they were called to testify, and that convictions were based on mindless fear rather than on fact, Miller chose to write a play which would reveal to Americans the injustice that was occurring. Since McCarthy was on a "witch hunt," Miller set his play, <u>The Crucible</u>, in Salem, Massachusetts, in the year 1692, the time of the infamous Salem witch trials. Americans had long realized the travesty of justice that overshadowed the trials. In his play, Miller shows how petty people, specifically Abigail Williams and her followers (substitute Joseph McCarthy and his committee), following their own agenda (the desire for power and recognition), were able to disrupt society and convict innocent people of witchcraft (substitute Communism) on the basis of unsubstantiated evidence. The parallels that could be drawn between the two time periods, the motivations of the accusers, and the subsequent results of the false accusations gave Americans the opportunity to reflect on their attitudes and actions. Just as Abigail's quest to gain John Procter was unsuccessful (her accusations resulted in his being hanged), and just as she lost her power in the community (she fled to Boston after stealing her Uncle Proctor's money), so, too, did Senator McCarthy ultimately lose his power and credibility. Though it would be difficult to prove that Miller brought about McCarthy's fall from power, Miller's protest against mindless fear and false accusations is still viewed today as a powerful work which is able to let people view the folly of such actions.

Just as Miller chooses a setting in the past to distance his audience from the action, and to allow them to analyze the actions of "those people," so, too, does Bradbury choose a setting that is not of his time. Bradbury's story, "The Other Foot," is set in the future and on the planet Mars. Through his writings about the settling of Mars, Bradbury is able to focus on different aspects of the folly of people. In the story, "The Other Foot," Bradbury protests racism. Basing his work on the premises that minority groups have resettled on Mars and that the Earth must be evacuated because of the effects of nuclear war, Bradbury at first shows the members of the minority society (the dominant society on Mars) preparing to treat the white people from Earth, who are seeking sanctuary, as they once were treated. Signs are made which will be used to denote "white" facilities. Whites have to sit in the back of the bus. This reversal of situation at first is viewed as a great opportunity to "get even." This attitude soon disappears. In the end, the white evacuees are received on Mars as fellow members of the human race. The reader is left with the concept of a society developing in which there will be true equality. By setting his story on Mars, Bradbury is able to emphasize that the once arrogant whites had nowhere else to go, as their comfortable home planet was soon to be uninhabitable. They would have been forced to become slaves if the residents of Mars so demanded. Fortunately, the minority settlers of Mars chose not to treat members of a different race in such a way.

Both Miller and Bradbury were able to protest the injustice and ignorance they perceived in their society. Each attempted to change the attitudes of Americans to bring about positive change. Obviously, Miller did not stop the fear of Communism, and Bradbury did not bring about the end of prejudice. Each, however, took a stand. Each gave Americans the opportunity to reexamine their beliefs.

Here's an explanation of the top-score essay.

This essay receives full credit (6 points) because it provides a valid interpretation of the statement provided in the Critical Lens, agrees with the statement as interpreted by the writer in the discussion of two literary works, and supports the writer's opinion with specific references to the works. The writing task requires test-takers to discuss two literary works from the perspective of the statement provided in the Critical Lens. The task is complete in this essay.

In the essay provided, the writer provides an interpretation of the statement provided in the Critical Lens by stating that "American authors often have served as agents of change in their society" and discussing how the two literary works are protesting things—the dangers of anti-communist hysteria and racism, respectively. The two literary works discussed are Arthur Miller's play *The Crucible* and Ray Bradbury's short story "The Other Foot." In the second paragraph, the writer provides a highly intelligent analysis of the political message of *The Crucible* and makes direct correlations between the Salem witch trials and the McCarthy era, illuminating Miller's message and substantiating the writer's interpretation of the Critical Lens.

In the third paragraph the writer discusses the way Bradbury addressed the problem of racism using a futuristic setting, and demonstrates with specific examples how this work supports the writer's interpretation of the Critical Lens. The student points out that both Miller and Bradbury used a setting that was removed from the time in which the work was written in order to "distance his audience from the action, and to allow them to analyze the actions of 'those people,'" a highly perceptive point of literary analysis. The examples from each work are clearly stated, coherent, and relevant to the main idea of the essay.

The writer provides an interpretation of the statement provided in the Critical Lens and intelligently supports the argument with a fine analysis of both literary works. The essay is well organized—the first paragraph introduces the two literary works the writer intends to discuss, the second and third paragraphs each discuss one of the literary works in detail, and the final paragraph brings the essay together by making connections among the two literary works. Also, the sentence structure in the essay is varied, the language is interesting and frequently complex, there are no grammatical errors, and the content is comprehensible.

ABOUT THE AUTHORS

Elizabeth Silas graduated summa cum laude and Phi Beta Kappa from Boston College's Linguistics program. She teaches, tutors, and trains instructors for The Princeton Review in SSAT, PSAT, SAT, SAT II Writing, and GRE preparation. As head of Research and Development of The Princeton Review Textbook Publishing, she investigates tests nationwide and develops materials for them.

Reed Talada began teaching for The Princeton Review in 1988. He has managed offices in both New Jersey and Boston and is currently General Manager of The Princeton Review's Textbook Publishing division. He graduated from Drew University cum laude in 1991 and currently lives in New Jersey with a brilliant cat named Tigger.